The Revolution Will Not Be Downloaded

CHANDOS INTERNET SERIES

Chandos' new series of books are aimed at all those individuals interested in the Internet. They have been specially commissioned to provide the reader with an authoritative view of current thinking. If you would like a full listing of current and forthcoming titles, please visit our web site **www.chandospublishing.com** or contact Hannah Grace-Williams on email info@chandospublishing.com or telephone number +44 (0) 1993 848726.

New authors: we are always pleased to receive ideas for new titles; if you would like to write a book for Chandos, please contact Dr Glyn Jones on email gjones@chandospublishing.com or telephone number +44 (0) 1993 848726.

Bulk orders: some organisations buy a number of copies of our books. If you are interested in doing this, we would be pleased to discuss a discount. Please contact Hannah Grace-Williams on email info@chandospublishing.com or telephone number +44 (0) 1993 848726.

The Revolution Will Not Be Downloaded

Dissent in the digital age

**EDITED
BY
TARA BRABAZON**

Chandos Publishing
Oxford · England

Chandos Publishing (Oxford) Limited
TBAC Business Centre
Avenue 4
Station Lane
Witney
Oxford OX28 4BN
UK
Tel: +44 (0) 1993 848726 Fax: +44 (0) 1865 884448
Email: info@chandospublishing.com
www.chandospublishing.com

First published in Great Britain in 2008

ISBN:
978 1 84334 459 9 (paperback)
978 1 84334 460 5 (hardback)
1 84334 459 9 (paperback)
1 84334 460 2 (hardback)

© The contributors, 2008

Typeset by Domex e-Data Pvt. Ltd.
Printed in the UK and USA.

Printed in the UK by 4edge Limited - www.4edge.co.uk

Contents

List of figures and tables … vii

About the authors … ix

Preface … xiii

PART 1: SCANNING THE SILENCES … 1

1   Access denied: reading, writing and thinking about techno-literacy … 3
   Kathryn Locke

2   Restless redundancy … 11
   Sonia Bellhouse

3   Wiring God's waiting rooms: the greying of the World Wide Web … 21
   Tara Brabazon

4   Cash for corporeality: international students and the wealth of transgression … 73
   Leanne McRae

5   Cultware: constructing the matrix of internet access … 89
   Mike Kent

PART 2: DOWNLOADING HARMONY … 101

6   He who pays the piper must call the tune? … 103
   Mike Kent

7   The ultimate mix: try before you buy? … 115
   Carley Smith

8   Record companies vs technology … 123
   Felicity Cull

PART 3: UPLOADING IDENTITY   133

9   Putting their life on(the)line: blogging and identity   135
     Joanne Smith

10   Is it all bad? Japan's internet suicide subculture   145
     Joel Matthews

11   When home is away: re-thinking the travel weblog   153
     Rebecca Bennett

12   eBay: marketing the real body in the virtual world   163
     Angela Thomas-Jones

13   Cyber sluts: the new Victorians   171
     Melinda Young

14   The I in community: it's all about ME in gaydar's global gay diaspora   187
     Luke Jacques

PART 4: PACKET SWITCHING RESISTANCE AND TERRORISM   199

15   Information at the speed of thought   201
     Valentin E. Fyrst

16   Keeping an eye on Big Brother   205
     Garan Lewis

17   Dot-com, dot-bomb: (cyber)terror on the internet   213
     Christina Lee

18   Conclusion: What do you do with the other one in a duo?   223
     Tara Brabazon

Index   229

List of figures and tables

Figures

2.1	Survey of First Click participants	18
3.1	Microwaving change	47
3.2	Domesticating technology	50
3.3	The complexity of access	52
3.4	Technology in the lounge room	53
3.5	The 'digital shed'	56
3.6	A war over space	57
3.7	Barriers to access	59
3.8	A mode of exclusion	61

Tables

3.1	Computer and internet usage by seniors	32
3.2	Origin of overseas-born seniors in Western Australia, 2001	34
3.3	Eastbourne senior population by age group	40
4.1	International students in Australian higher education	79

About the contributors

Sonia Bellhouse is a mature student currently studying English, communications, cultural studies, and social history in Western Australia, with a view to extending her research profile through higher degree scholarship. She is an avid reader of all literary genres and a prolific writer. As coordinator of the Perth-based Westfield Reading Group she enthusiastically inspires others to extend their reading repertoire and writing expertise.

Rebecca Bennett has completed a PhD in cultural studies and backpacker tourism. She is the convener of the tourism hub in the Popular Culture Collective, a sessional lecturer at Curtin University and a part-time administrative manager of the student guild at Murdoch University in Western Australia. She has spent many years overseas in the UK, Europe and North America, but has returned to settle in her home city of Perth, Western Australia.

Tara Brabazon is Professor of Media at the University of Brighton, UK and director of the Popular Culture Collective. She is the author of nine books including *Digital Hemlock* and *The University of Google*. Her interests include media education, cultural history, creative industries strategies, sonic media and postcolonial theory. A former national teaching award winner, she teaches students from first-year to doctoral level and is the course leader for the Master of Arts Creative Media.

Felicity Cull has a BA (Hons) in communications and is a PhD candidate at Murdoch University. She is the rhythm and movement hub convenor for the Popular Culture Collective, and a sessional academic at Curtin University. Her academic interests include the role of music in cultural and political resistance in conservative times, masculinity studies and creative industries.

Valentin E. Fyrst has a background in business administration, psychology (clinical and organisational) and French. He is employed as a business consultant within the Strategy and Corporate Affairs Division of Western Power (Western Australian Electricity Networks Corporation). Before joining Western Power, Valentin worked as a project officer within the Electricity Reform Implementation Unit of the Western Australian Office of Energy where he had extensive involvement in the development, drafting and approval processes underpinning the restructure of the vertically integrated Western Power Corporation into its four successor entities (Western Power, Synergy, Verve Energy and Horizon Power).

Luke Jacques is currently working for the Australian government. He writes articles and commentaries for Australian queer free street press and is beginning a PhD in 2008. His research interests are in the convergence of postcolonial and queer theory.

Mike Kent is based at the University of Brighton, where he is a researcher for the Art Design and Media Subject Centre of the Higher Education Academy. He is also the critical digital hub convenor for the Popular Culture Collective. Mike has been actively involved with the internet since 1996 when he co-founded an internet service provider. His research is focused on the impact of new media and communications technology on society.

Christina Lee is Lecturer in Media and Cultural Studies at Curtin University of Technology, Western Australia. Her areas of research are youth cinema, Chinese cinema, nostalgia and memory in film, and gender studies. She has published on a wide range of topics in publications such as *Continuum*, *Cultural Studies Review*, *Images of the 'Modern Woman' in Asia: Global Media, Local Meanings* and *Liverpool of the South Seas: Perth and Its Popular Music*. She is editor of *Violating Time: History, Memory and Nostalgia in Cinema* (Continuum Books, 2008) and is writing a book on youth iconography and politics in cinema (Ashgate Publishing).

Garan Lewis is presently living in Perth, Western Australia. In 2006 he completed a bachelor of arts degree, majoring in political science, with a minor in cultural studies. He is currently finishing a diploma of education at Murdoch University. He is interested in developing participatory democratic ideas, tackling social justice issues and considering ways of moving towards a more egalitarian society.

Kathryn Locke works in the area of urban regeneration and arts management. She is also completing a doctorate in cultural studies at

Murdoch University, Western Australia. Her research and published work encompasses topics ranging from city imaging and the political economy to literacy theory and education policy.

Joel Matthews completed his undergraduate degree at Murdoch University, Perth, Western Australia and is currently a postgraduate student in the Graduate School of Intercultural Studies at Kobe University, Japan. He specialises in cultural studies and Japanese studies, currently focusing on contemporary Japanese media culture, popular culture and suicide practices.

Leanne McRae is a senior researcher and creative industrial matrix convener for the Popular Culture Collective. She is a teacher of media studies, cultural studies, screen studies, creative industries and mobility studies, with specialist expertise in the instruction of international students. Currently, her research interests include popular cultural studies, mobility and the media, pedagogy and men's studies.

Carley Smith has a BA (Hons) in communication and cultural studies and is a PhD candidate at Murdoch University in Western Australia. Her early academic interests revolved around fans and fandom and her dislike of patronising ethnographic and anthropological 'studies' that pathologised fan behaviour. Her doctorate investigates the propaganda and populism operating in and around Michael Moore's film-making and writing. She is currently working for the Australian government in an industrial relations advisory field.

Joanne Smith is a PhD student at Murdoch University in Perth, Western Australia. She is interested in the history of Australia and New Zealand and the political, economic, social and cultural relations which have manifested within the region. Her thesis investigates the negotiation of postcolonialism in the Antipodes through the analysis of popular culture.

Angela Thomas-Jones is a part-time academic at Murdoch University, Western Australia and editor of the Popular Culture Collective's community and hub projects. Angela's passion is writing and her publications include book chapters, and website and magazine articles. These research pieces focus on different aspects of popular culture such as fashion, body politics, the creative industries and youth.

Melinda Young is a PhD candidate at Murdoch University. Previous degrees include BPsych and BA communication and cultural studies with first-class honours. Her PhD research examines leisure and its condition in post-work Australia, with attention to how the relationship between class, (post) work and leisure is applied to obesity. Additional research interests include feminism and the contemporary representation of femininity, fatness, food discourses, post-industrial consumption, popular culture and class. Publications range from work on feminism and fatness, consumerism, post-work, leisure, food and class. Melinda works part-time for the Commonwealth and Federal Business Enterprise of Australia Post. She is also the body works hub convenor of the Popular Culture Collective.

The authors may be contacted at:
E-mail: *t.m.brabazon@brighton.ac.uk*

Preface:
passing the digital door bitch
Tara Brabazon

The first thing you should do whenever you hear anything stated confidently is to say, 'Wait a minute. Is it true?' (Noam Chomsky)[1]

Most things make me nervous. Going into clubs makes me nervous. I always think that I'm not going to get into the club. All my childhood, it was always stressful about whether you're going to get in or not. I was the classic person on the receiving end of, 'You can't come in trainers', or 'Sorry, it's members only night'. (Chris Lowe)[2]

The last 20 years have seen an explosion in the night-time economy. Dance music and dance clubs have boomed out their wares, punctuating the atmosphere with beats, smoke and mirrors. But before punters can push through into this sensual Narnia, hopeful partiers must pass the fashion muster from bombastic bouncers and demanding door bitches. Even Chris Lowe, one half of the style-lifing Pet Shop Boys, expressed his nerves in negotiating with these arbiters of identity and taste.

This analogue world, of shoes and nightclubs, membership and belonging, has edges, borders, exclusions and inequalities. Access and entry has always been exclusively granted to the empowered, the fashionable and the affluent. When the internet entered popular culture through the early 1990s and the World Wide Web interlaced with social life in the 2000s, the dreams of Howard Rheingold[3] and Sherry Turkle[4] appeared to reach fruition. The incomplete revolution of May 1968 suddenly found a platform for renewal. Democracy would finally be possible online in a way that had never been realised in our clubs, homes and workplaces. Yet these dreams have not been fulfilled and there have been sick twists in this narrative of cyber-topia. The democratic availability of information has been undercut by the auctioning of data. For example, 3G mobile phones allow owners to listen to music, watch television and video, take photographs, send and receive e-mails and play games. Yet Victor Keegan, technology journalist with *The Guardian*, recognised the profound disadvantage of this 'revolution', even for the digitally literate and employed:

> The biggest drawback was finding that a full month's bill was more than three times as much as usual. My operator's shop failed to explain why. Wireless uploads to my Flickr site (supposed to be around 7p) were varying between 2p and more than £1, even though they were on lowish resolution. It was also impossible to distinguish between uploading snaps and downloading from other sites. This is a real problem. Operators are trying to recoup their £22.5bn auction outlay by charging as much for data as they can get away with. Until they adopt something like the broadband model – more or less unlimited usage for a flat fee – they should be unsurprised at low uptake. The web-on-the-move revolution has yet to happen.[5]

One more 'revolution' has failed to deliver, and such a failure is not a surprise. The 'trickle down' theory does not work in economics: the affluence of the wealthy does not *inevitably* move millions to the minions through taxation. Similarly, this 'trickle down' effect does not *inevitably* transform elite sporting success into a physical culture appropriate for a sedentary and increasingly obese 'general' participation. Assuming – without policy intervention and regulation – that competition will *inevitably* ensure that all can share in the digital 'revolution' is naïve and fails to learn from the consequences of earlier technological transformations. When one application reduces its price, the next 'innovation' is introduced at great expense to the consumer.

To address the costs and consequences of these cycles of obsolescence and techno-enthusiasm, the title of this book was chosen with care. *The revolution will not be downloaded* tracks how far we have travelled through the narratives of e-ducation, online shopping, digitised music and cyberterrorism. We probe how the promises of the digital age have perpetuated analogue injustices. In sampling and remembering the popular cultural intervention by Gil Scott-Heron in his 1970 song, 'The revolution will not be televised',[6] the researchers in this collection affirm that digitisation – like the earlier media platforms of newspapers, books, radio and television – transforms and fractures community allegiances built through time and space. Indeed, 'the revolution will be live'.[7] Intriguingly, the journey and influence of this song shadows many misunderstandings of the media and politics since the track was released. Smoove, the British acid jazz group, were filled with the potentials of computer-generated imagery, sponsorship and branding, and sung that the 'The revolution will be televised'.[8] The same slogan was used by Apple upon the release of Apple TV. NOFX's song 'The Marxist Brothers' attacked the left-wing politics within which Scott-Heron's song may be placed and updated media, confirming 'The people's revolution is going to be a podcast'.[9] The Brooklyn-based Funk Essentials were more pessimistic and elemental: 'The revolution was postponed because of rain'.[10] Yet the influence of this lyric, rhythm, phrase and sentiment has seen the track recorded in Welsh,[11] French[12] and Spanish,[13] and become a title for a documentary on the 11 April 2002 Venezuelan coup against Hugo Chávez. Forty years on, the song has been re-recorded, remixed, shredded of irony, migrated onto digitised platforms and inverted in its politics, but remains a testament to the desire to cut through mediations, hyperbole, displaced blame, advertising and pseudo-neutrality.

Taking inspiration from Scott-Heron's courage, insight, intervention and influence, an array of writers from the Popular Culture Collective, a global community of researchers, writers, film makers, musicians and media activists,[14] has deployed a range of research methods, including interviews and surveys, to enter the spaces and places often forgotten by the digi-elite. The goal has been to seek out the defiant, the difficult and the dissenter. Music is important to any technological in(ter)vention as it can transform a platform from a work-based utility used by a few early adopters into the foundation of leisure and pleasure for many. We have explored the controversies of downloadable music from three perspectives. First, Carley Smith enters the community of music downloaders to monitor this group's behaviour and attitudes to law and copyright. Felicity Cull probes how musicians are 'managing' the benefits and costs of online music, and Mike Kent summons the cliché of 'he who pays the piper calls the tune' to determine how both 'the piper' and 'the paying' has transformed the role of the record company. Moving from music to fashion, Angela Thomas-Jones wheels the virtual trolley to find the literacies required to negotiate eBay. Leanne McRae enters the community of international students, letting them speak and have a space beyond the financial role written for them by university managers and marketers. She explores their attitudes to online education, and how digitisation has transformed the value of the education they receive.

All revolutions are selective. A radical few lead a radical few more with an objective to create change. Yet a key question remains how far digitisation has permeated into the lives of the many. Early adopters of digitised music, shopping and education require access to money and equipment, and assume these facilities are held by others. Less frequently investigated is how skills, knowledge and literacy hamper a movement from analogue to digital living. Building on the literacy model introduced by Kathryn Locke and the concept of cultware deployed by Mike Kent, writers in this collection investigate the consequence of digitisation empowering the already empowered and further disconnecting particular groups from not only governmental representatives and services, but families, friends and their community. My chapter investigates senior citizens in two of 'God's waiting rooms' – Mandurah in Western Australia and Eastbourne in the United Kingdom. I probe how and why this group has been excluded from the online environment and why digital access is not an optional accoutrement to positive ageing, but a necessary part of online policy. Similarly, Sonia Bellhouse activates an extraordinary research project and service through interviewing courageous 'non-users' of computers who are taking their first gentle steps into a community-run internet course. Three chapters in this collection then move to apply questions of 'revolution' and 'dissent' to the information landscape and world news. Garan Lewis sketches the narrow range of ideas that circulate through mainstream channels and how the web can both enhance and inhibit the range of informational options. Valentin Fyrst creates the concept of a 'cybernaut' to convey a voyage through data, and the consequences of this non-linear journey through space and time. Christina Lee, summoning our fears of violence, shows how digitisation is implicated in the so-called War on Terror.

No book on the web or internet can be either representative or encompassing. We are interested in how our daily lives are being agitated, challenged and – perhaps – transformed. Throughout the making of this collection, we have – with intent – sought out under-researched, ambivalent and troubling sites of digitised social life that transcend the conventional topics of music and shopping. With some bemusement, we have researched new forms of digi-love. These chapters go beyond the 'earnest middle-aged loser gets dumped by bored housewife' tabloid exposé of a decade ago.[15] Melinda Young, in summoning the ghost of Jane Austen, uses interviews to ask how and why the online environment is 'a route to a root'. Luke Jacques takes us on a journey through Gaydar, the 'global' gay meeting place, to show the disappointments of online 'love'. Joanne Smith studies blog spots and asks why these writers present intimate details online, and describes the consequences of their disclosures. Rebecca Bennett follows bloggers when they travel and travellers when they blog, revealing the profound political and cultural consequences when shallow ideas about race, religion and power are 'published' for an audience. Building on Bennett's study of difference, Joel Matthews explores the Japanese rituals of synchronised 'online' suicide. Therefore, the topics we summon in this book can never be symbolic or illustrative of the entire web or capture all modes of revolution and dissent, but the case studies chosen by these writers capture the heat of sex and the ice of death in the midst of constructing an i-dentity, along with occasional attempts to build community and download democracy.

Back to the future: Web 2.0

The Revolution Will Not Be Downloaded also has a subtitle which captures the trajectory of our argument: dissent in the digital age. Our goal in this book is to attack the often implicit and damaging assumption that 'everyone' is online and that 'everyone' is using online resources within the parameters specified by employers, the government and national laws. Put another way, we are adding a sociology to the web, asking who is using particular applications, how and why. This remedial work is required. For example, not 'everyone' is downloading music. According to one study from the British Phonographic Industry, 96 per cent of the money spent on music downloads is derived from men, and nearly 40 per cent of these men are aged between 35 and 44.[16] How such a sociological profile transforms online shopping, the music charts and the acts signed to recording companies is yet to be fully revealed. The pretence that 'everyone' is part of the downloading 'revolution' is not only mistaken, but damaging to e-commerce strategies and the plurality and diversity of popular music.

The concept and label of Web 2.0 is part of this problem in generalising and universalising the availability and applicability of the online environment for all groups within society.[17] The term captures the desire for online collaboration and the sharing of information, termed the 'architecture of participation' or 'service-oriented architecture',[18] and is performed most publicly through blogs, podcasts and wikis. Other 'products' that capture the Web 2.0 ideology[19] include Google Maps, Facebook, MySpace and Flickr. Within this framework, websites no longer hold information but become a platform to connect applications with users. Yet the original – or at least popular – origin of this term is derived from O'Reilly Media[20] and MediaLive International. It became the brand and title for their annual conferences, with the first held in October 2004. Business applications have gained the most attention, including content syndication, but there are also political initiatives overlaying this project including open communication, the sharing of data and deep linking of web architecture.[21] As with the (now burst) dot.com bubble, Web 2.0 needs 'less noise [and] more signal'.[22] It is not only a buzzword, like the bubble and the bling, but – pivotally for *The Revolution Will Not Be Downloaded* – increases the online opportunities and applications for those already online, ignoring those still excluded from Web 1.0. Nicholas Carr captures the pseudo-religious disappointments of 'the first' web, and how Web 2.0 has – once more – been summoned as a promised digi-land:

> But as the Web matured during the late 1990s, the dreams of a digital awakening went unfulfilled. The Net turned out to be more about commerce than consciousness, more a mall than a commune. And when the new millennium arrived, it brought not a new age but a dispiritingly commonplace popping of a bubble of earthly greed. Somewhere along the way, the moneychangers had taken over the temple. The internet had transformed many things, but it had not transformed us. We were the same as ever ... Web 1.0 may have turned out to be spiritual vaporware, but now we have the hyper-hyped upgrade: Web 2.0 ... Like it or not, Web 2.0, like Web 1.0, is amoral. It's a set of technologies – a machine, not a Machine – that alters the forms and economics of production and consumption. It doesn't care whether its consequences are good or bad. It doesn't care whether it brings us to a higher consciousness or a lower one. It doesn't care whether it burnishes our culture or dulls it. It doesn't care whether it leads us into a golden age or a dark one. So let's can the millennialist rhetoric and see the thing for what it is, not what we wish it would be.[23]

The contributors to this book have answered Nicholas Carr's challenge to see the 'thing' as it is, not how it is sold or marketed. This book reveals not only who is using particular online platforms, but the costs to citizenship and democracy through that social profile. We do care about the consequences of online exclusion. We do care how citizens' lives are transformed through the shifts in production and consumption, work and leisure. Unlike Shakespeare's Brutus, we neither bury nor praise the web. Our aim is to add analogue texture and density to the words and policies of digitised decision makers.

While the cyberpunks and 'residents' of The Well were loopy optimists,[24] at least they were committed to more than just themselves. It is the banality, boredom and minutiae of Web 2.0 that has triggered this current project and the topics selected by contributors. As an example of the strange priorities of the digitised 2000s, a recent UK survey of 1,700 people asked them about the most stressful parts of moving house:

> The survey ... highlighted how the nation's dependence on the internet has overtaken simple things like the need for curtains or the convenience of a microwave. Less than a third of people could not live without their curtains and a mere 8.5 per cent could not survive without their microwave. This compares to a staggering 92 per cent of people who said that in the first month following moving into a new home, the one thing they wouldn't be able to live without was their broadband connection.[25]

Eclipse Internet has now developed a 'House Mover package', so that broadband access is available in the new home on the first day of arrival. This is extraordinary. My parents taught me that the most important preparation for moving is writing the word 'Kettle' on the box with the kitchen utensils, so that after a long day, the tired and dirty (un)packers can make a cup of coffee. With a house filled with boxes, answering e-mails is not a priority. But such an odd 'service' confirms the other interpretation of our title, the notion that digitisation is not a revolution, but only rebrands more banal activities.

The Revolution Will Not Be Downloaded brings the world back to the web and the interrelationships back to the internet. The aim is not to celebrate Wikipedia or the open source 'movement'. Instead, we throw a sliver of light onto the groups, collectives and communities who are doing it tough or doing it differently in this wired age. We also problematise the notion that Google encourages the democratic permeation of information. When confronted by an open search engine, most of us will enact the ultimate of vain acts: inserting our own name into the blinking cursor. Using Google is a self-absorbing action, rather than an outward and reflexive process. It is not a search of the World Wide Web, but the construction of an Individual Narrow Portal. It is addictively riveting to see how an identity is constructed through Google. For example, Paul Morley, one of the most iconoclastic and talented of popular cultural writers, put his own name into the blinking cursor:

> I decided to ... punch my name into the Google search engine to see how I have been gathered, collected, framed, defined on the World Wide Web. Who am I on the net? I figured that this would be a pretty good description of who I was, or who I have been. It would be accurate, neutral, and would sum up my achievements inside the media, as a writer, as a personality, as some kind of operator in arts and entertainments. The Google search engine raked in versions of myself from across the virtual universe, and from the results you could piece together a version of me that is as good a biography as anything. What you could see straight away, from the very first mentions, is that I did become famous as a rock-and-roll writer of all time. I say this, without believing it, while knowing it to be fairly true, and would say that, on various occasions, during the late seventies and early eighties, while writing for the New Musical Express, I did materialize now and then as the greatest but overall, in the lists of greats, I would just about put myself inside the top twenty. Well, inside the top ten. About seventh. Or sixth. All in all, I think I was the fifth-greatest rock-and-roll writer of all time. Maybe the fourth. Actually, the third. The greatest non-American, anyway. And I could take on the top two Americans any day of the week.[26]

Morley shows how the 'objective' ranking from Google easily slides into subjective meanderings of social worth. Using Google provides the mechanism for the subtle but continual weathering of community-building strategies away from the consensual and the status quo. The search has replaced research. To grasp alternative views and ideas – to test and validate the opinions of our political leaders – requires work and effort rather than the passive acceptance of the rankings from a Google search. It is important to be completely honest about the internet – let alone the web – that is being searched. The web is large, occasionally irrelevant, filled with advertising, outdated ghost sites and is increasingly corporatised. Only when technology has a social purpose and appropriate context is it useful. Internet and web literacy is not inevitably triggered by the availability of hardware, software or the

Google cursor. More information does not – intrinsically – create more effective and convincing evidence to commence a process of social change.

An early techno-celebrationist welcomed the web in education, believing that 'we can learn virtually anything from the very source of the information'.[27] Everything can be learnt from the web, except *how* to use it. Digital wallpaper has covered over the cracks of analogue injustice. While Google users, bloggers and Wikipedia's Jimmy Wales affirm the democracy being woven from their desks,[28] it is necessary to remove the digital burka and see those who are working in the adjacent analogue environment. When times are truly bad, we are drawn to the light, the frivolous and the stupid. This phenomenon – which could be called the Paris Hilton Effect – occurs where bored surfers fill their cursors and minds with irrelevancies. We lose the capacity to sift, discard and judge. Information is no longer for social good, but for sale.

Democracy, let alone digitisation, is not inevitable. Francis Fukuyama, in his movement away from neo-conservatism and his earlier arguments in *The End of History*, confirmed that democracy is not an inescapable by-product of 'modernisation' or 'progress':

> This belief in the imminence of democratic change was based on two things. The first had to do with an interpretation of the underlying cross-cultural appeal of democracy and with the contagiousness of the democratic idea at the end of the twentieth century. The second had to do with their belief in the centrality of American power and, in particular, the view that Ronald Reagan's policies had been critical to the demise of the former Soviet Union ... But a theory of democratic change emerging out of a broad process of modernization like the one laid out in The End of History suggests that democratic contagion can take a society only so far; if certain structural conditions are not met, instability and setbacks are in store.[29]

There have been many 'revolutions' and many information ages.[30] The mobility of paper-based printed texts, the speed of the telegraph, the interruptions in the private sphere through the telephone and the movements of sound and vision through space via the satellite, transformed identity, community and nation. Yet more than hope and hype is required to link digitisation with democracy. The writers of these pages do more than diagnose 'the problem', but offer policies and possibilities for their resolution. Like a digital door bitch, we ask difficult questions and probe the truths and attitudes of bloggers, wiki-editors and podcasters, suggesting that their fashionable confidence in their own value is misplaced. The 'we' is returned to the web.

Notes

1. *Distorted Morality*, directed by Eric Watson (Plug Music and Silent Films, 2002).
2. *Pet Shop Boys – Somewhere: Live at the Savoy Theatre*, directed by Eric Watson (Pet Shop Boys Partnership, 1997).
3. Rheingold, H. (1993) *The Virtual Community*, Reading, MA: Addison-Wesley.
4. Turkle, S. (1995) *Life on the Screen*, New York: Touchstone.
5. Keegan, V. (2006) 'I loved my 3G phone until I saw the bill', *The Guardian*, 26 January, Technology section, p. 4.
6. Gil Scott Heron, 'The revolution will not be televised', *Small Talk at 125th and Lenox* (Flying Dutchman Productions, 1970)
7. Ibid.
8. Smoove, 'The revolution will be televised', *Dead Men's Shirts* (Acid Jazz Records, 2005).
9. NOFX, 'The Marxist Brothers', *Wolves in Wolves Clothing* (Fat Wreck Chords, 2006).
10. Funk Essentials, 'The revolution was postponed because of rain', *A Compilation 3* (Dorado Records, 1994).
11. Llwybr Llaethog and Ifor ap Glyn, 'Fydd y Chwyldro ddim ar y Teledu, Cyfaill', *Hip Dub Reggae Hop* (Ankstmusic, 2006).
12. Experience, 'La révolution ne sera pas télévisée', *Positive Karaoke with a Gun / Negative Karaoke with a Smile* (Green Ufos, 2005).
13. Molotov, 'La Revolución', *Con Todo Respeto* (Universal Latino, 2004).
14. *The Revolution Will Not Be Downloaded* is the second book from the Popular Culture Collective. The goal of this not-for-profit global community organisation is to improve the calibre of popular culture and the writing about it. Our first book was Brabazon, T. (ed.) (2005) *Liverpool of the South Seas: Perth and its Popular Music*, Perth: UWA Press.
15. For example, Hugh, from Lower Hutt near Wellington in New Zealand, supposedly 'lost' his wife *because* of the internet: 'Hugh believed he was happily married – until he got home from hospital after a quadruple-bypass operation, to find his wife Leona about to leave him for her Internet love ... Hugh thinks it was a "lousy" way of cheating. "It was an affair on the Internet, and I still have difficulty understanding how it could be done"'. See Milne, J. (1998) 'Trapped in the on-line love net', *The Dominion* (Wellington), 11 July, p. 17.
16. See Bachelor, L. (2005) 'Upbeat about downloading?', *The Observer*, 1 May p. 4.
17. The impact of Web 2.0 as a term/concept/marketing device has also been felt in libraries, with Library 2.0 also emerging as a description of the new

library service that focuses on the delivery of content to users. The term was first used in Casey, M. (2005) 'Working towards a definition of Library 2.0', available at: *http://www.librarycrunch.com/2005/10/working_towards_a_definition_o.html* (accessed 11 December 2007).

18. Erl, T. (2005) *Service-Oriented Architecture: Concepts, Technology, and Design*, Upper Saddle River, NJ: Prentice Hall.

19. Paul Boutin, however, says 'Just call it the Internet. That way, everyone will know what you mean'. See Boutin, P. (2006) 'Web 2.0', available at: *http://www.slate.com/id/2138951* (accessed 6 November 2007).

20. O'Reilly, T. (2005) 'What is Web 2.0: design patterns and business models for the next generation of software', available at: *http://www.oreillynet.com/lpt/a/6228* (accessed 28 June 2007).

21. Rhodri Marsden offered a critique of Web 2.0's proliferation. He stated that 'there's no denying that these innovations are reshaping the social landscape of the internet, but the rise of Web 2.0 as a buzzword has, inevitably, led to it being abused. If anyone asks if a website is "Web 2.0 enabled", you can be pretty sure that they don't know what they're talking about, and what they probably mean is a) does it look pleasant, and b) can readers leave comments on it'. See Marsden R. (2006) 'What does Web 2.0 mean for the internet?', *The Independent*, 26 July, p. 9.

22. This phrase is part of a critique of Web 2.0 derived from Jeffrey Zeldman. See Zeldman, J. (2006) 'Web 3.0', available at: *http://www.alistapart.com/articles/web3point0* (accessed 28 June 2007).

23. Carr, N. (2005) 'The amorality of Web 2.0', available at: *http://roughtype.com/archives/2005/10/the_amorality_o.php* (accessed 28 June 2007).

24. Hafner, K. (1997) 'The epic saga of The Well', *Wired* 5(5), available at: *http://www.wired.com/wired/archive/5.05/ff_well_pr.html* (accessed 30 June 2006).

25. *Homes Sales & Lettings* (2006) 'Who needs curtains anyway?' *Homes Sales & Lettings* 137 (June): 28.

26. Morley, P. (2003) *Words and Music*, London: Bloomsbury, p. 118.

27. Classroom Connect (2001) 'Applications of learning', available at: *http://connectedteacher.classroom.com/tips/resources/communicating.htm* (accessed 16 June 2004).

28. Anderson, C. (2006) 'Jimmy Wales', *Time Magazine*, 8 May, available at: *http://www/time.com/time/magazine/article/0,9171,1187286,00.html* (accessed 3 June 2006).

29. Fukuyama, F. (2006) *After the Neocons: America at the Crossroads*, London: Profile, p. 57.

30. Given, J. (2003) *Turning off the Television: Broadcasting's Uncertain Future*, Sydney: UNSW Press, p. 65.

Part 1
Scanning the silences

Access denied: reading, writing and thinking about techno-literacy

Kathryn Locke

> Because we suffer from the scourge of information pollution, we find it difficult to imagine its even deadlier opposite – information starvation. (Arthur C. Clarke)[1]

> The same technology that simplifies life by providing more functions in each device also complicates life by making the device harder to learn, harder to use. This is the paradox of technology. (Donald A. Norman)[2]

Education sits on contested ground. Caught between economic rationalism, vocational training and literacy teaching, a precise determination of education's 'mission' has been lost. Running parallel to this confusion of interests and agendas is a rapidly mutating and expanding technological environment, or as Richard Wurman identified it as, the 'Age of Also'.[3] The relationship between the transformations of media and how schools, universities and workplaces adapt to the challenges to current literacies remains the core problem. While an emphasis is placed on technological adjustment (by the user, rather than the technology), the orientation towards skill-based courses geared to job training is being pushed to the forefront of university curricula aims.[4] Uncertainty remains as to how technology conflates with literacy and literacy teaching. There is an expectation that direct skills-related training correlates with employment. There is also an assumption that the teaching of technologically-specific skills will eliminate or correct other literacy deficiencies. Yet what both suppositions fail to acknowledge is that this technology-led solution is circumscribed by context. As soon as a new or improved technology or job requirement emerges, the specific skill-set that was previously acquired becomes obsolete. A deeper and more damning question quietly shadows these concerns with obsolescence: will a function-based literacy prepare students for a critical or meaningful engagement with their world? Although uncomfortable, the essential question educators must ask is about the relationship between text and context, literacy and society. Each debate on the digital divide, computers in classrooms or the literacy 'problem' raises the same wide-ranging and unanswerable question: what is the purpose of education?

Many educators and policy makers are still propelled by the techno-celebration which is engrained in mainstream narratives of progress and development. Within this discourse, technology aids educational 'excellence'. The internet provides unlimited sources of information and teaching computer literacy helps students find employment. The failure of the internet – or any technological platform – to moderate the exploitations of the casualised workplace or counter the rise of tabloidisation and an investment in the banal confirms that we are living in an information age without information literacy.[5] High illiteracy rates are not confined to new technologies or communication systems. The OECD reported in 2000 that between one-quarter and three-quarters of adults do not have adequate literacy skills.[6] A chain of events, causes and consequences are emerging in and through an illiterate information age. We are already faced with a large body of people who lack basic literacy. The onset of new technologies and additions to the criteria by which literacy is performed and evaluated is only enlarging the group labelled 'illiterate'. While educators and politicians stress the importance of producing techno-literate digital citizens, attention is diverted away from creating an integrated palette of analogue and digital literacies to be taught, learnt and deployed. The 'problem of literacy'[7] is a problem of literacies. The basis of these illiteracy rates – and perhaps the reason for their continuation despite governmental programmes and funding assistance – is a lack of understanding regarding the complexity, hierarchy and purpose of literacy.

In 2000, Bill Cope and Mary Kalantzis published *Multiliteracies*, a book that largely arose from the educational challenges triggered through the morphing purposes of technology. Concerned primarily with the future role of education in a shifting social, political and economic climate, Cope and Kalantzis focused their attention on appropriate methods for teaching literacy.[8] Their concerns may not have been unique – a large body of research exists that acknowledges the need for an adapted pedagogy in a complex and plural learning environment – but in the fundamental concept of 'multiliteracies' lies a crucial review and critique of contemporary understandings of literacy. Defined as the 'increasing multiplicity and integration of significant modes of meaning-making where the textual is also related to the visual, the audio, the spatial',[9] the term 'multiliteracies' recognises the complexity of sources from which we attain information in contemporary society. The internet is used as a primary example of how 'literacies' can be found in hybrid forms. Our process of obtaining meaning is adapting to a new diversity of texts. While e-mail was considered a 'new' means of communicating, it was primarily text-based, written on the screen rather than paper, and transported by a network of fibre-optic cables rather than a postman. While it involved adapting older literacies to a new modality, it did not create an entirely new literacy and was premised on the attainment and qualification of the older knowledge systems.

The primary problem within this model of multiliteracies is the lack of acknowledgment of a pre-existing hierarchy of literacies. What *Multiliteracies*, as a project and term, failed to recognise was the assumption that 'traditional' literacy is valued over other skill-sets. This absence overlooked not only the cultural and social values attached to literacy behaviours, but also neglected to demonstrate how other literacy formations mark the user within a power structure. They assumed that a multiplicity of literacies can occur without a hierarchy and that those 'multiples' can only exist as an extension of, and subsequent to, a mainstream literacy. As Macken-Horarick outlines, 'problemat[izing] the relationship between meaning making (reading and writing) and social processes',[10] is essential to the formation of a liberal education. The teaching of critical literacy can only be obtained once other forms and modes of literacy are achieved. Macken-Horarick refers to these other modes as everyday, applied and theoretical literacy:

> Management of a critical frame is dependent on adequate induction into specialised literacy. In other words, an effective critical intertextuality is dependent on adequate development of a specialised intertextuality.[11]

What this model offers to digital education debates is a literacy structure whereby the achievement of multiple – or specifically technological – literacies can only be considered once a level of competency with a text is mastered. Literacy is linear and chronological. Rather than generating a curriculum that endlessly celebrates the new, adaptations should be made to provide a broad literacy palette that allows the student to conquer a variety of different texts, technologies or life challenges. This is not only a theoretical model but a social and educational policy objective.

In the USA, current and past strategies employed to overcome 'the digital divide' by both the Clinton and Bush administrations are prime examples of how new technology, especially the introduction of the internet, have been addressed in education. Clinton attempted to eradicate the division between the 'e-haves' and the 'e-nots' by 'connecting all of America's schools to digital networks by the end of the 1990s'.[12] President Bush introduced the No Child Left Behind Act 2002, which premised the 'integration of technology into the classroom', with the assumption that technology would be 'learned' if embedded in everyday classroom activities.[13] Both these attempts to address the digital divide lacked the crucial connection between literacy and technology, assuming that simple exposure – ensuring all classrooms had computers and internet connections – would create technologically-savvy students. Longitudinal statistics generated by PEW's Internet and American Life Project indicate that internet use is not simply correlated with, nor eliminated by, internet connection. Relationships between race, socioeconomic status, age, education and internet use are more significant than issues of access.

In 2000 and again in 2003, PEW launched an investigation into internet access and usage. They were specifically concerned with a continuing 'digital divide' and why, when there had been extensive governmental intervention in establishing nationwide access, 42 per cent of Americans still did not use the internet. A decade of government funding aimed at creating 'access' to the internet for all citizens and especially young people. Imprecise discussions of 'access' have resulted in not only the perpetuation of a digital divide, but increasing barriers of exclusion. While the research projects undertaken by PEW were detailed and necessary – illuminating racial and financial discrepancies and the explanations offered by those who consciously choose to not use the internet – what was lacking in their research was interpretation of their valuable compiled statistics. A challenge remains to policy advisers, literacy theorists and educators to provide this critical interpretation. This book provides a beginning to this needed dialogue between technology, policy, pedagogy and citizenship. *The Revolution Will Not Be Downloaded* not only addresses a broad range of social, economic and political issues stimulated by the internet and its associated technologies, but provides some solutions. The fact that 83 per cent of those who did not graduate from high school reported that they did not use the internet[14] suggests a direct positive correlation between literacy achievement and 'techno-literacy' attainment. The world in which the 'net drop-outs', the 'e-nots' and the 83 per cent of those over 60[15] exist is rapidly necessitating digital intervention. The reasons behind global and local divides, between those who use the internet and those who do not, should not be dismissed as 'adaptive' variations or age anomalies. There are important correlations in these figures that point to much larger social problems than lacking a telephone connection.

Changes to work, education and government have generated an urge to get citizens 'up to speed'. In an accelerated age, the emphasis is on the new, the flexible and the fast. Yet as much as shifting technologies and workplaces must be learned and conquered, we must not neglect the teaching of critical literacy, the fundamental skill that underpins 'the very survival of democracy itself'.[16] Theorists such as Fulton argue that the internet poses new and significant challenges to students and citizens:

> Due to the rapid growth of the internet and the access it provides to vast amounts of information, concerns about the need for increased attention to information literacy are mounting. Unlike other forms of media, what is transmitted by the internet is 'undigested' information, offered by novices and experts alike. As such, students will have to become skilled in locating information from a variety of sources, evaluating data, and making critical judgments about the validity, reliability, and value of information.[17]

Theorists have stressed attention to terms such as 'digital literacy', 'computency' or 'technologised literacy' but have disconnected new technologies from literacy theory. In fact, the emergence of the internet and its associated technologies has only confirmed the well-established understanding that effective citizenship requires reflexive, creative and critical literacy.[18] A technology-oriented education is of little significance if the platform or tool cannot forge a better socioeconomic environment for the majority of users. At the base of both internet hyperbole and internet critique is a discussion about how this technology will aid social and economic development and foster critical citizenship. If, as the OECD reported, over 25 per cent of the population does not possess enough literacy skills for the challenges posed by daily life, why should their ability to blog or use Google be of primary concern? Before we create a population of disconnected individuals who can turn on a computer, use eBay or email but have difficulties managing intercultural differences, a focus is required on creating citizens that negotiate, communicate, criticise, interpret and make a difference regardless of the tool they use to do so.

Notes

1. Clarke, A. (1999) 'Technology and humanity', in A. Leer, (ed.) *Masters of the Wired World*, Harlow: Pearson Education, pp. 31–6.
2. Norman, D. (1990) *The Design of Everyday Things*, New York: Doubleday Currency, p. 31.
3. Wurman, R. (2001) *Information Anxiety*, Indianapolis, IA: Que.
4. Aronowitz, S. (2000) *The Knowledge Factory*, Boston, MA: Beacon Press.
5. See Brabazon, T. (2002) *Digital Hemlock*, Sydney: UNSW Press. Several publications discuss at length the value that the internet can bring to the classroom and its students yet they also suggest that more research, policy intervention and 're-training' is needed for it to be successful. As an example of this discussion, see Fulton, K. (1998) 'Learning in a digital age: insights into the issues', *Technological Horizons in Education Journal* 25(7): 66–70.
6. Adequate literacy skills are those considered to be of 'Level 3' ability, which provides sufficient skills for the citizen to cope with the demands of modern-day life and work. Statistics were gathered from 20 countries between 1994 and 1998. See Tuijnman, A. (2000) *Literacy in the Information Age*, Paris: OECD and Statistics Canada.
7. Giroux, H. (1987) 'Literacy and the pedagogy of political empowerment', in D. Macedo (ed.) *Literacy: Reading the Word and World*, South Hadley, MA: Bergin, pp. 1–29.
8. Cope, B. and. Kalantzis, M. (eds.) (2000) *Multiliteracies*, South Yarra: Macmillan.
9. Ibid., p. 5.
10. Macken-Horarick, M. (1998) 'Exploring the requirements of critical school literacy: A view from two classrooms', in F. Christie and R. Mission (eds.) *Literacy and Schooling*, London: Routledge, pp. 74–103.
11. Ibid., p. 100.
12. The number of classrooms connected to the internet increased from 3 per cent in 1994 to 63 per cent in 1999, while the number of schools connected to the internet increased from 35 per cent in 1994 to 95 per cent in 1999. See Gore, A. (2000) 'Digital opportunity in the new millennium: making the internet work for all Americans', *Business Perspectives* 12(3): 180–92.
13. US Department of Education, Government of The United States of America (2002) No Child Left Behind Act. See: *http://www.ed.gov/nclb/landing.jhtml?src=pb* (accessed 1 November 2007).
14. Lenhart, A. (2000) 'Who's not online', PEW Internet and American Life Project, available at: *http://www.pewinternet.org/topics.asp?page=2&c=2* (accessed 10 November 2007).
15. The term 'net dropouts' refers to those individuals who have used the internet some time in their lives but have since decided to no longer use it.

'E-nots' are all internet non-users; they include those who choose not to use the internet and those who simply do not have access. It was reported by PEW in 2000 that 64 per cent of people over the age of 60 do not use the internet. See Lenhart, op. cit.; Lenhart, A. Horrigan, J. Rainie, L. Allen, K. Boyce, A. and Madden, M. (2003) 'The ever-shifting internet population', PEW Internet and American Life Project, available at: *http://www.pewinternet .org/PPF/c/2/topics.asp* (accessed 10 November 2007).

16. Aronowitz, S. and Giroux, H. (1985) *Education Under Siege*, South Hadley, MA: Bergin and Garvey, p. 24.

17. Fulton, K. (1998) 'Learning in a digital age: insights into the issues', *T H E Journal (Technological Horizons in Education)* 25(7): 66–70.

18. Aronowitz and Giroux, op. cit.

2

Restless redundancy

Sonia Bellhouse

I don't want to change anything, because I don't know how to deal with change. I'm used to the way I am. (Paul Coelho)[1]

Exclusion is always difficult to monitor, particularly when the marginalised are unaware of the scale of their social disconnection. The internet and World Wide Web reinforce already existing inequalities, exacerbated not only by a lack of computer hardware, but the literacies required to enter the digital environment. Australian history, through convict origins and colonial struggles, has configured a popular ideology of egalitarianism, mateship and 'a fair go'. These national characteristics are exemplified in films such as *The Castle*,[2] where a family of 'battlers' is assisted by a QC – free of charge – in their fight to save their home from developers. It is an urban myth which repeats the popular discourse of the little guy winning out against powerful interests. From such popular cultural formations, the digital divide – between those who own and are proficient with computers and those who are not – is masked by already existing, but sublimated, analogue class structures.

To affirm democracy is to marinate social change in the language of rights and active participation to ensure a more equitable social and economic environment. Within such a discourse, those offscreen are disadvantaged. They are unrepresented. They are invisible to the powerful, ignored or scorned by the media and considered a 'digital underclass'[3] by those *on*screen. Consequently, their views remain unexpressed and their concerns unanswered. They cannot formulate opinions in a way that attracts the attention of the digital citizenry among whom they might find assistance in developing literacy. Groups who do not have access or capability to use the internet are generally older, economically disadvantaged or living outside cities. They are often ignored because they are not prolific consumers. One-quarter of Australians surveyed in a household survey stated that the reason they did not own a computer was due to the cost.[4] Lack of interest in computers or the internet was the most common reason given for not being connected. Yet, as suggested in Kathryn Locke's last chapter, a further reason may be that literacies to operate the platform or technological application were lacking.[5]

Additionally, reasons such as embarrassment at a lack of skill, gender/cultural taboos and even frustration with the complexity of the technology might be relevant.[6] A more complex intergenerational explanation for a lack of access has been described as 'level of parental education',[7] a socioeconomic issue seldom considered and difficult to track. These Australian findings align with research conducted by the PEW Internet and American Life surveys.[8] These 'gaps in internet access' were attributable to 'those with limited income, those with lower levels of educational attainment'.[9] In the data from this survey, many reasons were given to explain a disconnection from the internet. Fifty per cent said they 'did not want it' or 'did not need it'.[10] Only 30 per cent were prepared to say it was 'too expensive'.[11] Twenty-five per cent declared that the internet was 'too complicated and hard to understand'.[12] Such quantitative surveys, while incredibly valuable, do not reveal more intimate and ambiguous structures of exclusion. Many might choose not to reveal their financial or educational disadvantage. Some may prefer not to reveal their ignorance of what is available via the internet. Other may not wish to share their fear.

In America, 43 per cent of households with incomes under US$30,000 used the internet regularly.[13] In comparison, Australian statistics show only 20 per cent of those with incomes under A$50,000 accessing the internet at home.[14] For Americans with incomes over $75,000, the figure for those with access was an expansive 84 per cent. Similar results are revealed in Australia, with the Bureau of Statistics figures showing that in 2000, 57 per cent of higher-income households were connected to the internet and used it regularly. Familiarity with computers and ease of access help foster the development of computer proficiency. The children of these households are far more likely to develop computer literacy.

Behind these statistics are profound and dense social consequences and hardships, particularly for employment and training. Those made redundant by technological 'advances' are the least likely to embrace the technology that replaced them. They feel incapable of grasping the new platforms. Unless they find the incentive and funds to buy a computer, together with the dogged determination to learn how to use it, they may have effectively ended their working lives. They may manage to obtain work, but in a menial and low-paid capacity. This will still leave them unable to afford a computer system or training and professional development. It is because they have limited computer knowledge that they have little concept of whether a computer would be useful to them in social, economic and political terms. Some do understand, but feel so disenfranchised that the effort is beyond them. Others simply reject the digital domain and the possibility of raising their literacy.

One of the participants in my surveys and interviews for this chapter[15] recalled that in 1983 the Western Australian Premier's Department employed a woman in her fifties as a typist. She was immediately placed in the typing pool and instructed in the use of a word processor. She left work each day in tears. She did not want to use it. She doubted her ability to gain the knowledge to use the computer. She was also resentful that she had been deceived as to what the job entailed. Increasingly, government and business use computers and peripherals with the presumption that they are accessible to and understood by all. Call a telephone number and the recorded message will often direct the 'customer' to a website. Some sites are user-friendly, designed in a logical and coherent manner. Others seem designed to provoke frustration at their lack of accessibility.

Richard Wurman has argued that 'access signifies the ability to do what everybody else can do and make use of what everybody else can use'.[16] Accessibility for a person in a wheelchair is devised through specially-designed equipment and construction. There has been some concern for those with physical disabilities, with the goal to make facilities available to enable them to move through social spaces. These include wider doorways for wheelchairs and ramps to alleviate the need to use stairs. Larger-print texts, hearing aids and other specifically-designed devices offer assistance. Surprisingly – or perhaps not – citizens with disabilities are not well represented in computer usage, with only 38 per cent using computers, compared with the general population's usage of 67 per cent.[17] Designers have not succeeded in accommodating their negotiation through digitisation as much as through analogue spaces. The key to success in promoting computer access is to consider what a person might wish to do with this literacy:

> In the context of computer usage, access is more than having the physical ability to use a computer. Access is a willingness to engage with the process, an interest in doing so, and a belief that the

encounter will be productive or in some way beneficial. Access also presumes a certain literacy or competence in computer usage. Families with low incomes and lower education may not grasp how essential a home computer and internet access are becoming. Educators take the availability of these resources for granted, while parents in lower socioeconomic groups struggle with mounting costs.[18]

It may be difficult to convince these parents that a computer is becoming essential in education and employment, not a luxury, a toy, or simply for home entertainment. There is a large group of people, even in developed digitised nations, who do not own a computer and do not want to become connected to the internet. They are categorised as the 'don't want tos'[19] and further subdivided into what Wyatt, Thomas and Terranova describe as 'resisters' and 'rejecters'. There is also a group that are systematically expelled from empowered structures, the 'socially and technically excluded',[20] and those whose computer usage has been involuntarily disconnected through cost constraints or cessation of previous access.[21]

Through this matrix of exclusion, avoidance, inequality and fear, it is difficult to develop a cohesive social plan to cater for the marginalised. Digital disability and marginalisation is invisible and can be ignored. They are disabled by literacy. They cannot buy a computer because they do not know what to buy. They need advice as to what is suitable for their needs and within financial limitations. Simple programmes for computers could allay their fears. The rich and literate have access to experts who will solve their computing problems. They do not need to question or locate barriers of exclusion. For those without the time, literacy or persistence to query the assumptions of progress and digitisation, they are left in analogue ambiguity.

To enact change, the first goal is to demystify the process of buying a computer. The second imperative must be the creation of a supportive environment where attempts at digital access are validated, alleviating people's fears of 'the complexities involved as people try to adopt technology'.[22] If we empower citizens by providing the keys to computer knowledge in places that are unthreatening and familiar, such as public libraries and shopping malls, then change can take place. The goal is to teach 'new' literacies through the filter of older competencies, creating a network of comprehension in a familiar and relaxed context. Without intervention, those without expertise and access will be left even further behind. As Aspin states, 'a low income allows little room for flexibility or for the satisfaction of other needs and wants'.[23] Those on low incomes are unable to bridge the gap as they struggle to meet basic costs for analogue needs. They are the ones who pay proportionately the most in the 'user pays' society.

A computer may not seem to be a high priority for those confronting daily disadvantage. A low income precludes activities that more affluent groups take for granted such as meals out, sitting in a café or shopping for relaxation and leisure. Isolation encourages gradual erosion of confidence and with it a further withdrawal from society. It has been left to individual organisations, such as churches and social groups, to bridge these analogue and digital gaps. In Kelmscott, Western Australia, the Crossways Community Services group has been running computer courses with state government funding. The First Click and Second Click courses teach computer basics for unemployed women aged 40–54, seniors, youth, people with disabilities, indigenous peoples, citizens from regional areas and those for whom English is a second language.[24] I first contacted the group in April 2005 and asked if participants could complete a voluntary survey into their experience of computer usage. These surveys were returned in April and June of 2005. Responses were by either mail or phone. Interestingly no one completed a questionnaire online. Some preferred to remain anonymous.

My surveys tapped into a special group who were confronting a very specific problem. While the quantitative surveys cited through this chapter categorise non-users into categories, there is a dense need to add history, context and subtlety to these statistics. Researching this First Click community, a group who lack computer-based literacy but demonstrate both the courage and activism to overcome disadvantage, reveals functional strategies in not only labelling and managing the 'e-nots', but understanding and assisting their passage through digitisation. These plucky soon-to-be computer users add incredible insight into digital dissent and online access for this book. They are on a journey to – and through – e-democracy.

The survey (see Figure 2.1) was devised from my own comparatively recent memory of having minimal computer knowledge. I was a complete computer novice when I began my university studies in 2003, and did not own a computer at that time. It was easy for me to empathise with the anxieties of computer novices, such as a fear of 'wrecking' the computer and worrying about 'deleting important matter in error', even calling it 'a glorified adding machine'.[25] The group acknowledged what having some computer knowledge now enabled them to do, such as giving them 'some confidence' or encouraging contact with the younger generation. One felt it had become 'an essential for a business person, as much as a mobile phone'. For many it meant contact with overseas family and friends.

Asked about any negatives with their computer experience, responses varied, including:

- junk e-mail, like all those annoying phone calls;
- often slow and boring to sift through heaps of stuff to find what you want;
- the panic that sets in when something goes wrong;
- repetitive strain injury.

My own experience has shown me while writing this chapter that a lack of computer skills and hardware can hamper communication. For example, Tara Brabazon, the editor of this collection, had made comments on an earlier draft of this chapter. Due to the unsophisticated nature of both my computer software and my own limited knowledge, I was unaware of these questions or queries until a friend I had asked to read the draft told me about the comment boxes on the document, generated through the tracking function of Microsoft Word. In this case, the editor made assumptions about digitised text, software and hardware that was inappropriate for a contributor. There was no intention or malice in this assumption, but it had consequences. Each day, web-literate users make assumptions that they presume are shared and obvious. But like those comment boxes on my Word document, sometimes – through hardware, software or literacy – these assumptions are simply not visible to the inexperienced or excluded.

A general comment from those who completed my survey, and remembering that these were motivated non-users who wished to develop computer literacy, was that they felt a computer was a luxury but was increasingly becoming essential. One stated it was a 'dust catcher' and that they could 'give up tomorrow', but these views were in the minority. The question about internet access drew a similarly mixed response. An organic grower commented, 'It keeps me updated on the latest research in my area. I can access what I need and have no need to download the rest'. This view contrasted with a concern about the danger of website content: 'I have not accessed [the Web because of] stories of what is out there'. An evocative expression of this fear of connectivity was the sense that 'I have just given "someone" the keys to my mind'. Another contributor enjoyed the information and movement through the web: 'my favourite part of usage. I learn about other countries, politically and geographically, I also do historical research'.

The respondents to my survey had two clear interests in using a computer: for work or research. Most used e-mail for quick contact and sharing photos. For others, the ability to research varied topics and find medical information was important. Some used the game-playing options such as solitaire, crosswords and jigsaws. One stated emphatically, 'no personal banking or financial details on line'. Most felt more confident and better able to understand their children or grandchildren. A few commented that they felt closer to their family because of this, rather than left out and ignorant as they had been previously.

No one begins with competency, expertise or knowledge. This develops over time. It is only 'when you can admit you don't know, you are more likely to ask the questions that will enable you to learn'.[26] People – teachers – who are skilled and tactful communicators, need to be employed. Such people are more useful to the digitally inexperienced if they remember the terror of being placed in front of the computer screen for the first time as their fingers and brains froze in incomprehension and terror. Specialised vocabularies are useful and important but do become jargon for those excluded, and a marker of those who belong, disempowering those who do not.

Computer novices require modes and nodes of translation. Greater attention is required on how hardware and software designers 'teach' their product or programming not only to their customers, but also citizens. Such a project is part of what Graham Murdoch confirms is the new definition of citizenship. He states that 'today, the idea of citizenship has broadened to include all of the rights and access to resources which guarantee full membership in a society'.[27] As computer usage and internet communication has been woven into the fabric of our daily lives, it is becoming essential to citizenship and full participation in society. Providing tuition in computer use would benefit companies by ensuring an ongoing flow of additional consumers for their products. Consumerist discourse is framed by what we have, what we can buy, what we possess. For those without the 'right' products and services, their identity – their citizenship – is compromised.

The computer course participants had mixed feelings about the benefits of computers. One stated, 'a computer can be a very overwhelming machine. Everything *must* be done its way'. The most considered response came from Richard:

> Well, it's gadgetry. I feel that it is destroying an aspect of life in the young, as they have become consumed and commodified. Their whole lives are controlled by a specific utensil [the computer] to

seek media entertainment. They are not living life. They seem to have less capacity to enjoy life. No camaraderie, less physical life, less physical contact.

While acknowledging that computer usage was essential to his business, Richard was sorry for the losses he perceived his grandchildren and others experiencing. Their way of life was foreign to him.

Equally, many respondents felt the language of computing was a foreign tongue. The ability to participate was limited by their difficulty in translating this language into their own. Techno-science has discarded them as irrelevant consumers. Forget Marx's restless masses, today we have the restlessly redundant. This digital detritus is of no further use to the system. They are redundant in life as their purchasing power is limited and their ability to gain recognition of their problems is restricted by both their lack of access and their invisibility. Data from a survey

Figure 2.1   **Survey of First Click participants**

I had no knowledge of computers before I enrolled as a mature aged student at university. If you had told me that I had to use the computer all the time, I would probably have given up on my dream right there. I am self-taught and still experience 'the black screen of death' and numerous panics.

Please complete my survey, and express both the positives and negatives that you have experienced with computer usage.

1. How did you feel about computers before you had computer knowledge?

2. What has having computer skills enabled you to do that you could not do before?

3. Are there any negatives to computer use for you?

4. Do you feel that having a computer is essential/a luxury/A toy/very important/not too important/could not do without one now?

5. Do you access the internet and web regularly or do you plan to? How important a part of computer usage is this to you?

6. What is your main interest in having/using a computer?

7. Any other comments?

conducted by the Smith Family's *Learning for Life* programme drew a response rate of 61 per cent.[28] They were disadvantaged school-aged children either from 'low income, lack of English language fluency, low educational attainment and high unemployment'.[29] Unsurprisingly, those from one-parent families generally had less computer and internet access.[30] For the majority of those surveyed, the most likely place to access the internet was at school (67 per cent) compared with using a computer at home (27 per cent).[31] Those who relied on social security were less likely to have a computer at home.[32] These children are doubly disadvantaged and likely to continue to experience life as 'have nots'.

For those without the necessary resources, the future is looking increasingly bleak. Both government and industry validate computers and computer users because of the cost-saving benefits to organisations. Through such assumptions, the technological divide widens. Those off-screen are becoming more disenfranchised, less visible and with no effective 'voice' to be heard. But with ongoing support through successful programmes, they may be able to grab the figurative mouse by the tail and see a future on and through a screen.

Notes

1. Coelho, P. (1993) *The Alchemist*, San Francisco, CA: Harper Collins, p. 59.
2. *The Castle*, directed by Rob Sitch (Working Dog and Village Roadshow Pictures, 1997).
3. Kent, M. (2005) 'The Invisible Empire', PhD thesis, Murdoch University.
4. Australian Bureau of Statistics (1996–2000) *Household Use of Information Technology*, Catalogue Number 8146. 0, Canberra, ACT: ABS.
5. Crump, B. and McIlroy, A. (2003) 'The digital divide', *First Monday* 8(12), available at: *http://www.firstmonday.org/issues/issues8_12/crump* (accessed 27 June 2005).
6. Ibid.
7. McLaren, J. and Zappala, G. (2002) 'The "digital divide" among financially disadvantaged families in Australia', *First Monday* 7(11), available at: *http://www.firstmonday.org/issues/issue7-11/mcclaren* (accessed 11 July 2005).
8. Rainie, L. (2005) 'What people do online. Data for the Congressional Internet Caucus', PEW Internet and American Life Project, available at: *http://www.pewinternet.org/ppt/Stats_Internet_Caucus_2005.pdf* (accessed 10 November 2007); Rainie, L. (2005) '75 Million Americans do not use the internet', PEW Internet and American Life Project, available at: *http://www.pewinternet.org/ppt/Freedom%20to%20Connect%20Conferen ce%20Speech.pdf* (accessed 10 November 2007).
9. Ibid.

10. Ibid.
11. Ibid.
12. Ibid.
13. PEW Internet and American Life Project (2005) 'Data for congressional internet caucus' (accessed 9 January 2005) and 'Digital divide disability', available at: *http://www.pewinternet.org* (accessed 3 March 2005).
14. Australian Bureau of Statistics (2002) 'Measuring Australia's Progress (2002): The Supplementary Commentaries – Communication and Transport', available at: *http://www.abs.gov.au/Ausstats/abs@.nsf/94713ad 445ff1425ca25682000192af2/5338D62935241FCDCA256BDC00122420? opendocument* (accessed 11 November 2007).
15. V. Gowlett, personal communication, 2005.
16. Wurman, R. (2001) *Information Anxiety 2*, Indianapolis, IA: Que Publishing, p. 21.
17. Fox, S. (2006) 'Digital divisions 7', PEW Internet and American Life Project, available at: *http://www.pewinternet.org/pdfs/PIP_Digital_Divisions_Oct_5_2005.pdf* (accessed 11 November 2007).
18. McLaren and Zappala, op. cit.
19. Crump and McIlroy, op. cit.
20. Ibid.
21. Ibid.
22. Mehra, B., Merkel, C. and Peterson Bishop, A. (2004) 'The internet for empowerment of minority and marginalized users', *New Media and Society* 6: 781–802.
23. Aspin, L. (1996) *Focus on Australian Society*, Melbourne: Longman, p. 108.
24. *The Examiner (Armadale edition)* (2005) 'News', *The Examiner (Armadale edition)*, 16 June, p. 4.
25. This and subsequent quotes (unless otherwise indicated) are responses from Crossways First or Second Click course participants.
26. Wurman, op. cit., p. 24.
27. Murdoch, G. (year unknown) 'Information citizenship', available from: *http://www.communications.org.au/cria-Publications/publication id 10 685271229html* (accessed 3 March 2005).
28. McLaren and Zappala, op. cit.
29. Ibid.
30. Ibid.
31. Ibid.
32. Ibid.

3

Wiring God's waiting rooms: the greying of the World Wide Web

Tara Brabazon

The story is densely sad. A 63-year-old man lay dead in a council flat for nearly six years before his remains were found. The fully-clothed body of Kenneth Mann was discovered in June 2004, lying on his bed in Walsall in the West Midlands of the UK. He had not been seen since a hospital visit in 1998. With housing agencies chasing unpaid rent, two living siblings, neighbours and a series of medical professionals who performed an electro-cardiogram on Mann at Manor Hospital and then released him to bed rest, he died without care, compassion or company. Gordon Lishman, the Director General of Age Concern England, could not mask his despair and anger:

> The appalling case of Ken Mann is extreme, distressing and shocking to us all. It is deeply concerning that many older people are isolated and excluded from society. Over 3.5 million older people live alone and many do not have regular visitors or any opportunity to get out of the house. Many vulnerable older people are at risk of simply being forgotten.[1]

Perhaps that is the greatest tragedy of a positive ageing policy. Those men and women who have lived a life and know so much are easily forgotten. Their knowledge, experience, passion and disappointments are lost without record or care. The response from Annie Shepperd, the chief executive of Walsall Council, was compassionate but demonstrated that such a case could happen again:

> Kenneth Mann died alone – friendless and isolated from his family. This is the sad and shocking story of the lonely death of a man

whose life was disintegrating ... The authorities also did not pick up this death and we are deeply sorry that this did not happen.[2]

This Eleanor Rigby effect disturbs policy makers and the citizens they service. To die alone is bad enough. To die alone and not be discovered for six years captures the quiet desperation and social isolation of our supposedly wired age. More attention needs to be placed on a policy to ensure connectivity and community. As family structures morph and urban environments spread, how we age and our expectations of growing older change.

The proportion and number of wired seniors is small. A grey gap punctuates the digital divide. The World Wide Web is not a panacea or salve for the isolation and ruthlessness of the modern age. Ken Mann had far more urgent needs than a Hotmail account. Yet e-mail addresses and the desire to wire those living, dancing, talking and thinking in Walsall and God's waiting rooms around the world provide one more safety net and social safeguard to collectivise the dispersed and dispossessed. Building on Kathryn Locke's discussion of literacy and Sonia Bellhouse's case study of community courses for non-computer users, this chapter investigates how older populations dis/connect from the digital environment. Commencing with international surveys monitoring web users, the study then drills down to regions with a high proportion of older residents, and finally settles within a single household, exploring if and then how seniors use the World Wide Web.[3]

The extraordinary characteristic of research on older people's social, cultural and intellectual lives is that there is so much data about health, income, ethnicity and regional distribution. There is even some information on their internet and computer usage. Yet this material is not linked to the answer of the simplest question: why are older citizens not internet-active? Throughout this chapter, the aim is to balance diverse research materials. The quantitative work from PEW, based in the USA – the most mature web-based environment in the world – is aligned with governmental policy documents, library and local government strategies.[4] While recognising the value of such data, silences remain. Through my work, the aim is to find the voice and views of wired seniors, alongside those who remain invisible through digitisation. These voices are important. Margaret Richardson, C. Kay Weaver and Theodore Zorn, for example, have noted 'significant gaps between the New Zealand Government's identification of the benefits of computing for older people and the benefits identified by older people themselves'.[5] In monitoring this gap, a more subtle and informed understanding of wired and unwired senior citizens can emerge.

Have you got a VD player?

Peter Kay, British comedian and pop ethnographer of the 2000s, uses his family as the basis of his stories. His grandmother in particular is the fount of much humour. Her use of technology is legendary: changing channels with a glasses case, becoming confused when confronted by an answering machine, and not talking while recording from the television because the chatter may be heard on the resultant video. When confronted with the digital replacement for her recorder, she could only respond, 'Have you got a VD player?'[6]

Representations of older people and technology are a hub of humour. Grandads driving cars (way) below the speed limit and grandmothers using video library cards in automatic teller machines (ATMs) are a trigger for a rolling of the eyes and a muffled chuckle. When the Australian government's Department of Health and Ageing released five pictures of seniors using technology, their choices were disturbing. All five featured men, while only two images had women even included in the image. The context for these photographs was also poorly chosen. While women are often associated with consumption and shopping, it was a man photographed using a chip-and-pin device and an ATM. It was as if older women had been displaced of daily functions when using technology – they were invisible. While the accuracy of these representations is debatable, of greater interest is not only their rationale but the outcomes and consequences of this selective iconography for older people when stepping up to the challenges of the new and the digital. The difference in life-expectancies between women and men means that there will always be more female than male seniors in the 65–69 age group, with the disparity increasing as they age. Therefore, senior women are particularly important when discussing web literacies for older citizens as they are the majority of beneficiaries.

Findings from the PEW survey 'Older Americans and the Internet' were reported in March 2004. They confirmed that 22 per cent of Americans 65 years and older used the internet. Such a proportion is not only low when assessed as a self-standing proportion in the most mature e-sector in the world, but particularly when compared with the figures in other age groups: 56 per cent of Americans aged 50–64, 75 per cent of those aged 30–49 years and 77 per cent of those aged 18–29 years are actively online. There are marked characteristics of these digital seniors. They are white, well educated and living on high incomes. There are also some distinct behaviours in these older users. They use e-mail more than their younger counterparts,[7] use instant messaging less, but are just as likely to go online daily.[8] Such immersion in the virtual environment only increases the gulf between the habits and practices of seniors on and offline:

> Most seniors live lives far removed from the Internet, know few people who use e-mail or surf the Web and cannot imagine why they would spend money and time learning how to use a computer. Seniors are also more likely than any other age group to be living with some kind of disability, which could hinder their capacity to get to a computer training centre or read the small type on many websites.[9]

The digital divide, when applied to American citizens over 60 years of age, is at its most overt when compared with other age groups. The services of e-mail and finding information about news, sport, health and government initiatives is of great use for those groups restricted in their physical mobility.

While the proportion remains small, there has been a rapid growth in internet penetration among seniors. When embracing the online environment, seniors are keen: their daily use of the internet demonstrates a saturation of technology and its applications in their life. In 1996, only 2 per cent of Americans aged 65 years or older were online, lifting to 15 per cent in 2000 and 22 per cent in 2004.[10] While this growth is remarkable, it is clear that this age cohort lags behind other groups. The other significant social change, which will become more relevant as this chapter progresses, is that between 2000 and 2004, older women became 50 per cent of the senior web users in the USA, matching the online gender distribution of the rest of the population.[11] While these figures are important, perhaps this growth has now reached its zenith. When assessing non-wired seniors, the results are clear: 'Eight in ten off-line seniors do not think they will ever go online'.[12] This is an important and serious result of the survey. There is a large group of older Americans who – with intent, justification and rationale – have disconnected from the World Wide Web. With consciousness and clarity, they see no use for it in their own lives.

There are profound barriers to their e-entry. This current generation of seniors was not in the workforce when computers became as standard as paperclips. Secondly, through educational or social isolation, they lack peer or family reinforcement to overcome the barriers of confidence, cost and skill to go online.[13] The characteristic of seniors who go online is that a family member encouraged their use. Without family involvement, community centres may fill in the gap but this is simply not as effective in smoothing the transition between analogue and digital lives. Through these challenges, it is clear that disability or vision difficulties remain pivotal in actively blocking the wiring of older citizens, regardless of their location, education or level of family support.

This PEW research is important because it separates the use of computers and the internet. Too often for non-users, all the functions of computer-mediated technologies are clumped together, justifiably creating the sensation of overwhelming and frightening newness. For example, in the 2004 survey, it was found that while 29 per cent of older Americans used a computer, only 22 per cent were online.[14] That means there is a 7 per cent gap between being literate with computers and using a modem. In such a small percentage of seniors who have made the digital leap, there is a proactive need to intervene and assist this group who have already learned so much, but require another skill to add on to their competencies.[15]

The value of this quantitative survey is extraordinary, particularly when moving from the USA and assessing international governmental policy interventions. In the lead-up to the 2005 election, the Blair government released their 'Connecting the UK' digital strategy. The language of this document was problematic. In his foreword with Patricia Hewitt, the then Secretary of State for Trade and Industry, the then Prime Minister offered the following overview:

> We have a range of measures to improve accessibility to technology for the digitally excluded and ease of use for the disabled including giving all learners on basic skills courses an e-mail address.[16]

The problems confronting the excluded generally, and the disabled specifically, require much more intervention than the provision of an e-mail address. Indeed, and as shown by the previous chapter, those groups attending basic skills courses are not the problem, but need to be validated and encouraged for their initiative and desire to learn new skills. The profound policy – and educational – question is how to attract and assist the digitally excluded, particularly senior citizens, to these courses in the first place. The PEW data demonstrate that family members are the greatest influence on wiring seniors. Yet the UK strategy does not provide concrete proposals or initiatives for groups that do not have this familial advantage. Instead, it deploys ambiguous language:

> Government has a clear role in helping to promote and increase public awareness about the internet and harness the economic and social returns in a way that benefits all society.[17]

Such a statement is marinated in third-way ideologies. Government does not initiate, offer leadership or intervene. Instead it 'helps' to 'promote' and 'increase public awareness'. Clearly such language, and the social policy that emerges from it, is not enough to encourage and assist those engrained in analogue modes of communication to take that enormous leap into digitisation. To create a context conducive to building computer and web literacies requires intervention, time, facilities and money. Words like 'helping' and 'awareness' are not actually helping. The focus in this UK document is children and ensuring that they hold the information technology skills in preparation for the workplace. There is also attention to delivering government services online, increasing 'choice, greater personalisation, convenience and flexibility'.[18] There is no sense that – post-Blair – there will be a transformation of this bland language of facilitation into action-oriented, interventionist agendas. The concern is that, as more public services are delivered online, the loss and cost increases for those citizens who are not online. As technological applications become ubiquitous, the consequences on those who are excluded become more serious. This inequity particularly impacts on seniors. Half of all non-users are over 50 years of age.[19]

Some governmental initiatives and interventions have been effective, such as technological assistance for rural and regional areas. In addition, considering the isolation of some older citizens and the role of family members in initiating computer consciousness, online centres have been developed:

> In order to tackle the clear inequality of access to the internet in 1999 we have invested in bringing the internet into every community. There are now over 6,000 UK online centres in the UK – places were [sic] people can access the internet in a safe, secure environment and where they also receive technical support and training. UK online centres have targeted areas where they are likely to have the most impact on inequality – they operate in all 88 Neighbourhood Renewal Areas and in 2,000 deprived wards. Centres are in diverse venues ranging from community centres to libraries, colleges and high street cyber-cafes. 95% of households are within 5 km of a centre and virtually all households in the UK are within 10 km of a UK online or Learn Direct Centre. Independent research has found that 96% of the population is aware of where they can access the internet.[20]

Again, the words 'awareness' and 'access' mask the profound difficulties in assisting those who are not sufficiently computer literate to take the step to switch on their first computer. While providing public centres for internet usage is important, even more significant is mapping and understanding the reasons why some citizens choose not to digitise their lives. The UK report tracks the reasons given for not using the internet, with respondents submitting several of their most relevant explanations. Reasons for not using the internet are given as follows:[21]

- no interest: 46 per cent;
- no connection: 40 per cent;
- lack of knowledge or confidence: 35 per cent.

While the lack of connection – 40 per cent of the sample – can be solved through community centres with classes and internet access, the other two categories of exclusion listed in the survey are far more difficult to address. Consciousness and awareness of online content, with family support facilitating reasons for connectivity, may assist the 'no interest' group. It must also be noted that in recent years the web has been increasingly corporatised, transforming much content into a virtual shopping mall. For the disempowered and poor, who wish to 'use' the web rather than 'consume' on the web, the marketisation of the digital environment remains a barrier.

The group that requires the most initiative and effort in teaching, learning and literacy strategies is the 'lack of knowledge or confidence'. While the report does not map other social variables like age, gender, race and class over such data, all three categories must be monitored when assessing the reasons for senior citizens not entering the web. Focusing on the direct and rapid benefits to be gained in the online environment for seniors may be significant. In a UK survey, 66 per cent of people aged 55 and over who are computer users found it of positive benefit.[22] Certainly there is evidence for this value:

> Online forums can provide a 'lifeline' to people suffering from debilitating conditions, depression and insomnia. For example a symptom of Parkinson's disease is insomnia – the Parkinson's disease online forum attracts a high proportion of visitors at night-time, when other forms of support may not be as readily available.[23]

This forum is valuable not only for sharing information but also the building of social connections during difficult times. Parkinson's disease can shred family relationships, impacting on mobility, language and even the most basic of functions like eating and toilet habits. Asynchronous and synchronous communication provides comfort and advice when it is needed.[24] However, the outreach work that is required to give these groups confidence must confirm that the content is of relevance and the internet gateway is both stable and safe.

An important tactic for seniors is to stress the continuity between the off and online world. They have a lifetime of literacies, competencies, experiences and knowledge. Their lives should be enhanced by digitisation, not erased. Users bring analogue interests to the digital landscape. Yet there are systematic exclusions enacted through the online environment. We still meet older people in our analogue life when buying groceries, in exercise classes, leisure activities and playing sport. But we are far less likely to meet seniors online. The internet is an ageist environment. The screen is a barrier.

All literacies are based on confidence, and that includes web-based literacies. The key recognition to make is that each skill, competency and literacy is based on that which preceded it. Actually, the current generation of senior women has a skill that is frequently underestimated: touch typing. They gained this ability during a period where women were secretaries not managers and in the typing pool rather than the boardroom. This inequality has bestowed a gift: a high-level competency and awareness of a keyboard. Yet when all computer-mediated tasks are compressed into web-literacy, the specific skills that these older women possess are not recognised. There is no functional reason why a woman who has used a typewriter and paper cannot mobilise a keyboard and screen. They require the same base abilities. Working from this realisation, older women can gain computer literacy through an acknowledgment of the abilities they already possess. Once comfortable with the keyboard and screen, online experiences can be added, tethered organically to the abilities they already possess. Instead, women continue to have these skills undermined. For example, Carlo offered advice to Nev:

> Typing slower give you more chance to think anyway. Most of the people I have seen including myself, don't touch type, but just use a couple of awkward fingers that appear to move over the keyboard surface with a movement that looks a bit clunky at first, but it gets better as time goes by ... But it doesn't matter that you type slower, because as I said, many people are slower typists. Doing things on the internet is usually a lot of mouse work at any rate. Though you can use keyboard shortcuts for some things, depending on the browser you're using.[25]

Literacies are based on familiarity. Learning new skills is best tethered to the skills we already hold. Yet the ignorance and depreciation of the time, effort and expertise required for the development of accurate touch typing is sexist and devalues the ability of others. The disrespect of this skill held by older women is also ageist. If policy makers focused on respecting and acknowledging the value of keyboard skills, and demonstrating how this ability makes computer use simpler and faster, then a greater number of older women would go online. Instead, women have seen men get away with two-fingered pecking at a keyboard, pretending that they are typing. By not gaining these literacies themselves, these men are – implicitly – disrespecting typing skills, which are mainly held by women.

Positive ageing is an odd phrase, attempting to reprogram and shift the ideologies and discourses involved in getting older. Too often, these policies focus on the window dressing of representation, rather than dense assessment of the quantitative data to trigger a recognition of the wide-ranging interventions required to make a difference in the social lives of the ageing. In Australia in particular, seniors are talked about, and not to. When reviewing federal and state government policies, technology is used to 'manage' and 'control' the lives of seniors, not to grant them agency to live differently and defiantly. For example, in 'A Guide to the Western Australian Active Ageing Strategy', a goal was established:

> The Active Ageing Strategy promotes policies and programs to encourage employers to attract and benefit from older worker's skills and experiences. It assists employers to retain older workers' skills and experiences. It assists employers to retain older employees through innovative workplace practices, phased retirement and life-long learning. It assists mature employees to maintain and develop their skills and to profit from and contribute to the workplace as they age.[26]

This is a significant and troubling aim. The value of seniors is as 'older workers'.[27] Their right to retire, enjoy leisure, play sport, use government services and gain respect for simply being citizens is outside the definitions of 'active ageing'. The government is imposing masculine truths on these seniors. While half of Western Australian senior men between the ages of 60 and 64 years are in the workforce, only 25 per cent of women the same age are at work.[28] This statistic has significant consequences for computer and internet use. Most people's experience of technology is derived from the paid workforce. Senior women are excluded from this skill base. Most offices have a computer on a desk. For seniors where this wired desk was not available through their working lives, such embedded skills were not easy to develop in the home.

Such home-based technologies are even more difficult to obtain when reviewing the low income level of older citizens. The median weekly income for Western Australian seniors is A$245. Once more, older women are more vulnerable than men. Forty-five per cent of women aged 55–69 years of age have no superannuation, compared with 17 per cent of retired men of the same age.[29] By focusing on seniors as a unified group, there is no recognition that the needs of a 60-year-old married couple are distinct from an 85-year-old widow.[30]

The proportion of seniors in Western Australia can be broken down as follows:[31]

- 60–64 years: 27 per cent;
- 65–69 years: 21 per cent;
- 70–74 years: 19 per cent;
- 75–79 years: 15 per cent;
- 80 years and over: 18 per cent.

When moving from work to health policy, the problems become even more damaging. The Australian Department of Health and Ageing released their 'Interim Report for Clinical IT in Aged Care'. Their goal was to link up aged care services with integrated information technology, to support and improve the collection and access to data, thereby facilitating the support of clinical decisions for the aged.[32] While the goal of improving the flow of information across the health sector is important, the anomaly in this strategy is the non-participation by the senior patients themselves. Within the health discourse, technology is used 'on' old people, not 'by' old people. As long as they are controlled and supervised by employers or doctors in the workplace or in aged care, then policies towards old people are 'positive'. Yet policies involving older people making active decisions about leisure, health or employment are far more difficult to find. There is a clear need for this proactive independent decision making, as demonstrated by a message posted on the seniors.gov.au site:

> I'm a retired male, 69, extremely bored, and interested in hearing your ideas/thoughts/suggestions on ways to fill my days. I like to use my head (although I am not a quick thinker), have rather good

verbal skills, and am a bit of a loner. Reading is all very well, however there must be something more challenging. I have no interest in making anything with my hands. HELP, please.[33]

Instead of addressing the needs and goals of these seniors, researchers spend far too much time with language selection, and not enough time thinking about how to create space and choice for older people. As a case in point, consider the following extract from a Community Services report:

> For policy makers the term 'healthy ageing' was considered appropriate, and while the term 'positive ageing' was viewed as acceptable it was not preferred, and there was no support for replacing the term 'healthy ageing' with 'successful ageing'.[34]

Not only are there age and culturally-specific determinations of meaning, jurisdiction and application of the term 'healthy', but such phrasing once more embeds seniors into the medical discourse. Individuals can rarely class themselves as healthy. Instead empowered institutions bestow that term on others. Such a statement is confirmed when reading the report reviewing healthy ageing research in Australia: 'the need for targeted information to be provided to older persons (of all ages) themselves is self-evident'.[35] Who determines the scale, scope and spread of this 'targeted' information? These data are provided 'to' older persons, not for or from seniors. There is little value given to the words, experience and needs of the aged. Policy is applied – and imposed – on them. There is no feedback, discussion or dialogue between policy makers and policy users. While they remain concerned about whether 'healthy', 'positive' or 'successful' ageing is the correct term, there is no evidence presented from seniors themselves to express not only their needs, but their knowledge. While wishing to reorient perceptions and representations of ageing, the reality and lives of these seniors remain administered by others, not lived and enjoyed by themselves. The goal of technology by governments is to tag the aged electronically, not facilitate the building of community and information sharing which may lead to the development of new ideas, skills and relationships. There is much proactive and important work to accomplish, providing the facilities, literacies and space for different seniors to live lives in different ways.

The Australian senior population exhibits different patterns of distribution in computer and internet use when compared with the USA and UK. While 50 per cent of online seniors in the USA are women, in

Australia the age divide is also a gendered divide. In all age categories, senior Australian men are more likely to use computers and the internet when compared with senior women (see Table 3.1). However, a social variable not considered within these tables, and with clear reason, is indigeneity. The life-expectancy at birth for indigenous Australians is nearly 20 years less than for non-indigenous peoples. Indigenous men, on average, live to 56. Indigenous women live to 63. This is startling, particularly when compared with the life-expectancy figures of 77 years of age for non-indigenous men and 83 for non-indigenous women.[36] There are profound social justice issues to be addressed for indigenous seniors beyond computer usage. Yet, this suite of statistics renders Australian seniors different from their American counterparts. Older Australian women face particular disadvantages. Nonetheless, the pattern in all the international data is the younger the senior, the more likely they are to be online.

The major reasons seniors give for not using the computer is because they see no need for it, the start-up costs are too high, or they are not interested in the services it provides.[37] As we get older, there is an increased chance of us living alone because of the death, illness and disability of a partner. Almost one-quarter of all Western Australian seniors live alone. The need – in some way – to connect these citizens not only to services but to each other remains an imperative. The infantalisation of seniors, the assumptions of dementia, sickness, limited

Table 3.1   Computer and internet usage by seniors

Age group	Male (%)	Female (%)
Computer usage		
60–64 years	29	23
65–74 years	19	12
75 years and over	9	4
Total seniors usage	19	12
Internet usage		
60–64 years	25	17
65–74 years	13	7
75 years and over	5	2
Total seniors usage	14	7

Source: Perth Department of Community Development (2004) 'A profile of Western Australian seniors', Topic Sheet No. 4.

mobility and stupidity punctuate policies. In moving from national policies and the quantitative data from PEW, it is important to assess the goals of local governments and community organisations within those areas populated by seniors. It is here that the citizens within God's waiting rooms start to be heard.

Regional, creative, but (not) old

American studies show that older citizens are much less likely to be online than the rest of the population and also less likely to be motivated to move to the digital environment. Urban users are also greater in number than rural users. Significantly, offline men are more likely than offline women to be confident that they will eventually be wired.[38] Internet penetration is also uneven, differentiating by region, age, education and income. The PEW studies show that in rural and regional areas, internet access and use is far lower. Particularly the southern states – Louisiana, Mississippi, Tennessee, Alabama, Arkansas and Kentucky – are the regions that show the lowest level of internet penetration among adults.[39] Obviously, considering the geographical expanse of both the USA and Australia, regional areas are less wired than urbanised areas. These problems are less serious in the UK because of the nation's size and geography. Getting broadband to Roebourne or Emerald in northern Australia is far more difficult than spreading the connection to Preston or Blackpool in northern England. When assessing policies in the UK and Australia, seniors are valuable when working or are compliantly manageable within healthcare. This section of the chapter drills down from national policy, focusing on two regions known for their senior citizens: Mandurah in Western Australia and Eastbourne in East Sussex in the UK.

Mandurah is a coastal city with azure waters, chalk-white sand and a Mediterranean climate. It is a place of fishing, crabbing, swimming, surfing and recreational cruising. Time moves more slowly. Leisure is embedded in daily life. Mandurah is located 72 kilometres south of Perth, the capital city of the largest state in Australia. Granted city status in April 1990, a local government authority serves 54,000 residents. This number has boomed through the last decade, increasing 67.7 per cent between 1991 and 2001.[40] There are no figures in Mandurah for the proportion of seniors who were born overseas, but the state-wide figures provide an indication. Derived from the 2001 Census of Population and

Housing, 41 per cent of Western Australian seniors were born overseas. This is the highest proportion of overseas-born seniors in all the Australian states. Table 3.2 presents the origin of overseas-born seniors in Western Australia.

Besides the 41 per cent of seniors in Western Australia having been born overseas, 60 per cent of seniors had one or both parents born overseas. This means there is a connective tissue linking the lives of older Western Australians with the rest of the world. The advantages of asynchronous communication, particularly e-mail, in initiating and continuing these familial relationships are important. David Morley's research in home-based media found that first-generation immigrant women are particularly reliant on and engaged with satellite and cable broadcasting from their country of origin.[41] In this way, isolation in the home is palliated through televisual transcendence into alternative and mediated geographies. Obviously, this capacity is increased through e-mail and instant messaging.

Table 3.2   Origin of overseas-born seniors in Western Australia, 2001

Place of origin	(%)
United Kingdom	49
Italy	11
Netherlands	4
India	3
New Zealand	3
Germany	3
Poland	2
Ireland	2
Malaysia	2
South Africa	1
Myanmar	1
Federal Republic of China	1
Singapore	1
Birthplace not stated	7
Born overseas, but place not precisely described	10

Source: Perth Department of Community Development (2003) 'Western Australia's Seniors', Topic Sheet No. 2 (2nd edn).

One user of seniors.gov.au writes:

> I love my computer, I belong to four groups that are with MSN, one group is called 'Poms Down Under', we are all here in Australia originally from the UK, it is a fun group, and we are more or less the same age.[42]

The sense of geographical distance is shrunk through technological proximity. Yet this group who could most gain from virtual movement, particularly through the geographical isolation of Australia, does not have the literacy or infrastructure to use this capacity.

Mandurah is a city of retirement, a tourist destination and holiday town. It has recreational and sport facilities, cultural centres and public halls. It is a place where leisure and lifestyle are marketable commodities. Mandurah also has the highest proportion of seniors in all Western Australian localities. While, by the June 2001 figures, people aged 60 and over comprised 15 per cent of the general population, in Mandurah, the equivalent proportion was 24 per cent.[43] Mandurah's population over 65 years of age was 17.6 per cent.[44] Like all new cities conscious of its image, slogans try to name and brand the place. One of the more awkward was 'a regional city reflecting community values'.[45] Perhaps of most interest is the title of the current Community Charter and Strategic Plan: 'Mandurah Vibrant City: Innovative – Creative – Diverse'.[46] Even though Richard Florida has never visited this regional hub, his ideas certainly have. The remaking of Mandurah as a creative city, with rapid growth and an industry base, is peppered by phrases like 'innovation and partnerships', 'vibrant and sustainable community', and 'trust, vision and creativity'.[47] Florida's ideology of cities naturally conflates youth, diversity, creativity and excitement. Obviously such connections and affiliations are ageist, but do offer an explanation of why the age profile of Mandurah is not mentioned in the Strategic Plan. 'Diversity' is noted, but it is a word that is imprecise in its meaning and clouded in interpretation.

What is unstated is frequently more important than that which is stressed and publicised. The notion that Mandurah's age profile may chip away the creativity of the city remains a lasting impression of this document. In this plan, learning is encouraged beyond the limits of formal educational institutions.[48] Such an affirmation is important in Western Australia. Six per cent of seniors are currently studying in a formal institution. Yet the enthusiasm for learning is strong. A fact sheet from the Western Australian government reported that 'a large proportion (88 per cent) of seniors stated they were studying but gave no further description on the type of institution they were enrolled at'.[49] While it is difficult to determine where these seniors are undertaking their education, many may be attending community centres, University of the Third Age or senior citizens' organisations. Win reported how and where she gained computer and internet literacy:

> Win didn't take up the computer until her early seventies. As a volunteer she needed the skills for her work so she undertook a course for the 'mortally terrified' run by Council of the Ageing WA and hasn't looked back since. Ten years later Win is regularly online sending e-mails to friends and families overseas, buying products and using tutorials to increase her skills. Her latest challenge is to master Adobe Photoshop so that she can tweak photos for a family history she is writing. 'The internet really stretches my creative abilities, it is a stimulating hobby and there is always something new to learn.'[50]

Win's story is inspirational, but unusual. Her use of the word 'creative' to describe her deployment of the digital environment should be noted and applauded. Of interest to my current study is that the 2001 Australian census, for the first time, recorded the population's use of personal computers in the home, revealing results by age. Mandurah's results show how the PEW results in the USA are not matched in contemporary Australia. According to the data, only 38.1 per cent of the total population of Mandurah – at any age – had used personal computers in the home. This proportion was then split into age categories:

- 1–19 years: 14.0 per cent;
- 20–44 years: 13.1 per cent;
- 45–64 years: 8.6 per cent;
- 65 years and over: 2.4 per cent.

Pivotally, the census data recorded computer, not internet, use. In reading such figures, senior computer users are a minority of a minority. In addition, because of the data collection method, the '65 and over' category was not further specified in terms of those between 65 and 84, and 85 and over. With such a large proportion of Mandurah's population in these categories, the data would have been significant.

Before Mandurah tried to brand itself as 'Creative', it used the slogan of 'WA's leading education city'.[51] The focus was on social cohesion, economic regeneration and development. Mandurah became a Regional Education City. Focusing on diverse educational initiatives from books for babies through to the University of the Third Age, learning was the policy focus. It was a way to recognise the strategies commenced in the Regional Australia Summit in 1999, to build networks of learning between business, education, local government and community sectors. There was a focus on particular groups in the Mandurah community:

> Young and older people will particularly feel the benefits of lifelong learning. Older people are a vital link in the learning chain due to wealth of experience. Young people become informed from a very early age at school about the post-compulsory and beyond education and training opportunities that are available and the benefits of expanding their learning horizons.[52]

Within this learning community document, there was a recognition that the lack of employment and industrial sector was reducing the potential for growth. When the next strategic plan was written, the focus moved from learning to creativity.

The Chief Executive Officer of the City of Mandurah, Mark Newman, was both forthcoming and open in his presentation of the goals and initiatives for his region. I asked him about the challenges Mandurah may face.

> TB: What specific policy and planning challenges do you believe will confront the City of Mandurah in the next 5–10 years?
>
> MN: Employment creation, including quality jobs, pathways from school to training and employment, and proactively managing the issues associated with Australia's emerging skills shortage are all in the local strategic focus.[53]

The sheer growth in population in Mandurah makes the residents difficult to administer. Newman noted that 'some 30 new families [are] moving in to Mandurah every week'. Intriguingly, Mr Newman did not mention the older citizens of the city without my direct questions about the cohort.

> TB: Are there specific issues that need to be addressed by local government because of Mandurah's relatively high proportion of senior citizens?
>
> MN: While – in our view – the prime responsibility for facilities and programs for meeting the ageing demographic lies with the Australian and state governments, Council will play an increasing role in matters such as disability access, fitness and diet and

associated wellness in a population health context, and in its urban planning process – endeavoring to persuade developers and aged care providers that aged accommodation should be considered in the wider community planning context, rather than in 'gated', purpose-built villages and the like.

To carry his metaphor to the digital environment, it is obvious that the internet is a gated community, with seniors isolated on the other side of the e-wall. I then asked the Chief Executive Officer about the specific policies Mandurah has in place for the development of senior web literacies.

MN: While Council has not necessarily seen a direct role in ensuring that seniors have access to the internet and/or the literacies required, this is part of the Learning Community objectives – not only for seniors, but for the wider community. Our Library services and Senior Citizens Centre activities reflect this, with the addition of a computer room in the Centre and a variety of programs from both facilities including 'First Click' programs and the like. Interestingly, a recent survey of Senior Citizens Centre members indicated that only some 20 per cent utilized the computer room facility. Forty per cent indicated they were not interested, and 20 per cent indicated they were too busy with other activities, together with a variety of other reasons including those who had access to computers at home.

Lacking this 'direct role', Mr Newman still reported interest in why only 20 per cent of the senior citizens who actually use the centre utilise the computer facilities. As more materials are only available online, particularly for health, education and transportation, this 20 per cent level becomes significant. These are proactive older citizens – the joiners. They have left their home and joined a community. Yet only one-fifth of this group uses the room. Therefore, to increase the wiring of seniors needs more than a computer facility. New strategies and programmes for teaching and learning are required.

Access is only part of the problem. There are also infrastructural challenges confronting those Mandurah residents trying to connect their home computer to the internet. The broadband rollout has been slow and patchy. Mandurah is not alone in this infrastructural absence:

In a national review carried out by the Commonwealth Government it was identified that of the Regional Telecommunication Services and Telecentres Network, only 22 per cent of the sites overall had access to ADSL. Of that national average, Western Australia represented the smallest percentage of 13 per cent.[54]

If seniors need to be convinced of the value of online content, then broadband is a necessary service to improve the availability to integrated mixed-media digital platforms. Yet Australia, because of its size and geographical challenges, has failed to ride the momentum of broadband rollout. Regional and rural Australia has been left behind in high-speed internet readiness. This problem not only affects seniors. But for a group that needs to be convinced of the value of online materials, broadband is pivotal to improve the content that is available to access.

Local and federal governments have not been proactive and interventionist in their respect and care for the full life and experiences of senior citizens. When they are sick, health services are available. To mask the lack of superannuation in these older populations, there is a 'positive ageing' strategy to keep them in the workforce. Still, the city of Mandurah has managed its older population quite well. The Mandurah City Senior Citizens Centre, opened in 1990, is run by seniors and for seniors. A range of activities and services is available, from bootscotting to yoga, from legal advice to hairdressing. Significantly, on 4 July 2002, the computer room was opened, providing classes with qualified tutors. Yet it remains a minority interest. How and why this facility is used by few senior citizens needs to be explored.

For older immigrants, content and language is relevant. The importance of gaining sports results, international news and reading online newspapers adds value to the web for seniors in particular. For women, e-mail is important. As a 2005 report acknowledged:

> People use e-mail to deepen their connection to the people they like and love and increase the volume of communication they have with them. E-mail users, especially women, feel they are working on relationships and tending to their social networks as they exchange e-mail.[55]

The Mandurah case study reveals both the strengths and problems with a local government stressing learning and creativity in strategic plans, providing the computer rooms but not exploring what other interventions and solutions may be required. The value of e-mail for senior women must be stressed. It may not be 'creative' and is a basic function of the internet, but it remains 'the killer app' – the breakthrough application that (often surprisingly) transforms a minor innovation into a major intervention. Furthermore, broadband is not required for e-mail to operate effectively. In this regard, the key comparison to Mandurah is Eastbourne in East Sussex in the UK. Eastbourne's population is 89,667, of which 12,499 are aged 75 and over. Eastbourne provides a snapshot of Mandurah's future, and the lessons to learn in terms of library services and the transformations of a city when it ages.

Table 3.3 shows the senior population of Eastbourne by age group. Unlike the population of seniors in Western Australia, where a sizeable proportion are born overseas, the overwhelming majority of UK seniors are born in the country of residence. Eastbourne has a much longer and more established history than Mandurah. An elegant resort town located at the foot of the South Downs in Sussex, it is a gothic God's waiting room. There has been no rapid and recent growth which serves to place excessive demands on services. The Eastbourne Seniors Club was founded in 1954. It features activities from darts to crafts but also daily computer classes. Their website confirms that 'Eastbourne Seniors Club specialises in tuition for older people and teaches a wide range of skills on various software'.[56] Computer access is available between 9:30am and 4:30pm weekdays, charging 50p per hour for use of a computer and £1.50 for the first 30 minutes of internet usage, with 50p for each subsequent 30 minutes. The daily computer classes remain invaluable, placing the digital environment within the context of other more familiar analogue activities.[57] Educational activities and the development of skills are placed in the context of leisure, not work. Quality of life becomes the imperative. In such an environment, computer skills and the internet are embedded into the life of seniors,[58] offering new opportunities that

Table 3.3	Eastbourne senior population by age group

Age group	Number	Percentage
0–59	62,915	70.2
60–64	4,584	5.1
65–69	4,665	5.2
70–74	5,054	5.6
75–79	4,748	5.3
80–84	3,743	4.2
85–89	2,465	2.7
90 and over	1,493	1.7

Source: 'Census 2001 – Profiles – Eastbourne', available at: http://www.statistics.gov.uk/census2001/profiles/21uc.asp.

are tethered to their already existing needs and goals. Similarly, the local education and library services are delivered by the East Sussex County Council, showing a smooth level of integration between these facilities and institutions. Through this synergy, lifelong learning is not only a cliché, but a realisable initiative. In Mandurah, indeed in Australia more generally, there is a separation of universities, which are administered at federal level, primary and high schools, which are administered at state level, and libraries, which are the responsibility of local governments.

The difficulty with providing knowledge and assistance to senior web users in Eastbourne is a question of resourcing. Sally Parsons, a librarian in Eastbourne, explained the areas of highest demand:

> We also have a heavy demand for large print and spoken word resources and housebound services. Internet-wise we have a demand from customers for help with enquiries and accessing the internet where they lack IT skills. This can be time consuming in a single staffed reference department. We have also had some IT problems with the initial installation of internet based catalogues for the library service, and self reservation, but the bulk of customers pick it up very quickly – possibly quicker than younger people who have not so much leisure to visit and learn.[59]

The Eastbourne library system is not a service provider for computer classes. The Sussex Careers Service, run by the County Council, runs free and small-fee courses for eight weeks. They use the People's Network computers in Eastbourne Central Library and the Polegate branch, including 38 terminals. Most of the participants in this service are seniors. These graduates then return to the library with increased computer skills. I asked Parsons about the web literacy of the senior men and women she sees in Eastbourne's library.

> TB: A survey of American internet users found that older women in rural and regional areas are excluded from World Wide Web usage. Have you seen this problem emerging in Eastbourne?
>
> SP: Our older ladies seem well able to access the technology if they have any wish to do so. I think it is a choice issue, not a capability one, as most of our seniors fall into the well-educated bracket and are busy with all sorts of pursuits, not just IT.
>
> TB: Who are the most regular senior users of the library – older men or older women?

SP: In lending, women, but I would say it is about 60 per cent to 40 per cent and lots of them take material for their husbands. In the reference department, it is about 85 per cent male, 15 per cent female – reading papers, checking answers to questions of fact, or looking up companies to complain about things!

TB: Do men and women approach the library, the web-based catalogue and web-based searching differently? Do you have to mobilize specific strategies to assist older men and women in developing internet-based literacies?

SP: Men complain it's not working or it doesn't do what they want and make the staff help them. Women quietly get on with it or ask the staff anyway rather than use the catalogue. (I think this is just the usual difference of the sexes.) It may be the men do use the system more, or they just make more fuss when doing it.

I was also particularly interested in how libraries address issues of mobility for senior citizens, and their proactivity in ensuring that services continue through social or physical isolation.

TB: Are there groups who do not come into the library? For example, do you see many senior citizens who speak English as a second language? What about those with mobility issues? What about senior citizens who have lost a spouse? Do husbands and wives go to the library together?

SP: Certain minority ethnic groups do not use us so much – but we have a very small minority ethnic base here. We see few of the Chinese or female Asian community. We do see a fair number of East European seniors – they are often practising English reading via the children's stock. Mobility issues are addressed by a volunteer scheme or a housebound book box service to homes – we have reduced the use of the mobile library to town locations, although this was a successful service, because of resource cutbacks. Husbands and wives do visit us together in the majority of cases. Widows and widowers use us just as much as before, or maybe more, if they were regular users, because they read more and seem to enjoy the contact with familiar staff.

The web and print facilities of the Eastbourne library are fully used. Resourcing could improve their service for groups confronting immobility through health or social isolation. As Eastbourne is a resort town, Parsons reported a remarkable change in the pattern of internet usage in the library during summer months.

> SP: Eastbourne has a huge use by non-British summer visitors wishing to contact home or use enquiry facilities in their own language. Internet access is essential for them and we have 29 terminals fully booked 60 hours a week, with about 80 per cent non-resident usage. It may be that we get used by those who would feel an internet café is well out of their comfort zone, and I guess these may be older residents, especially women.

This prompts the question as to what happens to the residents' internet use during the tourist high season? That tourists use the library to check their e-mails seems a curious notion, and does not seem effective or efficient for those who have made their lives in Eastbourne on a permanent basis.

Finally, in the context of this chapter, I asked Sally Parsons about how her purchasing and policy decisions would change if resourcing was not a concern.

> TB: If money was not an issue, what services would you provide in the library for Eastbourne's senior citizens?
>
> SP: More spoken word material, increased housebound service, weekly mobile library service to outlying parts of the town or reopen the town branches for local communities (both with internet facility aboard to bring it to those who want it), regular internet services with trained staff to help with enquiries, better browsing areas with seating to improve their book selecting experience, and more copies of the books they want, more bookstock generally. This is what we get asked for all the time, never mind the internet!

Her answer demonstrates that with all the attention to lifelong learning and positive ageing, the most basic of facilities and improvements are still required. Spoken word books, a mobile library service, seating and more books are easy analogue additions to a library, but require funding. Until these basic facilities are provided, web facilities and literacies must remain an afterthought. Conversely, an internet-based solution – of e-books that can be augmented for different visual capabilities and audio-streaming of MP3-based spoken word materials on portable listening devices such as the iPod – may also provide options.

Confirming Parson's argument and views, Tim Coates has diagnosed wider problems in British libraries:

> There is a simple reason why libraries have declined over the past two decades while bookselling has boomed. Anxious to be accommodating, accessible and inclusive in an age where high standards of design are to be seen in every public building, both librarians and booksellers need to find a way to make their premises cheerful and welcoming. Their responses are instructive. Booksellers invented the Borders style: large, bright, comfortable shops with a wide range of stock on a huge variety of subjects but with places to sit and feel at home. It was a realization that a dusty collection of old books in dark premises can be forbidding. Librarians, meanwhile, decided to reduce the emphasis on books ... senior managers became enthralled by computers. They anticipated that all information could be organized in an accessible way. Not only was the electronic future technically innovative but it was also attractive to young people. Computers were introduced to libraries and book collections were allowed to fall into neglect. As a consequence, demand dwindled.[60]

'Learning community' is a phrase tethered to the development of the knowledge economy and creative industries. Through these changes in rhetoric, public libraries quietly maintain their role in building education programmes for active citizenship and community development, along with employability and economic benefits. Charles Leadbeater, for example, wished to stress the role of libraries as part of a social network. He suggested that libraries should be based in shopping centres to combine learning and leisure.[61] Before reaching this goal, much greater attention and funding is required for libraries. A learning community without a well-funded library is like a shark tank with dolphins: it is interesting, but misses the point.

Eastbourne and Mandurah, with a high proportion of seniors, do not recognise them or value them as much as they should. As a social fact, it should be stated overtly that the proportion of senior citizens in these cities is high. Currently, it is not part of the integrated city imaging framework or strategic plans, because it may harm the claims for creativity and innovation. Obviously, this is ageism.[62] In economic terms, this ageism is blocking a proactive recognition of the value in digitising leisure and lifelong learning. Education, learning and textured literacy environments for the post-work population are sites of future commercial opportunities. The final part of this chapter moves from local governments and greying regions to the wiring of a single household.

I clean around it

> Tara Brabazon: Is Kevin's office part of your home?
>
> Doris Brabazon: Yes, I make sure that it's clean and tidy.
>
> TB: So you clean the computer, you don't use it?
>
> DB: I don't clean the computer. I clean around it.

David Morley commenced his *Home Territories* with the story of his mother, repeating her reprimand that, as he left for university at 18, he had little understanding of any home.[63] It seems an effective homage to Morley to conclude this study of the greying web by returning to my parental home. My interest in this topic actually commenced while monitoring the remarkable division of e-literacies between my parents. The social consequences of this division capture all the structural fears, policy dilemmas and problems raised throughout this research. While we commenced this chapter with national studies and continued with a regional emphasis, the study concludes with a single home in Mandurah.

Doris and Kevin Brabazon were married in Broome, a regional pearling hub in the northwest of Western Australia, in 1950. A son was born in 1954, and a daughter in 1969. I did not move out of the family home until 1994, and only then because I was leaving the country for my first academic appointment in Aotearoa, New Zealand. In other words, my parents have been raising children for 40 years and we liked them (and their homes) so much that we stayed (too long). There are only two houses that have been acquired for their own needs and purposes. Their first shack, rather than home, was in Broome, with a veranda sleep-out and old boiler hens scratching around the red dust. The following 14 homes were all purchased and organised with children in mind, children who never seemed to leave. They sold that final family home in 2001, and moved to Mandurah, God's waiting room. They bought a house without stairs to assist mobility as they aged. They could use all the rooms for their own purposes, without decorating them the Abbaesque taste of their son or pseudo-Gothic fixations of their daughter. What is interesting to me, in light of the research enacted in this chapter, is how these late 70-somethings have managed not only digitisation and the World Wide Web, but the divisions of labour and power in their home. As both a physical outsider to their current home and familial insider, I observed how the digital divide operates within a household run and lived in by seniors and for seniors, and applied the quantitative and policy analyses discussed in this chapter to a single domicile. I interviewed Kevin and Doris separately but on the same day. I asked them the same questions, recorded on the same iPod, but in the rooms in which they are the most comfortable. Doris was interviewed in the kitchen. Kevin was interviewed in his 'computer room'. These spaces are important to both of them, and are significant to their comprehensions of technology.

Doris was fascinating to interview. Like so many women, she believed at the start of the interview that she had nothing to offer in the way of information for the project. Her answers were short at the start, but gained confidence as the process progressed. From the first question, she offers a remarkably clear realisation of why women doubt their skills in technology.

> TB: When I say the word 'technology', what sort of image or idea appears in your head?
>
> DB: Computers and televisions and phones. Everything that is electronic.
>
> TB: Interesting definition. Let's look around your kitchen. Do you see technology?
>
> DB: No not really.
>
> TB: Is the microwave technology?
>
> DB: No.
>
> TB: Is the refrigerator technology?
>
> DB: Not really.
>
> TB: Are they electronic?
>
> DB: Yes.
>
> TB But you don't see those as technology?
>
> DB: No.
>
> TB: Do you see a car as technology?
>
> DB: No.
>
> TB: Isn't that interesting. I wonder why that is?
>
> DB: It is just ordinary. Ordinary people manage that rubbish.
>
> TB: So I'll repeat this back to you. If ordinary people can use it, then it is not technology, but if it requires special skill, then that's technology.
>
> DB: Yes. Yes.

Figure 3.1 **Microwaving change**

This was the complex response to the first question. I thought it would be an easy one. Instead, her answers revealed how she was becoming trapped and limited by her own definitions of technology. While she manages technology every day, these appliances are not included in her definition.

The great advantage of oral history, particularly with disenfranchised groups such as senior citizens and women, is that they can be probed in greater detail, and their answers qualified. Doris, after being questioned about the contradiction in her own definition of household items being both 'electronic' and yet 'not technology', realised that the label of technology was not invested in the item, but in the literacy of the user. What I found remarkable when probing Doris's definitions of technology is that she continually underplayed her own skill, and overestimated the ability of others.

> TB: Can I be controversial and suggest that you think technology is that which requires skills that you don't have?
>
> DB: Yes. That's absolutely right. I never get involved until I've got the knowledge to back me up.
>
> TB: You've mentioned knowledge a lot so far. Do you feel like you've not got the knowledge?
>
> DB: No. No. Not at this point, anyway.

For Doris, technology is not the object, but the skills necessary to use the object. She uses two microwaves and two refrigerators. She manages a reticulation system that would trouble most landscape gardeners. Yet she continually normalised and discredited her own ability with domestic technology, to render those with computer-based literacies far beyond her expertise. Within her words is the explanation for why only 20 per cent of senior citizens use the computer room in Mandurah. Access to the technology is not enough. Confidence, knowledge, skills and literacy are the key. On the Australian government site – seniors.gov.au – already wired older users ask each other how to improve their online knowledge. One online contributor, McGuiries asks:

> How did you learn to work with digital pictures on your computer? Trial and error; self taught (ie trials and error plus additional info). Do you think a 'how to do it' course of a few lessons written by a retired person for other retired people might be helpful?[64]

McGuiries offers a range of possibilities to build web literacies for older citizens. Yet he offers opportunities for those who have already taken the first steps online. Those who are yet to wire their world are not able to read his words, or take up his options.

One of my favourite research tasks is to ask those who have never used a particular technological application – the World Wide Web, iPods or a DVD – what they actually think the object does.

> TB: What is a computer?
>
> DB: It is something that works faster than if you were writing it all by hand. It gives you information that would take you ages to get out of books.
>
> TB: So you think it is like a typewriter that works faster?
>
> DB: More. More. It's got a library.

For Doris, it was the speed that was fascinating. As an outsider, it was the rapidity of the typing that interested her and the notion that there is a body of information – which she termed a library – available. Importantly, she used older technologies, such as pen and paper, and older institutions like libraries, to explain the definition of these new innovations and applications. While Doris was very quick to determine the relationships between old and new media, she very sharply decried her capacity to use this fast typewriter with a library attached.

TB: Do you use a computer?

DB: No.

TB: Why not?

DB: I haven't any knowledge to use it. I haven't got the knowledge.

TB: Very honest answer. Does that worry you that you don't have the knowledge?

DB: Does a bit. Does a bit.

Access to a computer is not Doris's problem. There is one in the house. Her concern is that she lacks 'the knowledge' or the literacy to handle the object. The repetition of phrases in this interview extract is significant. The tone of her voice conveyed concern, like there was something important going on and she felt like she lacked confidence and skills that she required to be part of it. Her repetitive use of the word 'knowledge' throughout the interview is important. This focus aligns with her definition of technology as being much more than what 'ordinary people' (like her) can use.

TB: I'll probe you a bit more. Why does it worry you?

DB: Well if anything happened to Kevin, I'd be unable to get into my bank account...

TB: You're reasonably isolated here, living in Mandurah, a long distance from Perth, a long distance from me.

DB: But the computer keeps you in touch...

TB: So explain it to me. Your husband, my father, runs the banking, the insurance, the household accounts on the computer.

DB: Yes. But I run everything that does not involve the computer.

TB: But he runs the finances?

DB: With my approval.

TB: If anything happened to Kevin what would you do?

DB: I'd learn. I'd have lessons.

TB: Would you be frightened of doing that?

DB: No. No.

TB: The question is then, why haven't you done that already?

DB: Because I haven't had the opportunity. He doesn't care if I know about it or not.

TB: Why is that?

DB: I don't know. I think he likes to be in charge and the computer is his life and he doesn't like anyone hopping in ... It's the money that worries me. If it was a different time, it would all be on paper. But now it's on the computer, and I don't know anything about it. The knowledge is there. If I didn't have him, I'd have the knowledge.

A strong example of digital codependency has been forged here. She justifies her lack of computer knowledge with the rationale that 'he likes to be in charge' and without him, she would learn. She also believes that Kevin does not care about her lack of literacy. While his interview revealed that the opposite is true, there are myriad structural barriers in the house to facilitating Doris's disengagement with the computer, as it is located at the furthest point away from the kitchen.

The greatest challenge for those who do not possess literacies is to create structures and methods to show them how these skills could be obtained, and how they would slot into their current life. Throughout the interview, Doris offered different options.

TB: How would you assess your skill level with computers right now?

DB: Nil.

TB: How would you – how would you – improve those skills?

DB: I would get a tutor in.

Figure 3.2   Domesticating technology

TB: You would get someone into the house?

DB: Yes.

TB: Would you leave the house – for example the Mandurah Library puts on a programme – would you go?

DB: Too right. Yep, I'd go.

TB: So you would use that opportunity if it was available.

DB: Yes, definitely.

TB: And then you'd be able to go into his computer...

DB: ...his territory

TB: and use it.

Her correction of me is significant. Not only does she see the computer as owned by Kevin, but that it is in a space that he has also claimed: *his* computer room. She spatialises technology. It is, in her words 'his territory'. Therefore Doris's problem is not an issue of technology and access, but space and power.

While concerned about her lack of access to financial records, there are few motivations to encourage her jump over the digital divide.

TB: Do you think you need to understand computers to live a full life?

DB: No. No. I don't think they come into lifestyle at all.

TB: You don't think they improve lifestyle?

DB: No. Perhaps they do the reverse. I really do. There are more things in life than computers.

TB: Are you frightened of new things?

DB: No, I love new things.

TB: Can you use the mobile phone?

DB: (pause) No. Not really. Not really.

TB: Does that worry you?

DB: No. I could put it in the bin.

TB: Would you like to learn how to use the mobile phone?

DB: No.

This is significant. She – in reality – believes that computers and mobile telephones interrupt her life. She does not believe that her life would be improved through their use. Other media in which she is already literate allow her access to the world.

> TB: What about television? Is that invasive of your privacy?
>
> DB: No, I love television. I love to watch what I want to watch.
>
> TB: What do you get out of television?
>
> DB: Everything that's going on in the world.
>
> TB: You listen to radio too?
>
> DB: Yes, all night. It keeps me informed about what's going on in the world.

Doris is probably not sufficiently motivated to use a computer. She gains enough connectivity from television and radio. Only the online banking and disconnection with family finances worries her.

Intriguingly, she is technologically-savvy when she wants to be. I made this realisation when Kevin installed a new home entertainment centre that required the use of six remote controls. He even built them their own box (Figure 3.3).

This was a disaster of a 'system'. It took at least five minutes to set up the system to get a picture. I still find it incredibly difficult to work the multiple

Figure 3.3 The complexity of access

remotes. But Doris wanted to watch television. So within two weeks, and while Kevin was down in the computer room and not answering her pleas about how to work the system, Doris learned how to operate the television on her own. It was not using his method, but she got the system working. She was motivated, and she was not prepared to wait for him to organise her viewing. As she stated of television, 'I love to watch what I want to watch', and she is prepared to negotiate any obstacle to do so.

By the end of the interview, the specific barriers blocking her access and literacy in computers and the internet were obvious.

TB: Would you leave the house to do a computer class?

DB: I would after I had the knowledge of someone teaching me about the computer. I'd want someone to come in and teach me everything and I'd write it all down as he went. I'd need to know exactly what I was doing.

Figure 3.4   Technology in the lounge room

TB: Even though the class at the library is titled 'Introduction to the internet'?

DB: That wouldn't worry me. But I'd want my knowledge in the first place.

TB: So if you were the Mayor of Mandurah, it is not only classes at the library that would matter, but a mobile tutor service may actually give people literacy.

DB: Yep.

While, in an earlier question, she stated that she would go to classes, it became obvious that her lack of 'knowledge' is actually a lack of confidence. Without confidence, she would not attend a class to help her gain that 'knowledge'. By the time she had that knowledge, she would not need the internet class anyway. Her revelation demonstrates that for this group of computer avoiders, public classes may not be the answer to this problem. Motivation and confidence are required. Doris has managed six remote controls that are far more complex than Google. Yet she is reticent to connect her existing skills in typing and screens with a keyboard and technology to other applications.

There are reasons for this reticence and some of them involve her husband. Kevin is not only computer or web-literate: he is positively pioneering. Importantly, he has gained confidence through his son Stephen. They spend hours together in 'the computer room'. Kevin therefore gains continual feedback on his skills, abilities and literacies.

TB: How would you assess your skill level with computers?

KB: Typing very poor. I'm developing some knowledge of the websites. I can chase through Google or I can chase up websites. I've learnt all the accounting facilities on it. Steve doesn't know Excel, but I've learnt that one. Publisher – don't use it at all except to do greeting cards. I can design artwork on Publisher.

TB: So in review, you feel quite confident in your web searching skills. You're very good with particular programs in the Microsoft suite. You're quite confident with Word functions.

KB: Yes, I can edit. I can edit documents. But nothing like Steve. The other day, I took the cover off that [Hard drive tower]. Six screws at the back. And there was a great lot of gunk in there. And Steve said that slot has got to go there, and we've got to put this in because you don't have one of those. And a lot of people can do stuff like that that you wouldn't have expected. You know, the average person doesn't take the carburettor from his car, strip it down and work on it. They'd be too fearful to do that. But Steve goes in there and puts in a slot card.

TB: Do you wish you could do that?

KB: No. No.

TB: So this is the hardware–software divide. You're very comfortable in your use of software. You can't fix hardware, but it doesn't worry you particularly.

KB: No. No. In fact we were having trouble, and I said don't bother, we'll buy a new computer. (laughter) He had to take the network card out to put the USB2 card slot in and now we want the networking card because we've got to take your computer and before we download supplement two we've got to download your contents just in case we lose it, and we can't do that without the network card. We've got to go in there and take out the third slot for the modem, put in the network card and then use an external modem sitting on top of the machine.

TB: So even though you're saying you don't do the hardware work, you're aware of it.

KB: Oh, I'm aware of it, but I'm too frightened to do it.

TB: But that fear doesn't worry you.

KB: No. If Steve doesn't do it, I'll take it in and get someone else to do it, or I'll buy a new machine.

The number of 79-year-olds who grasp the capacities of USB slots with this level of confidence are few. His literacy is of a high order, and he continues to learn from – and with – his son. Such testimony confirms the PEW data that wired seniors are oriented in the online environment through family members.

Doris does not have that level of digital contact or experience because 'the boys' are in the computer room while she watches television from the family room and kitchen. These problems of literacy are spatially determined within the home.

TB: How do you define home?

KB: Home is where the heart is. Home is where you go when you're drunk. Where would you go? You wouldn't go to a park and lay on a bench. (laughter). No, it's our stability. It's our fort.

TB: You do like this room. Tell me what's going on in this room [Figure 3.5]?

KB: This is my computer room. I do all my accounts. I do my editing. I type letters to people.

TB: Do you feel comfortable in this space?

KB: Yeah, it's great. This is more than I could hope for. It's the second largest bedroom in the house and it's my office. It's almost like my shed.

The computer is placed 'in Kevin's room'. A digital divide has been created in this house. Doris avoids the computer because she can, and Kevin has the space to explore, enjoy and learn new information in his way, at his speed and on his terms. The internet has become his digital shed.

Kevin has also spread out his interests throughout the house. He does not only stay in the e-shed. While Doris is not at home in the computer room, 'her' pantry has been colonised by Kevin's other new interest: wine (Figure 3.6).

This pantry demonstrates that Doris has also lost control and ownership of 'her space', the kitchen. This is one of the few places in the house that was demonstrably hers. Now that Kevin shares an interest in wine with his son, the racks have taken half of her storage space.

Figure 3.5 The 'digital shed'

Figure 3.6 A war over space

What this photograph and the pantry do confirm is that they are a good match: both are as ordered and obsessive as the other. I wish I had inherited this trait for rigid ordering and pedantic placement. Revealed through these photographs is that there is an undeclared space war in this house. Technology is only one of the battlegrounds.

Through the daily use of e-mail and search functions, Kevin has embedded the digital applications into other areas of his life.

TB: What is a computer?

KB (pause) Don't really know. It's only what I've read, that it was an interchange between universities and it's been used by the armed forces, but you don't think about that.

TB: What is a computer for you then?

KB: It's e-mails, it's research on something that you want to know about. We've just looked up the [Australian Rules] footy score. Collingwood beat St Kilda. If you can't get it off the television you can generally find it here. And it is a means of storing photographs and music. That's about all: e-mails, information and storage.

TB: Great definition. So for you, the computer is the applications – what you can do on it?

KB: Yeah. Yeah.

To paraphrase Doris's earlier definition, this is 'ordinary people' managing 'rubbish': football scores, music, photographs and e-mail. It is Kevin's confidence that is not only remarkable, but also intimidating for those without his level of skill.

> TB: If you wanted to, how would you improve your computer skills?
>
> KB: Oh, I'd do a course. I'd go down to TAFE [Technical and Further Education] or do a course at the Senior Citizens. They run a programme. I think it's heavily subsidized. I think it costs about 30 or 40 dollars for a six-week course. But I just haven't bothered to do that. They'd go back too early. I wouldn't like to sit through how to do a Word document. But I wouldn't go into the advanced class because they'd start to teach me how to take out a hard drive. I don't want to sit in a room with people who have never seen a computer before in their life. I wouldn't go to the advanced one because I don't have the confidence.
>
> TB: Is there a computer skill that you wish you did have, that you could do?
>
> KB: Yeah. Type.
>
> TB: Your wife can type. I can type. So why haven't you learnt to type?
>
> KB: I can do all I really need to do on a computer. I don't really want to learn how to do any more.
>
> TB: Would you – really – front and go to an internet class?
>
> KB: No.

He is satisfied with his current web literacy. While he would like to type, he has not desired this skill enough to learn it, even though he has seen his wife and daughter touch type. The fact that Doris may actually use word processing programmes with greater speed and effectiveness than him has not crossed his mind. What is significant is that neither Doris nor Kevin would – actually – go to a computer class. When probed, they both admitted that they would not attend: Doris because she lacks confidence at the most basic level, and Kevin because he would be bored at this basic level of knowledge. His home setup is not only advanced, but expansive: he scans, he prints, he burns, he uses memory sticks and iPods.

What I learned through the interview is the breadth of Kevin's knowledge. While I had known of his software ability, his awareness of hardware was a surprise. Continually, when asking about web literacy, he corrected me and asked for specificity.

> TB: Do you think you need to understand computers right now to live a life?
>
> KB: What do you mean – use them or understand how they work?
>
> TB: No. No. Just be able to use one.
>
> KB: Oh yeah. I couldn't exist without the computer. With e-mails. With websites. With music. Whatever you want to know, I can find out on here.

Both interviewees became even more fascinating when they started to talk about each other. Their focus in the finances, the paying of bills, and e-banking surprised me. Both of them mentioned it in great depth. There was a reason for my surprise. While attention is placed on the 'content' of the internet for senior users, more attention should be placed on services. Their interest is in how existing analogue practices can be facilitated online. Only 4 per cent of Australian seniors use the internet to pay bills or transfer funds, with 2 per cent using it to purchase goods and services, like accommodation and travel.[65] Kevin is in that 4 per cent and does not understand why his enthusiasm is not shared by others.

Figure 3.7   Barriers to access

TB: What do you think happens to the people who are not internet literate?

KB: They don't think they're missing out, but just like I'm too frightened to tackle the inner workings of that computer by pulling it apart, your mum's too frightened to press a button that says enter. She's nervous. She doesn't want to do it.

TB: Does that worry you that she thinks like that?

KB: I keep trying to tell her. All our accounts are here. I could be ripping her off right, left and centre and she wouldn't know. (laughter) See that's another very important thing, internet banking. Hell I wouldn't know the last time I went down the post office or paid an account. I put all my accounts on Visa and pay it online once a month

TB: Do you think Doris will ever be web literate?

KB: I'd like to think she would be. Doesn't seem to want to learn.

TB: How would you help her learn?

KB: Well, teach her. I say, come on, we'll have a half-hour session about how you go to Bank West and see what's in the account.

TB: Why do you think she hasn't?

KB: I think she's frightened. I think she thinks I try to teach too hard. She doesn't even like driving the car. If I fell off the perch tomorrow, it would be great to think she could ... Steve [their son] would have to come around and show her how to get on to Bank West. But she wouldn't learn. She'd have to get Steve to do it. Don't know.

TB: Does it worry you?

KB: Does a bit. I think she'd do what the others are doing. Get a passbook and walk down town and stand in a queue and get some money out

TB: Then there's the issue with the car.

KB: Oh she'd drive the car. I think she'd drive it now if I got into the boot.

TB: So she won't learn from you. We don't know if she'd learn from Steve.

KB: And she wouldn't go down the Senior Cits and learn either.

TB: So you have no idea about what she thinks she would do?

KB: I don't think she wants to.

Kevin's high level of web literacy has created a gulf of misunderstanding so that he cannot comprehend why everyone is not matching his ability. The nature of literacies is that we all forget – once we have attained the skill – the effort, confidence, fear and confusion required to develop those abilities in the first place. The idea that a woman who has done nothing except clean around a computer may be able to go online, use passwords and deploy internet banking is converging keyboard, computer and web literacies. His screensaver does not help, either (Figure 3.8).

This is not a welcoming site/sight for the unfamiliar or the under-confident. 'The computer room' is labelled with ownership. The first stage in managing this disconnection must be a familiarisation with the keyboard – with which she is familiar through touch typing – and orienting her to a screen that is not a television. Once she is able to use a computer, then web awareness can develop. Yet we all forget the pain and effort required to develop literacies.

> KB: I don't know why women will go down to the Senior Citizens and do aerobics exercise and step up and stuff, but they won't go to the Senior Citizens to learn how to use a computer. I don't know why.
>
> TB: So you don't really have an answer to your own question.

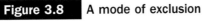 **Figure 3.8** A mode of exclusion

KB: No one's really promoting it, saying come down to the Senior Citizens and we'll teach you how to use a computer. They're saying, come down to the Senior Citizens and do some aerobics exercise. And they think that'll be good. It will do me good. They're mixing with people their own age and feel confident and happy about it. But the same people don't go down and do a computer course.

Implicitly, Kevin has realised that confidence in the present is derived from confidence in the past. Women exercise because they have experience with it. It is an incredible leap to learn new knowledge at any age. Kevin, through the interview, warmed to the need for intervention from government.

KB: Why would Mandurah City Council want to promote internet literacy in their senior citizens? It does nothing for them.

TB: I'll give you a reason. In rural and regional areas there are less facilities to pay bills and for utilities.

KB: But why local government? Why not state government? What about the Ministry for the Aged?

TB: I'll give you another reason. Libraries exist in local government jurisdictions.

KB: Yeah. But would libraries take it upon themselves to be responsible to educate old people? Somebody's got to say, that's our function. And really, it should be the Minister for the Aged who should be setting up programmes. I don't see anything coming from the state government. There's no statement from them saying, let's teach old people computers.

TB: I wonder why that is? Do you think it's ageism? Someone is saying even to themselves – look, these old bastards will die?

KB: It wouldn't be a bad initiative. They put money in ballet or music. A bit of money teaching old people how to use computers in their homes wouldn't go astray.

He is right. 'Somebody' must take responsibility for this project. Hoping that senior citizens will gain this skill without intervention is an error. The difficulty that has been raised through the national, regional and home-based information presented throughout this chapter is how to enact this intervention. The Australian government is putting material online for seniors – *www.seniors.gov.au* – yet how to 'encourage' or 'facilitate' this usage is unclear. More attention, care, respect and funding need to be developed to explore the educational opportunities and goals of those who are post-work and without major family responsibilities. In an age where education is reduced to training for the workplace, the learning goals for those who require internet and web access for reasons of citizenship and social justice are more difficult to justify. Older people are marginal and marginalised in educational policies. Ageing is a disease to be managed and a problem to be administered, not a focus for positive and proactive policies for citizenship and learning. Older people are not 'them' to be handled by 'us'. Increasingly, as our population ages, we are all becoming 'them'. Senior citizens are diverse and heterogeneous in their needs and goals. As the post-work period lengthens, this time of life can be refashioned as a time of renewal, rebuilding and reconsideration of life's priorities. There are obvious health benefits in encouraging social, mental and physical mobility for older populations. Yet this group also has the right to access and use educational opportunities.

The World Wide Web is part of an electronic landscape of instability and flux. The changes in communication networks have permitted a highly mediated and de-territorialised social environment. In such a time, the understandings of home shift and morph. Privacy, the moderation of access and the border between public and private spaces, is continually in flux. Not only terrorism but viruses infiltrate the home and the homepage, the corporeal self and the digital avatar. Through mobile telephony, the boundaries of the home are permeable at all times. With the home connected to powerful systems and structures, such as banks, utilities and work via technology, it is no longer a space apart from the hassles of life. The layers of mediation and barriers that block full access of home-based media from non-literate household members are significant. Increasing barriers – through remote controls and passwords – disrupt the routine constructed by media and technology built through television, radio and the telephone. The dispersal of screens throughout the house, from multiple televisions, computers and mobile phones, can set up barriers and new literacies that members of the household do not have. Concurrently, the domestication of technology could trigger democratisation, feminisation and commodification. Women use particular technologies and appliances more than others. Ann Moyal reported that:

> A pervasive, deeply rooted ... feminine culture of the telephone in which 'kinkeeping', caring, mutual support, friendship ... and community activity play a central part ... which ... contributes

substantially to women's sense of autonomy, security, participation and well being.[66]

For women, the telephone is a technological platform strongly integrated into social life and social behaviour. It is used to create a community separated by location. It would seem logical that e-mail was an extension of this feminine culture of community. Yet in Australia, the use of computer-mediated applications is underutilised by older women.

The PEW Internet Project showed that 20 per cent of non-internet users live with someone who uses the internet.[67] This second-hand connection may be creating as much access as these non-users require, or one member of the household may be dominating the online environment.[68] This domination and submission of the online context is not gendered in a predictable way. For example:

> Two men we interviewed said that among their circle of friends, it was the wives who used the computers to e-mail each other, and that the men did not use the internet. Men in their social circle do not use the internet, they said, often because their wives knew more about the internet than they did. They noted that they did not want to be embarrassed or told what to do by their spouses or children.[69]

This embarrassment is significant as older users invariably require family support to provide a context and environment for online activity. However, this American example is distinct from Australia. In the USA, women and men equally use the internet in all age groups, including the seniors. In Australia, older women lag behind their male counterparts. Therefore, if domination of the computer by one partner occurs, then it is likely to be a man.[70]

This chapter concludes with a home in Mandurah. It started in a flat in Walsall where a fully-clothed man was found dead. This mobility and connection between spaces is important. The vista presented in the digital world is frequently narrow. Images and experiences often value the world view of people from European backgrounds, the young, the financially secure, heterosexual and masculine. These circulated images of normality construct communities that exclude difference.[71] Powerful groups impose their readings of the world on the social space. Through digitisation, cultural literacies – or the literacies of others – can be repressed. An aim of Blair's third term in government was 'changing the middle-class character of the web',[72] to ensure that all families with children had computer access by 2008. As the calendar clicked through this year and Brown replaced Blair, shopping and surfing were still more important than consciousness and community. While such a goal was election-time politicking, at least there was recognition that handing out computers or broadband does not create digital literacies. A grey revolution has not been downloaded. As Michael Cross reported:

> When aiming at the socially excluded, content is the key, not connection. The success of digital television and mobile phones shows that people will go digital when there is something in it for them.[73]

While such awareness is significant, there must also be an acknowledgment that internet literacy is not inevitable, triggered by the availability of hardware, software or content. Questions of motivation, confidence and context, rather than access and content, need to be addressed.

Perhaps the most profound, yet unsettling comment made by my father was that the 'problem' of non-wired seniors will die with them. Inevitably, those men and women who see no use for the web in their lives will die. Policy makers are already waiting for 'the silver tsunami'[74] – the Baby Boomers who were immersed in the digital environment at work and, upon retirement, will continue to be wired. When the current generation of 50-somethings retires, the archetype of Peter Kay's grandmother changing the television with her glasses case will dissipate. Wired seniors will be the normal state. The web will be greyed.

For those of us who take the issues of social justice seriously, there are two challenges: social change and dissent. Firstly, such an argument about the inevitable death of the problem could not be sustained in health policy – denying older citizens access to hospitals or medicines because they are going to die anyway. Secondly, societies and their citizens are judged, not by the wealth of their most successful businessmen, but by the treatment of those people who stumble or are challenged physically, socially, culturally or economically. To avoid the digital divide festering into H.G. Wells' dystopia of Eloi and Morlocks, with older people left in analogue isolation as families move away, government services move online and banking services become automated, intervention is required. Waiting for a problem to die with the people who do not comply with new digital 'reality' is cruel and unjust. It also reveals a problem for the policy punter. When will these people die? We would all live our lives differently if we knew the precise day of our funeral. Whenever the choice is to do nothing and hope the problem will disappear, or dissent and intervene in a plan that may fail, we must choose action. It is possible to remake Eleanor Rigby into Nannanet. If we do not, then more Kenneth Manns will continue to die alone. We will – years later – discover many fully-dressed skeletons in bed. And we will continue to wonder why. There is an answer and the solution is in our hands. Kenneth Mann's death must remain in our minds.

We conclude this chapter, not with Kenneth Mann's skeleton, but an even more tragic death. It confirms again, how the digital darkness in which the aged find themselves is only a symptom of wider social isolation. In 2005, a 94-year-old woman and her 66-year-old son were found dead in a Sydney home. The post mortem showed that the son had slipped and died in the bath. However, this dark story has an even more macabre ending. His dependent elderly mother starved to death, bereft of care. Both mother and son remained dead in their house, separated yet together, for one month before their bodies were found. The investigating police officer stated that 'from what we have established, she was dependent on him for everything. They owned the house and, from what neighbors have said, it seems that they shunned contact with their neighbors. It's very sad.'[75] This banal reportage does not capture the rage, disgust and horror that such a story should provoke. When I first read this newspaper article, my immediate thoughts went to the elderly mother. It appears that she tried to walk when she realised something had happened to her son, but actually died a few steps from her wheelchair. This poor woman must have known her son was in trouble, but could not reach him. She did not die in peace, but in confusion, frustration and grief. We need to remember her, and note that proactive policies for digital justice must break these cycles of analogue isolation and inequality.

Notes

1. Quoted in Dodd, V. and Hussain, A. (2005) 'Forgotten man lay dead in flat for six years', *The Guardian*, 6 April, p. 11.
2. Ibid.
3. For this chapter, I note the remarkable case studies of senior computer, internet and web users. For example, see the New Zealand based study of Richardson, M., Weaver, C. K. and Zorn, T. (2005) 'Getting on: older New Zealanders' perceptions of computer', *New Media & Society* 7(2): 219–45.
4. The PEW Internet Project is based in a nonprofit, non-partisan think tank. While assessing the social impact of the internet, they are not advocates for a specific position, but provide quantitative data and general analyses, but without policy recommendations.
5. Richardson et al., op. cit., p. 219.
6. *Peter Kay, Mum Wants A Bungalow Tour – Live at the Bolton Albert Halls* (Goodnight Vienna/Phil McIntyre Entertainments Ltd, 2003).

7. Ninety-six per cent of online seniors use e-mail, compared with 91 per cent of 18–29-year-olds using e-mail, according to the PEW Internet and American Life Project (2005) 'Internet: the mainstreaming of online life', available at: *http://www.pewinternet.org/pdfs/Internet_Status_2005.pdf* (accessed 15 November 2007).

8. Fox, S. (2004) 'Older Americans and the internet', PEW Internet & American Life Project, available at: *http://www.pewinternet.org/pdfs/PIP_Seniors_Online_2004.pdf* (accessed 15 November 2007), pp. i–ii.

9. Ibid., p. ii

10. Ibid., p. 1.

11. Ibid.

12. Ibid., p. 11.

13. One strategy to overcome this lack of direct family support is found in the EarthLink programme. It is a strategy based on linking generations through high schools and senior citizen centres. The students learn skills in teaching, and seniors gain internet literacy and confidence through a six-week programme. Annamaria DiGiorgio affirmed that 'the success of GenerationLink is largely due to the remarkable connections technology made happen between two groups that probably wouldn't have met in the first place'. See DiGiorgio, A. (2004) 'EarthLink program bridges the generation gap with technology', *T H E Journal* 31(6): 8.

14. Fox, op. cit., p. 11.

15. A fine example of this reinforcement occurs through magazines such as *Australian Net Guide*. Distinct from the Generation X-inspired *Wired*, this magazine offers step-by-step guides to sonic and visual media, free software and multiple letter columns for readers to ask for advice. Senior citizens are well represented in this magazine. For example, Vanya and Paul Bryant wrote to the magazine's 'InBox', 'Thank you for the terrific digital camera we won in the "picture of the month" contest. We are delighted with it! Your publication has given two computer illiterate oldies the confidence in "give it a go" with amazing results; we are now hooked'. See *Australian Net Guide*, November 2005, p. 10.

16. Blair, T. and Hewitt, P. (2005) 'Connecting the UK', London: Stationery Office, p. 3.

17. Ibid., p. 6.

18. Ibid., p. 7.

19. Lenhart, A. (2003) 'The ever-shifting internet population: a new look at internet access and the digital divide', The PEW Internet & American Life Project, available at: *http://www.pewinternet.org/pdfs/PIP_Shifting_Net_Pop_Report.pdf* (accessed 15 November 2007), p. 8.

20. Blair and Hewitt, op. cit. p. 17.

21. Ibid., pp. 24–5.

22. Ibid., p. 28. I particularly wish to note that this figure is not as convincing as it may appear. The definition of 'senior citizen' varies through much of the quantitative and qualitative data utilised in this chapter. In Australia, the data refer to those over 60 years of age. Much of the data from PEW refer to those either over 60 or 65. In this UK report, there is a moveable definition of senior citizen. Particularly considering that this figure refers to those

over 55 – and knowing that Baby Boomers are far more web-active than their parents – there is no clear determination of the reality for those not only over 60, but over 70 and 80 years of age. An important task in further research is to be very precise in web research on the basis of age. In my survey of the already existing data, there is little differentiation between those 60 and 80 years of age, yet in terms of access to the web, there appears to be marked differences. The younger the person, the more likely they are to be online.

23. Blair and Hewitt, op. cit, p. 28
24. The role and place of blogging in this palette of asynchronous and synchronous communication is significant. Blog readerships increased by 58 per cent in 2004, providing an opportunity to tell personal stories and share information. However, when drilling down into this group of bloggers, we see that 57 per cent of blog creators are men, and 48 per cent are under 30. Further, 70 per cent of bloggers have broadband at home and have been online for six years or more. They are also well educated and live in reasonably affluent conditions. Therefore, considering these sociological variables, it is unlikely that senior citizens – even those online – are yet blog-active. As the blogosphere grows, the diversity of its population will also increase. See Rainie, L. (2005) 'The state of blogging', PEW Internet and American Life Project, available at: *http://www.pewinternet.org/pdfs/PIP_blogging_data.pdf* (accessed 15 November 2007).
25. Carlo posting on seniors.gov.au 'Meeting Place', 15 April 2005, available at: *http://www.seniors.gov.au/internet/seniors/meetingplace/main.nsf/topiccont ributions?Open&ID=0BD85773F972FACDCA256FDC002546E4&Start =1&Count=10&Order=oldest&* (accessed 27 July 2005).
26. Department of Community Development (2004) 'Generations together', in *A Guide to the Western Australian Active Ageing Strategy*, Perth: Department of Community Development, p. 4
27. Such a goal was also expressed by the Equal Employment Opportunity Network of Australasia. They found that '32 leading employers had found business needed to wise up and start holding on to a valuable asset ... Most employers were yet to realize older workers were adept at developing new products and marketing to their own age group'. See *The West Australian* (2005) 'Business must "wise up" to older women', *The West Australian*, 23 July, p. 58
28. Department of Community Development (2004) 'A profile of Western Australia's seniors', Topic Sheet No. 4, Perth: Department of Community Development.
29. Ibid.
30. As the Perth Department of Community Development (ibid.) confirms, the gendering of old age is a significant variable to consider: 'Senior men are more likely to be in a registered marriage than senior women, however this is partly explained by the higher widowed rate for women. Women tend to marry men older than themselves, and have a higher life expectancy, therefore many outlive their spouses'.
31. Ibid.
32. Australian Department of Health and Ageing (2003) 'Clinical IT in aged care', Interim Report, available at: *http://www.health.gov.au/internet/wcms/ Publishing.nsf/Content/ageing-rescare-clinitrep.htm/$FILE/clinitintrep.pdf*

(accessed 15 November 2007). This report particularly noted the low use of information technology in aged care homes, with the systems used primarily for administration and accounting. Obviously, the potential of the patients and residents themselves using technology and computer applications is not even considered. The value of seniors using computer-mediated systems and platforms to improve their own health is also not mentioned in this report.

33. Anonymous posting on seniors.gov.au, 15 July 2005, available at: *http://www .seniors.gov.au/internet/seniors/meetingplace/main.nsf/topiccontributions* (accessed 27 July 2005).

34. Kendig, H., Andrews,G., Quine, S. and Parsons, A. (2000) 'A review of healthy ageing research in Australia', Report prepared for the Community Services Ministers' Advisory Council, Health and Aged Care, available at: *http://www.health.gov.au/internet/wcms/publishing.nsf/Content/ageing-ofoa-research-haresrch.htm/$file/haresearch.pdf* (accessed 15 November 2007), p. 14.

35. Ibid., p. 12

36. Department of Community Development (2003) 'Western Australia's seniors', Topic Sheet No. 2 (2nd edn), Perth: Department of Community Development.

37. See: Australian Bureau of Statistics (2006) 'Statistics from household use of information technology', available at: *http://www.ausstats.abs.gov.au/ ausstats/subscriber.nsf/0/B1A7C67456AE9A09CA25724400780071/$File/ 81460_2005-06.pdf* (accessed 15 November 2007).

38. Lenhart, op. cit., p. 17.

39. Spooner, T. (2003) 'Internet use by region in the United States', PEW Internet & American Life Project, available at: *http://www.pewinternet.org/pdfs/PIP_ Regional_Report_Aug_2003.pdf* (accessed 15 November 2007), p. ii.

40. These dates were chosen because these were the years of the Australian census. There had actually been an increase of 18.7 per cent between the 1996 and 2001 census.

41. David Morley reported that in the United Kingdom and France he found 'a greater tendency for first-generation immigrant women to be confined to the house, and their consequently less developed skills in the language of their host culture, often leads to them being particularly attracted to satellite broadcasting in their language of cultural origin'. See Morley, D. (2000) *Home Territories*, London: Routledge, p. 168

42. Anonymous posting on seniors.gov.au 'Meeting Place', 19 July 2005, available at: *http://www.seniors.gov.au/internet/seniors/meetingplace/main. nsf/topiccontributions* (accessed 17 April 2005).

43. Department of Community Development (year unknown) 'Western Australian Seniors', Topic Sheet No. 1 (2nd edn), Perth: Department of Community Development.

44. Australian Bureau of Statistics (2006) 'Mandurah – 2001 Census Basic Community Profile and Snapshot', available at: *http://www.abs.gov. au/Ausstats/abs@census.nsf/4079albbd2a04b80ca2569d00208f* (accessed 17 April 2005).

45. City of Mandurah Local Government Authority (2006) 'A regional city reflecting community values', available at: *http://www.mandurah.wa.gov. au/council* (accessed 17 April 2005).

46. Mandurah City Council (2005) 'Mandurah vibrant city: innovative – creative – diverse', Community Charter and Strategic Plan 2005–2008, available at: *http://www.mandurah.wa.gov.au/news/charter/community_charter_and_strategic_plan_2005_2008.pdf* (accessed 15 November 2007).
47. Ibid., p. 2.
48. The Strategic Plan mentions the importance to 'Actively pursue increased educational participation for all our community' (ibid).
49. Perth Department of Community Development, 'A profile of Western Australia's seniors', op. cit.
50. Quoted in Perth Department of Community Development, 'A profile of Western Australia's seniors', op. cit.
51. Mandurah City Council (2004) 'Mandurah – A Learning Community'.
52. Ibid., p. 2
53. M. Newman, Personal correspondence, 24 May 2005.
54. Peel Broadband (2005) 'Assisting the Peel Region', available at: *http://www.peelbroadband.net/* (accessed 17 April 2005).
55. PEW Internet and American Life Project (2005) 'Internet: the mainstreaming of online life', available at: *http://www.pewinternet.org/pdfs/Internet_Status_2005.pdf* (accessed 15 November 2007), p. 64.
56. Eastbourne Seniors Club (2005) 'Eastbourne Seniors Club: Activities', available at: *http://www.cowbeech.force9.co.uk/ESC/activities.htm* (accessed 17 April 2005).
57. An outstanding analysis of the information literacy divide is Bundy, A. (2003) 'One essential direction', paper presented at eLit 2003: Second International Conference on Information and IT Literacy, Glasgow Caledonian University, 11–13 June, available at: *http://www.library.unisa.edu.au/about/paper/oneessential.htm* (accessed on 23 April 2004).
58. This embedding is referred to as 'a seamless world', in Wee Keng Neo, L. and Eng, C. S. (2001) 'Getting it right: enhancing on-line learning for higher education using the learning-driven approach', *Singapore Management Review* 23(2): 61–74.
59. S. Parsons, e-mail interview, 3 May 2005.
60. Coates, T. (2005) 'Think tank', *Society Guardian*, 7 September, p. 11.
61. Leadbeater, C. (2003) *Overdue: How to Create a Modern Public Library Service*, A Laser Foundation Report, London: Demos.
62. I am configuring an ideology of ageing from the work from M. Carolyn Thomas, Virginia Martin, Jeri Jo Alexander, Fannie Cooley and Averil Loague, who stated that 'older people often are viewed as frail, incompetent, inflexible, wedded to the past, sick, slow, helpless, dependent, depressed, lonely, physically limited, and boring'. See Thomas, M. C., Martin, V., Alexander, J. J., Cooley, F. and Loague, A. (2003) 'Using new attitudes and technology to change the development counselling focus for older populations', *Counseling and Human Development* 35(8): 2.
63. Morley, D. (2000) *Home Territories*, London: Routledge.
64. McGuiries, posting on seniors.gov.au 'Topic Contributions', 10 June 2005, available at: *http://www.seniors.gov.au/internet/seniors/meetingplace/main.nsf/topiccontributions?'* (accessed 27 July 2005).
65. Australian Bureau of Statistics, op. cit.

66. Moyal, A. (1998) 'The gendered use of the telephone: an Australian case study', in S. Jackson and S. Moores (eds.) *The Politics of Domestic Consumption*, Hemel Hampstead: Harvester, pp. 51–72.

67. Lenhart, op. cit.

68. Living with someone who dominated the online environment was listed as one reason why a person did not go online (ibid., p. 10).

69. Ibid., p. 12.

70. There is also another group that may be masked by this discussion of domination and subordination: net evaders, i.e. those who are offline in an online home. These people have opportunities to go online and are therefore actively resistant. Access and cost are not the concern. There is an agency and activity in this resistance.

71. Thomas Novak and Donna Hoffman studied the relationship between racial identification, income and educational level and internet use. See Novak, T. and Hoffman, D. (1998) 'Bridging the racial divide on the internet', *Science* 280(5362): 390–1.

72. Cross, M. (2005) 'Class consciousness', *The Guardian*, 7 April, p. 15.

73. Ibid.

74. Fox, op. cit., p. iii

75. Quoted in Kennedy, L. (2005) 'Woman 'starves to death' after carer son dies', *Sydney Morning Herald*, 25 October, available at: *http://www.smh. com.au/news/national/womn-starves-to-death-after-carer-son-dies* (accessed 4 July 2006).

4

Cash for corporeality: international students and the wealth of transgression

Leanne McRae

> It is densely ironic that universities have entered a period of crisis at the very time when women, mature-aged students and ethnic minorities are entering the institution. (Tara Brabazon)[1]

Tara Brabazon's words have special resonance. They mark the beginning of my own suspicions about online education. To borrow a phrase from Brabazon, I find it densely ironic that 'online learning' and 'access' to education have become catchphrases of policy makers at the time when neither are guaranteed. Interfacing with flexible education through e-learning is being framed as an important innovation for student success in higher education institutions. The ability to multitask, organise time and transgress traditional and tired models of classroom instruction is being advanced at multiple levels of educational management. Access to traditional learning infrastructures (on-campus lectures, tutorials and workshops) is no longer guaranteed by governments and universities. This intellectual poverty is masked by rhetoric that affirms that the best way to demonstrate social tolerance and advocate universal literacy in education is to disengage students from traditional instruction and digitise their dialogue with learning.

Within this modality of management, educational standards and systems are framed as old and obsolete. Staid university administration and dreary educational philosophies are implicated in the reduced respect granted to teaching and learning, feeding into government policy. As a consequence, the e-learning oeuvre is hailed as the funky future for flexible delivery and design. These ideas fit snugly into the creative economy where innovation is advocated, and educational institutions are encoded as inflexible and ill-fitting to the customised economy.

In an era that celebrates change, it is even more important to recognise that education demands structure and discipline. Learning requires rigour. Flexibility is a word that sustains inequitable educational reform. Educational ideologies that suggest access is best facilitated by e-learning mask the intricate and complex analogue meanings and methods of education. Effective pedagogy requires more than the interface of students with educational infrastructures. Generating analytical literacies requires a struggle over ideas. This tumultuous process cannot be contained in bullet-point PowerPoint slides or a tired textbook culture. Scholarship involves discomfort and strategies to rethink the self. Access alone is not enough. When educational reformers advance the benefits of flexibility, they fail to recognise the frameworks, operational protocols and paradigms needed to succeed at learning. This commentary also ignores the context in which 'flexibility' is advanced. It fails to spotlight the government decisions about funding that have resulted in shrinking income for universities, creating the need to rationalise education delivery and advance more manageable study options. Teachers are being asked to work more for less pay. Students are expected to direct their own learning. Access to education is being valued more than literacy outcomes, knowledge networks and applications of expertise. Students log into their learning and once they activate their avatar, literacy is their responsibility. Digital pedagogy is clean and uncomplicated. Teaching responsibility is reduced. Ideologies of access to more than a computer – to knowledge development and critical literacies – are stripped of their wider social justice accent and controlled by measurable and easily defined infrastructural outcomes. Constructing computer access presents a learning interface that deprioritises embodied and experiential classroom contexts. Creating corporeal contexts for scholarship and rigorous investigation of ideas offers deeper challenges for educational systems.

E-learning offers students a way to diversify their learning experiences. Programmes are now being written and curricula designed that make effective use of digital literacies and languages. Yet such strategies remain no more than a Band-Aid over the gaping wound of educational inequality. A clear division is emerging between those who have access to data and those who have access to teaching, learning and literacy. While students from the working class, women, mature age and ethnic minorities are told to log in and download their education, international students pay cash for corporeality. The place and function of a teacher in a classroom engaged in face-to-face instruction is a signifier of an integrated and invested learning experience. The ideology advocating online learning and flexible delivery masks this significance. International students demonstrate the importance of teaching and interacting in the flesh.

The lessons embedded in this chapter activate ideologies of literacy, e-learning, flexibility and the value of face-to-face teaching and learning. My argument affirms that in an economically-rationalist social and education system, wealth (financially and intellectually) can be measured through the capacity to be taught by a person. Online learning and its 'flexible' rhetoric is being activated at a time when there are more disempowered, working-class, immigrants, women, disabled and other minorities at university. The e-education hyperbole displaces the realisation that they are being disengaged from accessing traditional educational structures and therefore full entry into a critical capitalist economy. These students are told to stay home – to remain docile and domesticated. International students are afforded a wealth in transgression – able to move across social, economic and national boundaries via the affluence of face-to-face pedagogy. The money they pay for an onshore education coupled with the expense of moving to and living in a new country captures the value of a traditional education. These students are not logging in and downloading course material to study from home. They come to Australia seeking an expert education, embodied in teachers measuring and mentoring them in the classroom. Transnational styles of education demonstrate the significance of defining and re-encoding how we understand 'access' to pedagogy.

International education – both as a curriculum strategy and embodied in overseas students – has been marketed as the future for educational institutions. For example, different styles of transnational learning have been active in Australia since the early twentieth century. Student exchanges between higher learning institutions have continued since 1904.[2] However, within the last 20 years, 'export education' has become a catchphrase for university administrators and managers. The exporting of information is characterised by a series of 'institutional agreements [and] internationalisation of academic content'.[3] This market is comprised of international or overseas students who arrive to study at Australian higher educational institutions, students studying at an offshore campus – for example, Monash University Malaysia – as well as students studying online offshore.[4] Also included are private educational institutions specialising in educational delivery to an international market. For example, the Institute of Business and Technology (IBT) is affiliated with Australian universities and provides bridging courses into second-year scholarship.[5]

The ideology activating the increasing internationalisation of education is encased in the possibilities for economic growth in social and cultural diversification. Many commentators argue the benefits of international education by citing the 'changes in the labour market ... [that] call for different kinds of skills and knowledge, not least a deeper understanding of the languages, cultures and business methods found elsewhere in the world'.[6] The potential to learn and promote diversity within the curriculum is often cited as a fundamental benefit in a globalised information economy. Drawing connections within and between students from different national contexts can be productive in social and economic cooperation and cultivation. Masked by this ideology are the structural shifts that have required universities to look for outside funding sources to sustain educational delivery.

Universities are in crisis. More significantly, they are propelled by crisis management. Australian government funding has halved within ten years. The problem is so severe that in 'the year 2000, universities received less than half their income from annual Commonwealth operating grant allocations'.[7] Adding to this pressure, 'state government funding ... now constitute[s] 1 and 2 per cent of university budgets'.[8] As a result, universities must seek out alternative sources of revenue. Where domestic students cost universities money, overseas students earn money for universities. The importance of these financial shifts can be seen in the shifting demographics of university populations and budgets where 'international higher education enrolments now generate well over $1.2 billion for Australian universities'.[9] Overseas students are fundamental to the continued operation of the country's university sector. Increasing reliance on the 'international education dollar' has meant the diversification of operational protocols for universities, which now activate multiple relationships with off and onshore education providers and personnel:

> Almost all universities have multiple offshore partnerships, with a range of different kinds of organizations including public universities and colleges, private universities and colleges, hospitals, art galleries, professional associations and companies.[10]

These affiliations draw on shifting policies that are increasingly avenues for revenue raising, sponsorship and corporate funding for higher education institutions. A series of critical decisions at government level about the relationships between education, the economy and the internationalisation of Australia have stimulated these alterations.

Australia's delivery of higher education to international students has been spotlighted by national and international negotiations reframing the educational landscape. Student exchanges since 1904 had been normalised as an essential part of an outward-looking and intellectually-growing nation. When Australia became a signatory to the Colombo Plan in 1950, the motivations and intentions for overseas enrolments shifted. This international agreement was 'underpinned by recognition of the need to assist developing nations with economic development in order to promote peace and stability in the region'.[11] As a result, 'Australia agreed to fund sponsored student places for students from countries of the region'.[12] Undergraduates from the surrounding areas were brought to Australia to increase their levels of expertise so they could transport and translate this knowledge to improve the national economies of 'underdeveloped' countries. This arrangement continued until 1979. Fears about 'invasion' from Asia made the Department of Immigration 'impose a substantial visa fee on private overseas students'.[13] Yet the programmes designed to assist developing countries in the region were protected by the government. It was not until 1984 with the Jackson Report that education was marked as a major export industry. After this milestone, shifts in educational policy facilitated the growth of onshore enrolments for international students, the increase in transnational education and international education agreements. In 1988, the final barriers to full-fee paying international students were removed with the government sanctioning commercially-oriented universities. The Higher Education Contribution Scheme (HECS) was introduced in 1989 for domestic students and universities were permitted to seek out private funding. They were also not limited 'in the number of international full-fee paying students they could admit'.[14] As of 2005, universities were allowed to offer full-fee paying undergraduate courses as long as they did not make up more than 35 per cent of enrolments.

The changes since 1950 have been staggering. In that year, there were approximately 1,000 overseas students studying in Australia.[15] In the first semester of 2002, there were a total of 150,523 international students enrolled at Australian institutions, including on and offshore campuses.[16] In 1997, 'total annual overseas student fee income for public higher education institutions had reached $805 million'.[17] As of 2004, 'international students represented an estimated 16 per cent of the total onshore student population'.[18] The consequences of this growth in overseas student numbers altered the domestic market where from 2000 to 2001: '19,000 eligible domestic university applicants in Victoria could not be offered a university HECS place'.[19] The reason for this shortfall is in the high desirability for international students over domestic scholars. Most clearly 'there is a greater financial incentive for universities to enrol full fee-paying domestic students and international students, rather than marginally funded HECS students'.[20] The extent of this interest and investment in international education has spread across the higher education sector with 'each of Australia's 38 public universities now involved in providing offshore education'.[21] These relationships extend from educational partnerships to offshore campuses and online providers. The serious financial crisis of Australian higher education is increasingly defined by rising enrolments of overseas students on campus and movement towards cheaper e-learning and flexible delivery for domestic students.

The mantra of flexible delivery has entwined with e-learning protocols. The use of information and communication technologies (ICTs) is framed as a desirable method for modernising ageing educational systems. The terms 'flexibility', 'e-learning' and 'access' are converging. The confluence of these words is so seamless that 'in Australia, "flexible learning" is often used as a euphemism for technologically-mediated learning'.[22] Through this cycle of inward and self-reinforcing language, e-learning, WebCT and Blackboard are designated as the accessible interfaces between students and staff, learning and literacy, criticism and consciousness. As the rigours of a highly demanding economy monopolise individuals' time in the workplace, the possibilities for study become mediated through the ability to mould around other priorities and purposes. It is in this context that 'access' is mobilised in educational discourse as a digital interface. Access to education is complicit in the economic definitions of social mobility and success. The time, space and literacies required to develop knowledge and understanding are devalued in the consumer economy of accumulation without consideration. Flexible education is an effective metaphor for the shifting priorities and meanings of pedagogy. An education – financed by individuals and managed along(out)side of working hours so that it does not infringe upon capitalist accumulation and government rationalisation – is consistently legitimised within our current consciousness. The continual displacement of educational responsibilities onto individuals and away from governments fits snugly into a creative industries strategy where the 'innovative' skills needed for an information economy are embedded within the flexible learning mantra of universities:

> With great flexibility and expanded information networks, learning is fast becoming the new focus of work in the information

society. As the conventional factory-model of classroom learning becomes obsolete, skills in both self-motivation and group collaboration are seen as critical to lifelong learning and the vocational requirements of knowledge-intensive industries.[23]

The isolation of ideas and fragmentation of knowledge as a commodity is valued within such ideologies. Education is not seen as a fundamental framework for a healthy society, but as a tool for economic accumulation and capitalist expansion. When economic growth becomes the priority over social growth, then education becomes impoverished by influences that skew the nuances of knowledge that pedagogic practices problematise. The ideology of flexible learning through e-education holds little currency for those who do not have technological capacities and literacies. It also ignores the functions of the classroom and the disciplinary rigour of context management. For many students, flexibility is the last thing they need. For universities, a paradox emerges as the practices of students fail to match the e-education objectives. On-campus enrolments continue to increase. Online courses are undersubscribed. International students lead this trend by embracing the conventional and corporeal learning systems offered via the transnational education market.

E-education exists in tension with this sympathetic synergy between teachers, students and classrooms. This anxiety is reshaping the demographic makeup of universities. While domestic students are being placed behind the screen, international students are populating university campuses. These students actively reject online learning literacies and demand corporeal capital. They do not learn online. They seek face-to-face instruction. The collated data clearly demonstrate the trends towards classroom coaching for international students (see Table 4.1).[24]

Table 4.1   International students in Australian higher education

	Total	Onshore	Distance online	Offshore on campus*
International students, 2007	210,956	144,398	11,622	49,709
Growth from semester 1, 2006	3.5%	3.6%	n/a	1.3%

*This category refers to students enrolled in an offshore campus

E-ducation is unevenly conducted and consumed. International students prefer the face-to-face contact with teachers. In countries where the internet is accessible, indicators suggest resistance to e-learning.[25] Yet, onshore enrolments of international students in Australia continue to grow. By 2004, the greatest increase was in students who came from China, India, the United Arab Emirates, Japan, Hong Kong and Taiwan. Each of these countries – with the exception of India – has a vibrant and viable internet infrastructure. China had a 7.3 per cent online population penetration at this time, the equivalent of 94,000,000 internet users. United Arab Emirates has an expanding internet infrastructure with 29 per cent penetration; Japan has 52.8 per cent, Hong Kong 69 per cent, and Taiwan 50.9 per cent.[26] Despite the access to internet facilities and frameworks, these countries all recorded growth in the levels of onshore student numbers attending Australian universities.

These statistics become particularly resonant when an assessment is made of those countries with the largest growth in transnational education – those students either studying from home online (distance online), or enrolled in an offshore campus. The greatest growth in these numbers was represented by the United Arab Emirates, Vietnam and Sri Lanka. Vietnam has only 6.9 per cent internet penetration[27] and Sri Lanka 1.2 per cent.[28] The growth of private education providers in each of these countries indicates transnational students are enrolling in offshore campuses. The Australian College of Business and Technology operates a campus in Colombo, Sri Lanka and RMIT Vietnam International University is being developed in Ho Chi Minh City, 'with major loans from the International Finance Corporation of the World Bank and the Asian Development Bank'.[29] These offshore campuses are catering to local communities with face-to-face instruction and Australian affiliation.

This interpretation of data becomes obvious when noting that distance online enrolments have declined by 15 per cent, while onshore enrolments have risen by 11 per cent. The greatest decline in distance online enrolments can be found in Malaysian, Singaporean and Hong Kong markets – all of which have cutting-edge internet infrastructures. The Malaysian and Singaporean onshore enrolments have also decreased, indicating a plateau in the market which may be related to a series of factors from increasing expenses, improving local education and a stronger Australian dollar. These trends indicate a general retraction from international education by these countries. Yet onshore enrolments from Hong Kong have grown by 2 per cent, demonstrating a shift in the focus for Australian providers and teachers.[30]

What these statistics indicate is that when confronted with the choice of having a teacher or technology, most students choose the person over the portal. In nations like Vietnam and Sri Lanka, the offshore campus provides this embodied experience where students can have direct contact with pedagogic structures and synergies. What they are seeking from their international experience is a structuring framework embodied by the presence of an authority figure to shape their learning trajectory.[31] This need for discipline was activated in the responses to a survey I conducted among international students I teach. I asked them about their learning needs, specifically questioning their motivations for coming to Australia with the question: 'If PIBT [Perth Institute of Technology] had the facilities for you to do their courses online from your country of origin would you enrol? Why?' No doubt the question could have been better framed, but the range of answers revealed some curious trends in thinking. Some advocated the benefits of moving to a country where the standard of living is considerably higher than their own. They enjoyed the culture of wealth in which they were situated. Out of 28 students surveyed, only two affirmed they would enrol in a distance online course. Five were unsure and the remaining 21 declared they would not enrol in such a course. Those that responded about the benefits of the online environment recognised the costs involved in moving to another country and the sense of estrangement they felt. In response to the question, 'If PIBT had the facilities for you to do their courses online from your country of origin, would you enrol? Why?', two respondents answered as follows:

> Yes I'll enroll because when you come here it's different from what we were told by the representatives. And it is hard for international students to cope and adjust – pressure is too much and sometimes students will enroll by conditions which is hard for international students, e.g. failure, but student attend classes therefore in that case I'll enroll.

> I would definitely enrol for a course online because it would be even more cheaper cost point of view than coming here. Getting a degree from Australian university staying in own country would be a right thing because it requires a lot of time and hideous procedure to come here and settle in the new Australian environment. It would be 'PERFECT' doing an online course in my country and getting a PIBT certificate (degree).

The 21 students who said they would not enrol advocated the necessity of face-to-face contact for their learning. They recognised their need for discipline and their inabilities to measure and monitor their own time. Two responses to the same question were as follows:

> No, cos I think study between face to face is better. Also study online from my country is more hard to understanding. It is hard to ask a question online.
>
> No, because I believe that certain thing will be very difficult to understand online and you will need a teacher to explain to you. Even though questions can be asked online they may not be clear hence making it difficult for both the teacher and the student.

These answers are troubling. They are symptomatic of a student body that is underconfident and compliant to an uneven education system that values white, middle-class cultures over experiential, postcolonial and complex learning. That they viewed the teacher primarily as a disciplinarian rather than a guide or mentor captures their educational histories and habits. They relied on the implied or ideological intimidation of the teacher to provoke scholarship.

This survey demonstrated to me the chasm of expectations between teacher and students: I want them to think, they want me to tell them what to do. However, their answers to another question revealed a great deal more about their reflexive understanding of teaching and learning. When I asked them what they thought face-to-face teaching offered, they demonstrated insightful consideration of the experiences they had encountered in the classroom.

> I guess it helps in understanding. There are times when you can read something over and over but not understand it fully, but in a classroom situation you have a teacher to explain it, as well as class mates who might be able to explain it differently, so further understanding occurs.
>
> Well, it's more personal. You can see their body language and face to face is easier to relate or explain rather over the phone or by e-mail.
>
> Insight, lots of INSIGHT!!!

The value these students placed on multiple forms of learning demonstrates the function of teaching. They were not only interested in the content, but in how it was delivered to them corporeally – through facial expression, tone of voice, eye contact and gestures – all those extraneous and unpredictable engagements that communicate as much about the course as a lecture, the reading or an assessment structure. The energy, personality and persistence of the teacher are as important to the communication of knowledge as the structures of information and pedagogic framework. Learning involves experience, not just the assimilation of data. Knowledge must be felt and struggled over. E-ducation formats offer little space for such dynamic and discomforting processes. Unless the student is self-directed and disciplined, there is little motivation – except fear of unemployment – to inspire a rigorous interpretation of material. Indeed, many online advocates advance the integrity of the online student as a dedicated and motivated individual. These theorists assume that students are invested and engaged in their education – which they believe will advance them through the capitalist economy. They forget the disappointments of underemployment and the crushing callousness of work in late capitalism. Many students are pessimistic about their post-education careers. The overtures of online education have blocked this knowledge from challenging the theory and assessment of e-educational strategies. Learning is hard. If the rewards are spurious then there is little to inspire the instruction and motivate the learning. The need to engage bodies in a life of learning is activated by international students who come to our shores. They complicate teaching and learning to demonstrate to educational theorists and administrators that education is enfolded within strategic and political needs – not just economic value.

International students allow us to rethink the purpose of contemporary educational policies. By putting the postcolonial into education, they reveal the gaps and absences in learning structures. New languages and literacies emerge that translate learning methods and philosophies through transnational identities and experiences. Colonisation and capitalism intersect in the classroom. A new imagining of education must be activated if effective pedagogy is to prevail. The ghosts of colonisation cannot be ignored in a discussion of the impact and relationships between international students and education – particularly when the largest market for Australian universities and education providers is Asia, with the greatest enrolments originating in China, India and Hong Kong. It is not difficult to frame international education structures as neocolonial classrooms whereby the (post)colonised come to gain the great white education and entry into credentialed global cultures and exchanges. Education systems are gatekeepers for national growth and prosperity. Indeed, international education (in its current format) relies on the underdevelopment of educational infrastructures in the target countries to sell the advanced or advancing pedagogic policy of the administering country. The predictions for future enrolments reveal that little may change in the immediate period: 'the Global Alliance for Transnational Education (2000) estimate that demand for transnational higher education in Asian countries (excluding China) will rise to more than 480,000 students by 2020'.[32] The attraction of accessing information and knowledge industries is fundamental to selling international education to overseas clients. Open and operational access to scholarship and the rigours of instruction lies at the heart of educational credibility in a transnational context. Australian international education providers rely on the uneven activation of capitalism and postcolonialism in these markets.

International education is motivated by these ambiguities of access. In the case of overseas students in Australia, access is defined by the performance of bodies in space – not a computer or digital interface. This is a trend replicated in places where offshore enrolments are growing. Being taught by a teacher in a classroom is still highly desirable and 'existing patterns of teaching, learning and interacting are proving resilient'.[33] In Singapore, Malaysia and Vietnam specifically, these modes of teaching and learning are valued. Within these nations, online learning is neither feasible nor legitimised. It is the embodied experience that is sought:

> In Vietnam, where ISP costs are exorbitant compared with the costs of travel and accommodation incurred by international mobility, interest in geographical mobility continues to be high because the traditional view of international education in Vietnam appears to ascribe greater culture and vocational importance to face to face instruction.[34]

The face-to-face experience is crucial to social mobility. There is credibility attached to traditional models of pedagogy. This is not a matter of educational conservatism. It remains an effective model of instruction. It is not only Vietnam-based students confirming the needs and necessities of classroom experiences. Monash University Malaysia operates on the principles of face-to-face instruction. Their reputation as quality providers is based on this embodied delivery and the attendant fees reflect the expense and expertise of the education being distributed:

> The most significant feature of Monash University Malaysia for this study is its preference for traditional face-to-face teaching. Information technology is used extensively in administration and communications but in teaching and learning the campus has opted for a more traditional approach ... Monash University Malaysia is

able to charge higher fees than its competitors partly because it retains an emphasis on traditional forms of face-to-face delivery while other, less expensive providers, rely more on distance delivery techniques and part-time teaching staff.[35]

This institution performs the politics and the problems of international education. Monash University Malaysia clearly demonstrates the revenue potential in export education by activating and exploiting ideologies of traditional education in an era when 'access' to education is now limited to downloading a curriculum via digital technologies. For those prepared to pay, 'access' is able to mean much more. It is not only used to refer to course materials but access to cultural capital and social mobility through an operational and effective educational system. Ideologies of social justice are masked by a capitalist consciousness based in the exploitation of education-poor national contexts. Simultaneously, domestic students are enfolded into an e-education initiative that assures them better access to information if they remove themselves from the university campus and digitise. For these students, access to a computer and software is often the beginning and the end of their education.

The argument presented in this chapter is not intended to atomise domestic and international students. Nor is it designed to advocate the interests of local students over international ones. Rather, this chapter has demonstrated that terms like 'access', 'quality' and 'learning' are applied arbitrarily and inconsistently. Clearly, for domestic and international students, access to information and education are configured differently. These contradictions reveal how separate ideological frameworks are used to valorise particular educational choices at governmental and administrative level. For domestic students, whose place at university is often dependent on the level of government-funded places, the consequences of shrinking budgets have sparked the shifting rhetoric of educational providers to validate the benefits of an online education. At its core are notions of flexibility to allow students to fit study into their busy working lives. These ideals conceal the function of e-learning as a cheap alternative. For international students whose financial benefit to universities is growing every year, face-to-face teaching is essential to demonstrating Australia's quality as an educational provider. Flexibility is not the basis for marketing an education as a product or service for export. E-learning is often unfeasible or undesirable. These contradictory contexts reveal the varying ideologies influencing educational delivery and design. International students demonstrate the importance of face-to-face learning. They embody the transgressive potential of traditional models of teaching and learning. Meanwhile, domestic students are disengaged from such privileges. Their level of access to education and therefore social mobility and cultural capital is regulated by a screen and a keyboard. But scholarship is not being downloaded.

Access, flexibility and e-learning are the educational punctuation of universities. As bodies are being removed from learning contexts, the role of live and physical teaching environments is being sold more actively to international students. These pupils pay cash for corporeality and place the teacher at the centre of educational expertise. As a result, they valorise traditional ideologies of learning based in rigour, scholarship and struggle over meaning. Their understanding of education is founded not only in notions of value for money, but also in the nuances and meanings of embodied confrontations, discussions and debate.

Notes

1. Brabazon, T. (2002) *Digital Hemlock*, Sydney: UNSW Press, p. 4.
2. Harman, G. (2002) 'Australia as a major higher education exporter', paper presented at the Consortium of Higher Education Researchers 15th Annual Conference, Vienna, 5–7 September, p. 6.
3. Kameoka, Y. (1996) 'The internationalisation of higher education', *OECD Observer* 202 (October-November), Expanded Academic Index Database [full-text database], article A18802995 (accessed 8 December 2004).
4. Students studying offshore either on a campus or online are collectively referred to under the title of 'transnational education'.
5. The statistical data obtained for this chapter do not include measures for these styles of transnational institutions. They remain on the fringes of educational delivery.
6. Kameoka, op. cit.
7. Harman, op. cit. p. 8.
8. Bayley, S., Fernside, R., Arnol, J., Misiano, J., Rottura, R. and Williams, P. (2002) 'International students in Victorian universities', *Evaluation Journal of Australasia* 2(1): 58–61.
9. Harman, op. cit., p. 3.
10. Ibid., p. 13.
11. Ibid., p. 6.
12. Ibid.
13. Ibid.
14. Bayley et al., op. cit., p. 58.
15. Harman, op. cit., p. 6.
16. Ibid., p. 10.
17. Ibid., p. 11.

18. Brown, J. (2004) *International Students in Australian Universities – Semester 2 2004*, Deakin: IDP Education Australia, p. 7.
19. Bayley et al., op. cit., p. 59.
20. Ibid., p. 60.
21. Rizvi, F. (2004) 'Offshore Australian higher education', *International Higher Education*, Fall, available at: *http://www.bc.edu/bc_org/avp/soe/cihe/newsletter/News37/text004.htm* (accessed 14 February 2007).
22. Ziguras, C. (2001) 'Education technology in transnational higher education in South East Asia: the cultural politics of flexible learning', *Educational Technology and Society* 4(4): 8–18.
23. Walsh, L. (1999) 'Encounters with difference: In search of new learning spaces through internationalisation', Monash Centre for Research in International Education, Monash University, available at: *https://secure.ascilite.org.au/conferences/brisbane99/papers/walsh.pdf*, p. 4
24. Please note there is a discrepancy in these figures as they are only estimates. See IDP Education Australia, op. cit., for a more detailed assessment. These figures are only for university higher education and do not take into consideration international colleges and private education providers who cater specifically to international clientele. According to Professor Stephen Parker, the total number of international students in Australia in 2004 was 210,319, making approximately 22,000 students at private colleges; see Parker, S. (2004) 'Australian higher education: crossroads or crisis?', paper delivered at Taking Public Universities Seriously, Toronto, 3 December.
25. I recognise the ambivalence of these numbers. They do not mobilise any data on the effectiveness of the internet connection – whether it is reliable, stable or sufficient in capacity – all elements that impact on the integration of e-learning within a national context.
26. Internet penetration statistics are available from Global Internet Statistics, at: *http://www.internetworldstats.com/*.
27. The equivalent of 5,711,240 internet users out of a population of 82,851,971.
28. Only 225,000 internet users from a population of 19,466,567.
29. Harman, op. cit., p. 14.
30. The lacklustre scale of growth from 2003 to 2004 was blamed on the retraction of the traditional markets in Singapore and Malaysia. The decline in the statistics may also be related to delay in Australian providers and marketers adapting to this shifting focus.
31. It is important to recognise the paternalistic potential of this positioning. The possibilities of replicating colonial ideologies and relationships can also percolate through the international education experience.
32. Ziguras, op. cit., p. 8.
33. Ibid., p. 11.
34. Walsh, op. cit., p. 4
35. Ziguras, op. cit., p. 13.

5

Cultware: constructing the matrix of internet access

Mike Kent

Accessing the internet is an action performed alone at the computer screen. It is also significantly different in its solitary nature from many apparently analogous technologies, particularly television and radio, where the experience of access to the medium is often a shared one. This sharing is not only at the point of access, but across many isolated individuals who are all united in consuming the same textual material at the same time. Access to the internet does not follow these conventions. The same content may be downloaded by different users, but they are potentially spread in geography and time in a way that preceding technologies did not allow. This isolation has consequences for the way it is researched and understood. Other chapters of this book address how groups and individuals make use of the digital technology and content available through the internet and the implications of this activity. This chapter, positioned at the conclusion of the first section and opening out into digital applications and environments, offers the tether between theory and practice, or downloading and the revolution.

This chapter dissects the understanding of access to the internet. Before downloading can commence, a web portal must be opened. The familiar – if imprecise – terms of computer hardware and software are examined. Focus then turns to the less familiar area of wetware, which is the skills and experience of the person operating the computer. This literacy and context constructs the crucial final element required to make an individual point of access viable. The relative strength of each of these three components of hardware, software and wetware creates a matrix that will, at any one point, determine the strength and utility of access. If the computer screen represents a metaphoric gateway to the internet, then it is the combined value of this matrix that determines the size of that gateway and the benefit that can potentially be activated.

Having located this point of access for an individual, attention then turns to the broader context of that access both online and 'on-screen' – as part of the internet-mediated digital environment – and also 'off-screen' in the local social and physical space where that point of access is positioned. It is at this level that a fourth aspect to the matrix is introduced. Culture-ware – or cultware – describes the context in which the other three components in the matrix of access manifest. If the terms 'hard', 'soft' and 'wet' connote a sexual metaphor, it is cultware that gives them perspective and reclaims the romance from pornography. The focus on distribution of internet access is often most concerned with the tangible aspects of hardware and software, and to a lesser extent wetware. These are the components of access to which a monetary value is easily prescribed. Distinctly, cultware builds on Bourdieu's insights, to examine areas to which an easy conversion to currency is harder to determine, but which plays no less a crucial role.[1] The term includes the political and economic context in which the access takes place, the social and kinship networks of the individual concerned and characteristics of the online environment that access initiates.

Armed with such an understanding, this chapter turns its attention to how this broad matrix of access can be used to interrogate the conditions of those who are not able to meet the requirements of the threshold of access to the internet. In the context of this book, we show why the revolution cannot be downloaded and how dissent is necessary to create social change. The digital underclass is excluded from this increasingly pervasive area of contemporary culture. The research within the PEW Internet and American Life Project that has been discussed in the first part of this book found a significant number of individuals in America who lead lives completely disconnected both from the internet and anyone else who has access to the internet. This group has been labelled the 'Truly Disconnected'.[2] I examine how an understanding of cultware can be used to understand this position and facilitate intervention.

The matrix of access

Alone at the screen, the creation of internet access necessitates a marriage of discrete elements. The hardware of the computer meets with the software of its operating system. The melding of these two elements constructs the digital environment. These two components then interface with wetware, or the user's knowledge and literacies, to be mobilised at the screen. This convergence creates a matrix that determines if access is possible at that point in time and space. But more research and analysis is required that reaches beyond the point of an atomised individual and allows for this point of access to be understood in the context in which it occurs. To enact this project requires a fourth element – cultware – to enable a more complete conceptualisation of the point of access. The suffix 'ware' is derived from the old English word 'waru' meaning goods. In this case, each of these three initial wares can be seen as a distinct type of good or commodity with discrete qualities.

'Hardware' is a word appropriated by the information and communication technology (ICT) discourse. While originally used to refer to metal goods, it has been reinterpreted to represent the physical equipment associated with computing. In relation to the internet, this understanding can be extended further to the infrastructure of the communications network. Hardware can be defined as the equipment used to generate, transport, store and interpret digital data. Hardware – relative to the other components of the matrix – represents a traditional type of commodity. To generate computer and communications hardware requires a constancy of production. Each unit, once developed, requires the same resources to reproduce.

'Software' is a term coined by John W. Turkey in 1957.[3] It refers to the programs held in a computer's memory. At its most basic when applied to the internet, software describes the construction of the TCP/IP protocols and provides the matrix for bits – a collection of zeros and ones – to be translated by hardware. Typically, there are different layers of software running on a computer. At one level, they act as an interface with hardware to enable the computer to operate, and at another they act as the interface with wetware as it provides a platform of interaction with the computer user. Software in this context also includes the digitised content held in computer memories.

Software, both as a program and digital content, is starkly different from a more traditional commodity such as hardware. Computer hardware has a high component of its value determined by the development of the technology and knowledge required to design and initially produce that commodity. There are significant start-up costs to any production in addition to research and development. However, once this initial outlay and setup is achieved, there is a constancy of production that requires the same value to be spent to produce each additional unit after the first. For software, all the investment in its construction takes place in development and design. Once a piece of content has been digitised – for example the writing of a program or the digitisation of formerly analogue content such as a musical recording – there is no additional cost to make a perfect copy or a thousand copies of the original. This process requires the construction of no production facilities and the consumption of no extra resources to produce each unit.[4] The distribution of these copies will similarly be limited only by the size of the specific set of data and the bandwidth available for the transmission of that data. The value of software for its creator is maintained not by possessing and selling it as an analogue commodity. Rather, by an agreed understanding and implementation of their copyright, they receive a return each time a legitimate copy of their intellectual property is sold. The Downloading Harmony section of this book explores the potentially problematic nature of this type of 'agreed understanding' for the music industry.

'Wetware' is a term less widely deployed than hardware or software. It traces its relatively recent origins back to cyberpunk literature.[5] Rudy Rucker's book with this title won the Philip K. Dick Award for best science fiction paperback in 1989.[6] Also known as 'liveware' or 'meatware', wetware refers to a living organism and more specifically, the human operator of a computer. In this context, wetware is the knowledge and experience held by an individual seeking to access the internet, their ability to operate the computer interface at the screen and their literacy within the digital environment on the screen. Unlike both hardware and software, wetware manifests as an analogue rather than digital platform. Visual content from the screen and audio from speakers are interpreted through the eyes and ears of the user.

Wetware is a distinct type of commodity. It is often compared with software, only on a different type of operating platform, with information stored in a brain with analogue visual and auditory information 'processed' by the observer. While this might be true at a superficial level, wetware is significantly different from software in terms of its production. Unlike hardware, it has an inconsistency of production. Information literacy is not simply downloaded into a person. It has to be taught, learned and embedded in a social environment. Wetware consists of myriad literacies, developed through both formal and informal learning and experience. Producers of wetware span the education sector from kindergarten through to universities. Newly developed wetware is built upon existing literacies. Being able to read and write (and ideally type) is a prerequisite in learning how to use e-mail.

Another feature of wetware is that as well as being learned, wetware can be borrowed. If someone does not have the skills required for a task they can seek help. In some cases this may entail paying for a professional in the field, but often it will involve seeking an informal alternative source of wetware. Computer literacy within households is not evenly distributed. It is often separated by both age and gender.[7] One or more less literate members rely on the expertise of those with more literacy to establish and maintain internet access for them. In these instances, it is more appropriate to talk about a household, rather than individual, wetware. The reliance on one member for access can however be hazardous. A person without the literacy to activate access, who relies on another source of wetware such as an individual who activates access for them, is vulnerable to that access being curtailed if contact with that individual is lost. Children leave home, partners die. There is a difference between being taught skills and having someone 'do it for you' through facilitated co-dependence.

Quality of access

The screen does not provide a democratic gateway. The matrix of access does not present the same gateway to every person at every screen. Rather, the size of the gateway, the quality of connection at each manifestation, generates different levels and modes of access. The three components of individual access – hardware, software and wetware – intersect and communicate within this matrix. However, the ability to attain hardware, software and wetware are distinctly distributed. An awareness of how and where to attain these literacies requires the activation of cultware. Without an intersection between the three components, access is not possible. The size of the overlap then determines the size of the gateway and the quality of access. There is a threshold or point at which a potential matrix will not be able to generate a viable gateway. This can be due to any one of the components being absent or of insufficient intensity, or a combination of inadequate components. On such occasions, the computer screen (if one is present) becomes the point of the event horizon where, like its counterpart at the surface of a black hole, nothing traverses from the other side.

Hardware is the most obvious manifestation of the matrix of access. Without a computer of some sort and some kind of network to enable a connection, there will be no access. The utility of these devices will vary widely both in terms of raw processing power and also for the particular circumstances where they are activated. In some situations, a mobile phone with a low bandwidth signal that is able to operate on a battery and be easily carried will be far more useful than a powerful desktop computer with a high bandwidth fibre-optic data connection. Good hardware is potentially able to overcome limitations in both software and wetware, through both the design of the interface it presents and its enhanced processing and data storage capability.

Similarly, well-designed software can overcome some of the limitations of hardware and alleviate the requirement for a high level of wetware in a user. Originally, web pages were created by HTML programmers with basic text editors such as Notepad. The development of what you see is what you get (WYSIWYG) web authoring software such as Dreamweaver enabled people to focus their literacy on page design and content, rather than the raw code.

The original development of the World Wide Web software by Tim Berners-Lee in the early 1990s provided the foundations for the enormous growth in the population of people using the internet. The World Wide Web enabled a greater potential for access by eliminating modes of literacy that a user needed to access content on the internet. The web provided an easier way for information to be stored and navigated. Not only was the content organised in a way that facilitated easier access,[8] but the level of wetware or training required to use a web browser was much lower than for previous internet-enabling software. Software could be used to stretch the space for access, until that point limited by wetware requirements.

For access to occur at any point, a level of physical infrastructure must exist. There must be a telecommunications network and a way to access it. Digital content must be present along with other prospective communicators. Finally, there must be literacy to interpret this mode of communication. While the presence of hardware and software draws much attention from politicians and activists as the most obvious enablers, it is the additional requirement of wetware that remains of primary importance. These are the levels of access and understanding which form a network of encoding and decoding, downloading and uploading. The greater the range and literacy level, the greater the access. While it may appear a binary issue – literacy is present or absent – there are factors that affect the quality or the size of the gateway. A highly proficient user with developed wetware is able to extract more from hardware and software. They have expert knowledge in the use of this technology relative to a novice user. Once a person is within the digital realm, they choose to develop distinct translations and modes. In the first instance though, a threshold of literacy is also required to gain access to the internet. Without this threshold literacy, no other literacies can be developed. There is a difference between someone who cannot swim and a weak swimmer who falls into a lake. Without the literacy to use the internet, the content and technology to deliver that content is of little use.

An individual highly trained in the use of internet-mediated technology has an aligned and highly complementary level of wetware. Using this skill base, they are better able to make use of a given set of hardware and software than a user with less developed wetware. They are also able to expand the point at which access is available – the internet event horizon – by making better use of any marginal levels of software and hardware that are available. The types of wetware required to facilitate these two functions are not the same. Wetware, like hardware and software, is not homogeneous and varies in suitability to different tasks.

Unlike the other three components of access, cultware is a commodity that is hard to define and value. Pierre Bourdieu shadowed the concept of cultware when detailing his theories of cultural and social capital.[9] Bourdieu criticises traditional economic theory as being too focused on economic capital, or the capital that is most easily converted into tender. He has argued that a wider understanding of economic practice requires an investigation that encompasses more than simply a market-based study. This narrow understanding by Bourdieu is replicated in the analysis of ICT in general and the internet in particular, with the primary focus on hardware and software. Both comprise commodities that can be easily understood in terms of economic capital. Similarly, wetware – knowledge and literacy – is an increasingly commodified entity with a cost to obtain and a value to be realised.[10] Cultware comprises an equal if not more important field of understanding within the digital environment which is often overlooked.

Social capital for Bourdieu represents a personal asset that is developed through families, groups and individuals being 'connected', and providing these individuals with an advantage over others with less social capital. As Bourdieu infers:

> the aggregate of actual or potential resources which are linked to possession of a durable network of more or less institutionalised relationships of mutual acquaintance and recognition – in other words to membership in a group.[11]

The impact of different access to the shared added value of social capital needs to be discussed in terms of cultural literacy – the specific knowledge or wetware – that initiates the capital of cultware. It stretches across both the digital environment in which the multiple users of the internet dwell through the screen and the analogue environment in which those users find themselves off-screen. Within the matrix of access, wetware links literacy to identity. Cultware then provides context, linking identity to society.

The development of the World Wide Web increased access to the internet by making it easier to use and navigate, thereby reducing the wetware requirements. This development can be tracked as the driver behind the subsequent massive growth in internet penetration rates. That growth in population in turn caused the total potential value of the internet to increase. Each additional user on the network increased the total value of the network in accordance with Metcalf's Law.[12] This growth in the value of the network can be understood as a function of cultware. The online environment was enriched with more participants and its cultware value increased. Conversely, while the web reduced the level of literacy required to access the internet, it also generated a far more complex online environment that requires its own specialised literacies to navigate.

The digitised environment represented by the internet is a vast store of potential social and cultural capital, manifest in the wetware of other users and the software or content that is available through the network as well as the activated value of the hardware that supports the network. This grouping of resources, and the synergy within that grouping of different resources, is made available as a function of cultware. To access this capital requires a variety of literacies relating to all four components of internet access. Cultware often becomes embedded in social practice to the point where individuals forget their literacy levels and their early strategies in literacy development. This active or passive forgetting has the potential to create confidence, arrogance and social amnesia. The political consequences of such a conscious or unconscious process may be dire.

Cultware determines the potential for access in an analogue 'off-screen' space. There is a different distribution of wetware across households in mature internet environments in Australia, Britain and the USA. The level of cultware is a gauge of the access to technology and infrastructure off-screen. The off-screen cultware environment of Manhattan Island is significantly different from that of sub-Saharan Africa. Having a notebook computer with wireless-access capability would have very different utility for the average resident in each place. In each instance, an individual brings their unique context for literacy development, economic resources and social networks that will influence their prevailing level of cultware.

The digital underclass

Internet penetration rates have, following a period of rapid growth, begun to stabilise in developed telecommunications markets such as Australia, the USA and much of Europe. This period of rapid growth can be seen as a reflection of access being taken up by the majority of the population who, through their pre-existing access to cultware, were predisposed to gain that access. However as this growth subsides, those left outside of access – those with insufficient cultware to gain access – become a digital underclass. In 2003, a PEW Internet and American Life Project listed three different groups of individuals within the USA who did not use the internet: net dropouts, net evaders and the truly unconnected. This last group makes up nearly a quarter of the population in the USA. These individuals have no access to the internet and very little contact with anyone who does. Rather than actively avoiding the internet, it plays no part in their lives. It is this large group that lacks the cultware to engage with the internet.[13]

Each person at the screen faces that screen – the gateway to the internet – alone. This atomised engagement with the media platform means that this access, or more critically exclusion, is not performed in the view of others. Those within the digital environment have no perception of those excluded. The digital underclass do not manifest 'on-screen'. Similarly the digital underclass have no knowledge of the environment from which they are excluded. Off-screen, there are no obvious markers of gender, class or race to highlight membership of the digital underclass or those with access. The digital underclass is invisible, both digitally on the screen, and in their analogue environment.

Off-screen, the digital underclass and those with online access share physical space. While there are no obvious markings setting these two groups apart, the level of cultware in that environment affects the potential for translation and communication to occur between these two groups. Conversely, the greater the level of cultware, the more apparent and profound is the disadvantage of those without access. Race, class and gender manifest at the analogue side of the screen and it is there that the context of these markings becomes important.

The layers and levels of government in many nations have attempted to address digital awareness and availability. These strategies have varied greatly in their scope, form and ideology.[14] All these programmes have existed in a perceived environment of rapid growth in internet penetration. Internet growth is slowing and the proportion of the population online is becoming static.[15] The digital divide is becoming harder to cross for those on the wrong side. People left outside the gates of access to the internet are becoming a more definite and disadvantaged group. With the screen acting as an event horizon for those without access, messages cannot pass back from the other side. The digital underclass become invisible, having no manifestation on the screen. The consequences of this invisibility are ominous.

Now that the growth of internet penetration has stalled, there is a danger that those left outside of access will become a perpetual underclass. Their revolution will not be downloaded. The focus of previous political interventions in relation to the digital divide and the digital underclass have tended to focus primarily on the digital infrastructure of hardware and software, with less focus on wetware and crucially neglecting the role of cultware. This more complex matrix of internet access is intended to provide the intellectual tools to better facilitate any future interventions.

Notes

1. Bourdieu, P. (2005) 'The forms of capital', translated by R. Nice, available at: *http://www.viet-studies.org/Bourdieu_capital.htm* (accessed 10 October 2007). Originally published as Bourdieu, P. (1983) 'Okonomisches Kapital, kulturelles Kapital, soziales Kapital', in R. Kreckel (ed.) *Soziale Ungleichheiten* (Soziale Welt, Sonderheft 2), Goettingen: Otto Schartz and Co., pp. 183–98.
2. Lenhart, A., Horrigan, J., Rainie, L., Allen, K., Boyce, A., Madden M. and O'Grady, E. (2003) *The Ever Shifting Internet Population: A New Look at Internet Access and The Digital Divide*, Washington, DC: PEW Internet and American Life Project.
3. Turkey, J. W. (1957) 'The teaching of concrete mathematics', *The American Mathematical Monthly* 65(1): 1–9.
4. Obviously there will be a component of hardware system resources required to support each copy, but for all intents and purposes this cost is negligible.
5. The original notion of cyberspace is derived from science fiction, most famously from William Gibson's *Neuromancer* (1984) and Neal Stephenson's *Snow Crash* (1992). Cyberspace in these books is a virtual world generated by computers where people interact virtually with electronic representations of society, its computer systems and other users. Individuals are projected into this world as avatars, where their digital 'selves' are represented and they experience this world through a virtual reality interface which, to an extent, mimics the real world. The movie *Tron*

(1982) is an earlier, although less acknowledged predictor of cyberspace in popular fiction. The more recent *Matrix* trilogy also shares this conception of fictional cyberspace. Please refer to Gibson W. (1984) *Neuromancer*, New York: The Berkley Publishing Group; Stephenson, N. (1992) *Snow Crash*, New York: Bantam Doubleday Dell Publishing Group; *The Matrix*, directed by A. Wachowski and L. Wachowski (Warner Bros, 1999); *The Matrix Reloaded*, directed by A. Wachowski and L. Wachowski (Warner Bros, 2003); *The Matrix Revolutions*, directed by A. Wachowski and L. Wachowski (Warner Bros, 2003); *Tron*, directed by Steven Lisberger (Walt Disney Productions, 1982).

6. Rucker, R. (1988) *Wetware*, London: Avon Books.

7. Keightley, K. (2003) 'Low television, high fidelity: taste and the gendering of home entertainment technologies', *Journal of Broadcasting and Electronic Media*, June, pp. 236–9.

8. This was further enhanced by the development of various web-based search engines.

9. Bourdieu, op. cit.

10. Please refer to Tiffin, J. and Rajasingham, L. (2003) *The Global Virtual University*, London: Routledge Falmer; Newman, F. Couturier, L. and Scurry, J. (2004) *The Future of Higher Education: Rhetoric Reality and the Risks of the Market*, San Francisco, CA: Jossey-Bass; Teixeira, P., Jongbloed, B., Hill, D. and Amaral, A. (eds.) (2004) *Markets in Higher Education: Rhetoric or Reality*, Dordrecht: Kluwer.

11. Bourdieu, op. cit.

12. Metcalf's law describes the exponential growth in the value of a communications network that comes from each additional node. For every '*n*' number of connections the on a network the network's value will be *n* squared. See Gilder, G. (1993) 'Metcalf's law and legacy', *Forbes ASA*, 13 September, available at: *http://www.discovery.org/scripts/viewDB/index.php? command=view&id=41&printerFriendly=true* (accessed 15 November 2007).

13. Lenhart et al., op. cit.

14. In Australia, the success of these activities has been mixed. Of the funding made available to 'Networking the Nation' rural telecommunications projects by the Australian commonwealth government through the partial sale of Telstra, it is estimated that 80 per cent have stalled or failed. See Morris, C. and Meadows, M. (2004) 'Digital dreaming: indigenous intellectual property and new communication technologies', in G. Goggin (ed.) *Virtual Nation: The Internet in Australia*, Sydney: UNSW Press, pp. 156–9.

15. Studies in the USA indicate that internet penetration rates began to stabilise in 2002. Given that Australia is a similarly well-developed 'market' for the internet, it can be assumed that the penetration of the internet into the Australian population has similarly stabilised, or will do so in the near future. See Madden, M. (2003) 'America's online pursuits: the changing picture of who's online and what they do', PEW Internet and American Life Project, available at: *http://www.pewinternet.org/pdfs/PIP_Online_Pursuits_Final.PDF* (accessed 11 October 2005).

Part 2
Downloading harmony

6

He who pays the piper must call the tune?

Mike Kent

A cliché resonates in the ears of those who listen to downloaded music: 'he who pays the piper calls the tune'. For much of the twentieth century, the recording industry paid the various 'pipers' of popular music. The digitisation of recorded music has created an environment where music can be easily copied and distributed, both on compact disc and through the internet, by individuals and musicians who bypass the industry and established payment structures. The music industry claims that it is losing vast sums of money. But does this talk of economic disaster stand up to scrutiny? With the amount allegedly lost to piracy, one would expect to find closed signs over the doors of all the major record labels. Yet the industry continues to thrive. This chapter explores the economic reality behind the cost of file-sharing music, and the alleged suffering of those who pay the piper. I introduce this section on 'downloading harmony' by examining the changes to music that are taking place in the digitised environment, where it can be easily copied and distributed across the internet. These changes represent a radical departure from the music industry of the vinyl record and music corner store. The chapter examines both how music as a commodity has changed, and how the music industry – and the recording labels in particular – have reacted to this change and the factors driving this reaction. The supposed economic threat to the industry posed by the new digital single may not be the death knell it is made out to be.

Originally, the audiences for musicians were those who could physically listen to the performance. Recording music as a written text allowed the same tune to be performed by others and allowed for the transmission of music outside the range of hearing. Music thus became a string of information stored as the written notes on a page. These could then be reused in a new context by someone with the literacy both to read and perform the music. The written recording allowed tunes to travel through both time and space. The compositions of many great artists can be performed today by contemporary musicians even though the composers and performers of the notes are dead.

It later became possible to record an actual performance of a piece of music, initially through recording on an analogue platform such as a vinyl record, and more recently again as a digital file such as is found on a compact disc. These recorded performances have undergone a number of significant transformations to the way they are presented, from the pianola through to the gramophone, vinyl records (first as singles and then albums) and the compact disc. Each new technology is influenced by what it replaces. The vinyl single was superseded by the album. This format brought together a collection of individual songs that conformed to the protocols of length predetermined by the vinyl single.

The compact disc was first released in 1982. This medium represented a significant change in the way the sound was recorded as it was transformed from analogue to digital. However, it still drew heavily on the influence of the vinyl it was intended to replace. The data format chosen to record and store the music was of a size that allowed for a CD to contain a similar length of recorded sound to a vinyl record. The CD was broken into separate files for each song, replicating the tracks of the vinyl album, themselves mirroring the format of a collection of vinyl singles.

In a further development for digitised music, the MP3 or Motion Picture Experts Group-1 (MPEG) Audio Layer III compression technology was developed in 1992 as part of internet standards for video transmission. This allowed for songs to be stored in much smaller files than the compact disc format permitted. In 1998, the Napster peer-to-peer (P2P) file-sharing network was launched, providing an easy way to transfer music over the internet between individuals. The retention of the single meant that in this format the file size was sufficiently small to enable the relatively easy transfer of these files across the internet, even at relatively slow dial-up modem speeds. The peer-to-peer nature of the Napster network removed exclusive control of the distribution of music from the hands of the record companies, as individuals could download any of the music available on the network's computers. Napster used a centralised reference system to facilitate song sharing, and was therefore vulnerable to the legal sanction of the music industry, which eventually had the network closed. More recently, ad hoc peer-to-peer networks enabled by protocols such as Bit Torrent are more resistant to legal sanction than a centralised system.

Music recorded as a digital file is ultimately a series of zeros and ones that can be interpreted by a device capable of reproducing the analogue sound-waves for interpretation by listeners' ears. The digitisation of music has some significant effects on the type of commodity it represents. Vinyl records are a commodity not unlike many other manufactured goods. Resources are devoted to the initial design of the product – in this case the recording of the music – and then mass production occurs, reproducing the artefact to be purchased by consumers. The producer of the commodity, in this case the record companies, has a monopoly on the production of each record. In 1991, when recordable compact disc (CD-R) technology became available to the public, it became possible to create a perfect copy of the digital information recorded on a CD. At this point, the record labels then lost their monopoly on production. The CD-R mirrored the earlier loss of control experienced by the music industry in the 1970s with the advent of the analogue cassette tape, which allowed individuals to make (albeit imperfect) copies of vinyl records, and led to the famous 'Home Taping Is Killing Music' campaign by the British Phonographic Industry in the 1980s.

Information is not like other commodities. The ownership of information, such as the record company's control over a song, relies on copyright. Copyright is an entirely socially constructed value. It only has value if consumers give it that value. If everyone ignored 'the rights' of the producers, then those producers would cease to derive value from their creations. A digitised copy of something is different from a traditional analogue commodity. Owning ideas is not like owning apples. While both an apple and an idea can be locked in a box and no one can access them, both are deprived of the realisation of their value. The value of the apple is the eating. The value of the idea in a copyrighted world is that it can be sold (or denied) to others. Once the apple is eaten it is gone. However, once copyright for one copy is sold, then it relies on intellectual property laws to prevent that idea simply being endlessly recopied with no return to the copyright holder. Of course, these laws must be obeyed to be effective. The development of P2P distribution of copyrighted music files thus subverted these intellectual property constructions that benefited the music industry.

While it was once the master of the house who paid the piper, musicians who produce recorded music for sale are paid most directly by the companies that record and distribute that music. This industry has proven resistant to changes in consumer technology at every level, resisting radio broadcasts, the cassette tape, the CD burner and distribution of MP3 files over the internet. This resistance is examined more closely by Felicity Cull later in this section. The industry claims that sales have been in decline since the advent of the consumer CD burner, and more significantly since the development of P2P file-sharing networks. However, there are other factors that can also be used to explain declining sales. One of the great successes of the compact disc was not only its rapid adoption as a consumer item,[1] but for the music industry it produced a period where consumers 'upgraded' their existing vinyl record collections. By 2003, Lee Black of Jupiter Media noted that this CD upgrade cycle was coming to an end, bringing to a close the boost in sales that it had provided until that point.[2] The growth in the consumption of music and movie DVDs has also been a factor inhibiting CD sales, as the money people spend on home entertainment has become subject to greater competition. Finally the actions of the recording industry in relation to the type of product they release and the format on which it is released play a part in the declining sales. In 2003, the Australian music industry sold more than 50 million albums for the first time. Its press release was headlined 'Music DVD continues its rise while CD singles slide further'.[3] While this is an accurate statement, it is also misleading. The declining number of CD singles sold was also related to the reduction in the number of CD singles offered for sale.[4] Similarly, the data for the first half of 2005 released by The Australian Recording Industry Association (ARIA) noted a decline in sales of 7.54 per cent.[5] It did not comment of the reduction in the number of titles released (by 37 per cent from 2003 to 2005).[6] While a consumer might buy multiple unique CD singles, they are unlikely to buy more than one copy of the same music no matter how much they enjoy it.

How much is really lost?

The global music industry reported a decline of 7.6 per cent in 2003, the fourth straight year of declining sales. This same year was also a record year for music sales in Australia. Since this peak, however, Australia has followed the global trend.[7] This downturn is blamed by the industry directly on the effects of digital piracy, and the internet-based exchange of MP3 files specifically.[8] Does this allotment of blame stand up to scrutiny?

In 2003, Quantum Market Research estimated that 31 million homemade CDs were given away each year in Australia. This figure did not include online file sharing or homemade CDs that were not given away. As Peter Martin notes, this sort of hole in the sale of music should be easy to spot. Yet as music CDs in Australia reached their highest yearly sale of 65.5 million in 2003,[9] this expected interruption in sales was not apparent. While the music industry would like to equate each copied CD or downloaded song with a copy that they did not sell, this is obviously not the case.

In a perfect market, the ideal price is determined by the intersection of supply and demand. The supply curve measures the amount of a product that can be produced at any given price, tending to zero as the price is reduced. The demand curve measures demand for the product at any given price. In the perfect market, it is the intersection of these two lines that determines the ideal price. While this theory could be applied to the music industry when dealing with a commodity such as a compact disc, once the music is available for downloading the nature of 'supply' changes radically as each additional copy is produced at virtually no cost. In this circumstance, demand at a given price is determined for each product (in this case a recorded performance of a song) as a function of its demand curve. This curve will be unique for each song. More popular songs will sell more copies at a particular price.

When the song is available for free (albeit in breach of copyright), the price is effectively reduced to zero. However, the gap in price between what is asked and zero creates a space where individuals might download a copy of a song for which they would not have paid. These copies would not represent lost sales for the industry as they are sales that would not have occurred. It is only the potential purchased downloads that represent a true loss of income due to these breaches of copyright. While this theory obviously relies on a perfect market model that is distorted through questions of legality and consumer loyalty to particular artists, there are other issues that must also be considered. For example, the music industry delayed the provision of a legal option to download music over the internet. iTunes, the largest online music store, only launched in Australia on 25 October 2005,[10] and without any of the Sony-BMG catalogue.[11] This historical gap created a problematic environment for competition between illegal online digital downloads and CDs purchased from a retailer. Additionally, the online music store does not provide a direct comparison with what is available through the different P2P networks, as various digital rights management (DRM) systems produce files with less utility than an MP3 in an effort to protect the copyright of owners of the content.[12]

The single as a format for music sales, having initially been artificially maintained on CD,[13] has been phased out of production by the music industry in favour of the album. MP3 files are normally single songs, once again differentiating the two types of commodities. Contrary to the message of concern propagated by the industry, there have been a number of studies that show that the dissemination of songs through P2P networks may actually increase sales, acting as a free promotional tool for the artists and record labels.[14] A study by Oberholzer and Strumpf found that while some file-sharers purchased less music as a result, others purchased more.[15] The study found that while niche audience music suffered a small negative effect due to downloading, sales for large selling albums are actually increased. Despite this potential benefit, the music industry has sought to end the practice of sharing music files over the internet.

Within the USA, the Recording Industry Association of American (RIAA) has aggressively pursued file-sharing network operators, famously causing the Napster network to be closed down in September 2001. The industry has continued to pursue similar networks through the courts in different legal jurisdictions.[16] The rise in more ad hoc and transitory P2P networks enabled by software using Bit Torrent, which has in part been driven as a response to the recording industry's efforts, has proven more resistant to legal action. Partly as a response to these developments, although also preceding them, the music industry has employed a second, more controversial approach. Using provisions in the Digital Millennium Copyright Act 1998 the RIAA has searched the computer records of individual users and taken civil action, suing individual users, famously as young as 12 years old.[17] While this approach might seem excessive, it needs to be understood in terms of the industry trying to re-establish the socially constructed value of its copyright. Having resisted the technology, and crucially provided no legal alternative to music downloading, it has in part become seen as a legitimate and not unlawful activity. This ongoing legal action is an attempt to challenge this behaviour and ideology. The perceived morality of file sharing by users is more closely examined by Carley Smith in the next chapter.

Within Australia, the comically named MIPI (Music Industry Piracy Investigation), an industry body representing the major record labels, has tried similar tactics. In conjunction with the Australian Federal Police, they launched raids on the University of Technology Sydney in 2003, arresting three students for running a web page that served up music for downloading over the internet. Under Australian law, the students could have been fined up to $60,500 and been sentenced to five years in prison.[18] The three were ultimately sentenced to community service, despite the objections of the MIPI.[19] The Australian legal environment has some significant differences to its North American and European counterparts. Australian copyright law has no 'fair use' provision. It is not legal to 'rip' music from a legally purchased compact disc onto a computer hard drive or a digital music player such as an iPod. Until recently, the only content that could legally be played on these devices was copyright-free audio files. The music industry in Australia further enhanced this problem by resisting demands for legal downloads and withholding access to their catalogues from websites that catered to the Australian market. While more online stores have become active in this market, their catalogue is still limited. Even by 2005, the four top sites were missing between 32 per cent and 60 per cent of the top 50 songs.[20] ARIA's report for music sales in the first half of 2005 explicitly did not record online purchases.[21] While traditional recorded music sales in Australia declined, the industry continued to curtail the legal use of new technology.

A new twist

While freely shared MP3 files can be copied, burned to CD and transferred to digital media players, much of the music available for legal download comes with digital rights management restrictions that limit the owner's ability to perform these functions. Obviously, the aim is to protect the rights of the intellectual property holder. This may unintentionally stimulate demand for (easily 'rippable') CDs as consumers put a premium value on DRM-free digital music.

Although it is illegal to transfer the data from a CD into another format in Australia, some of the major music labels have tried to enact copy protection measures on CDs to physically prevent customers burning copies. The anti-piracy measures found on CDs released by EMI in 2002–03 meant that many albums could not be played through a home computer; of course, if the album was (illegally) copied to a blank CD, the illegal disc *would* play on the consumer's PC.[22] While these measures were designed to confront what the music industry perceived as the threat from CD burners on computers, Sony BMG's subsequent attempts at securing the content on their music CDs from their consumers were more damaging. Rather than simply not playing on computers with CD-ROM drives, the Sony discs were secretly installing invisible files within the computers' operating systems, potentially opening these systems to external attack through the internet. This 'rootkit' technique is similar to a virus, and was listed as malware or malicious software by many of the leading computer security firms, including Symantec and Frisk Software International as well as software manufacturer Microsoft. Once the nature of this software was discovered, Sony offered a 'patch' on its website that did not actually fix the security vulnerability.[23] Such attempts to limit consumers' control of content they have legitimately purchased have the converse effect of effectively adding to the utility and value of an illegally obtained MP3 with no DRM. In 2007, EMI became the first of the large record labels to offer music downloads for sale that contained no DRM.[24]

The online sale of individual tracks represents a transformation in music, a movement back to the single and away from the album. While the sale of CDs continues to suffer a limited effect – and may yet be stimulated by the development of single track file-sharing over the internet – the recording industry's predictions of doom and gloom may still prove to be true. While the music industry has focused its response to this threat to its business model on its own consumers, the real danger may in fact lie at the other end of the supply chain. In October 2007, the band Radiohead released its new album *In Rainbows*. The album could be ordered as either a digital download available immediately, or as a more conventional collector's boxed set of vinyl and CDs sent through the mail. The band released this music directly from their website, rather than through a record label. They also allowed the consumer to determine their own price for the downloaded version, from nothing through to £99.99.[25] This pricing model allowed the band to gain income from more points on the demand curve, both from dedicated fans who would pay the standard retail equivalent price – or sometimes more – through to those who would not have paid full price for the music, but were prepared to pay something. Of those who made early purchases or pre-orders, more than 75 per cent were prepared to pay some price for the download, with 25 per cent parting with more than £10.00.[26] The band used their existing fan base and previous success to effectively disconnect from traditional recording labels. It seems that the real threat to the recording industry may be from artists rather than consumers. As Thom Yorke of Radiohead notes:

> I like the people at our record company, but the time is at hand when you have to ask why anyone needs one. And, yes, it probably would give us some perverse pleasure to say 'F you' to this decaying business model.[27]

This example also shows how ingrained file sharing behaviour has become, with an estimate of more than half a million copies of the song being illegally traded over the internet in the first week after its launch, despite the album being available for free as a legitimate download.[28]

Music sold online is mediated in a significantly different way to its analogue counterparts. While CDs can be purchased through the internet, they are also available in the analogue spaces of the record store. Digital tracks do not have a physical manifestation. While many are still mourning the loss of the texture and imperfections and unmediated analogue sound quality of the vinyl record,[29] perhaps soon they will be able to add to that sense of loss the memory of uncovering an old classic in the back of a retail music store. Certainly, the internet provides a much easier environment for distribution. While on the one hand this makes the business of selling music more efficient, it also opens up the industry to those who previously lacked the resources to compete with the distribution mechanisms of a large record label. This creates a greater space for small labels and individual artists to get their music to a broader international market. The established music industry can still provide the money and media exposure that has allowed them to market their products successfully (sometimes in defiance of the quality of what is on offer). However, the ability to create and manipulate music reaches outside the expensive music studio and onto the domestic computer. The threat to the established recording industry may one day prove to be as dire as their predictions. However, even if a serious realignment of the production and sale of music occurs, it is the musicians who stand to benefit most from the disintermediation of large labels. The potential exists for a shift in the paymaster who calls the piper's tunes, and while it may become harder to make the obscene fortunes that are currently on offer for the elite few in the music industry, there will be greater opportunity for more musicians to share and be rewarded for their talent with a global audience of listeners.

Notes

1. In 1986, CD players were selling at a rate of more than 1 million units a year, making them, at the time, the fastest growing consumer electronic device ever produced.
2. Gibsen, O. (2003) 'Legal downloads won't make up for drop in CD sales record labels told', *The Guardian*, 30 July, available at: *http://business .guardian.co.uk/story/0,3604,1008594,00.html* (accessed 20 November 2006).
3. ARIA (2003) 'Australian record sales – 2003 full year figures – 12 months ending 31 December 2003', available at: *http://www.aria.com.au/pages/Australian RecordSales-2003FullYearFigures.htm* (accessed 20 November 2006).

4. Cannane, S. (2004) 'Music industry way off track with song and dance about falling sales', *The Sydney Morning Herald*, 29 March.

5. ARIA (2005) 'Australian recorded music sales for 6 months to 30 June 2005', available at: *http://www.aria.com.au/pages/news-halfyearsales2005.htm* (accessed 20 November 2006).

6. Malik, A. (2005) 'CD sales fall disguises a lack of choice: less is less', *The Register*, 15 September, available at: *http://www.theregister.co.uk/2005/09/15/oz_sales_fall/* (accessed 20 November 2006).

7. ARIA (2005) 'Sales by value for the years ended 31 December 1995–2005', available at: *http://www.aria.com.au/pages/documents/Table1.pdf* (accessed on June 20, 2006).

8. IFIP (2004) 'Global music sales fall by 7.6 per cent in 2003 – some positive signs in 2004', 7 April, available at: *http://www.ifpi.org/site-content/statistics/worldsales.html* (accessed 20 November 2006).

9. ARIA (2005) 'Sales by value for the years ending 31 December 1995–2005', op. cit.

10. While websites to online stores are available to anyone with access to the internet, the billing address on credit cards needed for payment is used to segment these into separate geographic areas.

11. Lee, J. and Higgins, D. (2005) 'Apple launches Australian music and video store', *The Sydney Morning Herald*, 25 October, available at: *http://www.smh.com.au/news/technology/apple-launches-australian-music-and-video-store/2005/10/25/1130006093720* (accessed 20 November 2006).

12. DRM can be used to limit the number of copies of a file made, or on what platform it can be played.

13. A CD single, rather than limited by the size of space to record, as with a vinyl single, is normally simply a full-sized CD with only one song.

14. See *The Age* (2003) 'Music downloads not affecting album sales: survey', *The Age*, 11 July; Smith, C. (2003) 'Illegal music downloads boosting album sales', *The Scotsman*, 10 July.

15. Oberholzer, F. and Strumpf, K. (2004) 'The effects of file sharing on record sales: an empirical analysis', available at: *http://www.unc.edu/~cigar/papers/FileSharing_March2004.pdf* (accessed 20 November 2006).

16. Deare, S. (2005) 'Sharman to appeal while record labels celebrate', CNET.com.au, 5 September, available at: *http://www.cnet.com.au/mp3players/musicsoftware/0,39029154,40056841,00.htm* (accessed 30 November 2006).

17. Vance, A. (2003) 'The RIAA sees the face of evil, and it's a 12-year-old girl', *The Register*, 9 September, available at: *http://www.theregister.co.uk/2003/09/09/the_riaa_sees_the_face/* (accessed 20 November 2006).

18. Pearce, J. (2003) 'Police raid Sydney University over alleged music piracy', *ZDNet Australia*, 30 May, available at: *http://www.zdnet.com.au/news/business/0,39023166,20274970,00.htm* (accessed 20 November 2006).

19. Pearce, J. (2003) 'Aust music pirates sentenced', *ZDNet Australia*, 18 November, *http://www.zdnet.com.au/news/business/0.39023166,20281145,00* (accessed 20 November 2006).

20. Ziffer, D. (2005) 'Sorry, but we can't hear you', *The Age*, 17 September, available at: *http://www.theage.com.au/news/technology/sorry-but-we-cant-hear-you/2005/09/16/1126750125395.html* (accessed 20 November 2006).

21. ARIA (2005) 'Australia recorded music sales for 6 months to 30 June 2005', available at: *http://www.aria.com.au/pages/news-halfyearsales2005.htm* (accessed 20 November 2006).

22. Varghese, S. (2003) 'When copy protection backfires', *The Age*, 13 May, available at: *http://www.theage.com.au/articles/2003/05/13/105259177 1111.html* (accessed 20 November 2006).

23. Bergstein B. (2005) 'Copy protection still a work in progress', *AP*, 18 November, available at: *http://news.yahoo.com/s/ap/20051119/ap_on_hi_ te/music_copy_protection* (accessed 20 November 2006).

24. Wearden, G. (2007) 'EMI and Apple in DRM deal', *The Guardian*, 2 April, available at: *http://buiness.guardian.co.uk/story/0..2048193,00.html* (accessed 17 October 2007).

25. On the band's website, there was a blank space next to the price. When the customer clicked the link, the prompt appeared, 'It's up to you'. A second click brought back the message, 'It's really up to you'.

26. Resnikoff, P. (2007) 'Radiohead sales estimates surface, new wrinkles emerge', *Digital Music News*, 17 October, available at: *http://www .digitalmusicnews.com/stories/101407radio* (accessed 17 October 2007).

27. Quoted in Tyrangiel, J. (2007) 'Radiohead says: pay what you want', *Time Magazine*, 1 October, available at: *http://www.time.com/time/arts/ article/0,8599,1666973,00.html* (accessed 11 October 2007).

28. A. Greenberg (2007) 'Free? Steal it anyway', Forbes.com, 16 October, available at: *http://www.forbes.com/technology/3007/10/16/radiohead-download-piracy-tech-internet-cx_ag_1016techradiohead.html?boxes= author* (accessed 20 October 2007).

29. While globally CD sales may be in decline, the sales of vinyl records have experienced a revival as consumers are drawn back to those textures and imperfections. Vinyl sales in the UK were up nearly 90 per cent in 2005, and continued to increase with seven-inch vinyl single sales up 13 per cent in the first half of 2007. See Dee, J. (2005) 'Plastic fantastic', *The Guardian*, 26 November, available at: *http://arts.guardian.co.uk/features/story/ 0,11710,1650966,00.html* (accessed 25 March 2006); Allen, K. (2007) 'Back in the groove: young music fans ditch downloads and spark vinyl revival', *The Guardian*, 16 July, available at: *http://business.guardian .co.uk/story/0,,2127381,00.html* (accessed 17 October 2007).

7

The ultimate mix: try before you buy?

Carley Smith

Before too long, it will be abundantly clear that trying to sell over-priced plastic disks to people who have ubiquitous online access to [an] entire vault of music will be like trying to sell snow at the North Pole. (David Kusek and Gerd Leonhard)[1]

Growing up in a small country town did not afford me access to the radio and television broadcasts my peers enjoyed in the city. My family and I listened to the radio when the atmospherics were in our favour and only received two television stations: GWN[2] and the ABC.[3] GWN did not provide much in the way of musical programming. The ABC did however give us *Countdown* and *Rage*. Essentially, *Rage* saved my life. Most weekends I would tape the programme, hook up our enormous ghetto blaster to the VCR, and make mix tapes. I had little money and no access to record stores, except on our annual trip to Perth before Christmas. This was how I 'listened' to music.

This type of music piracy did not – and does not – receive much media or legal attention. My earlier 'sonic' self is an extreme example, but less technologically-adept forms of music piracy are not that distinct from illegal online file-sharing. Downloading copyrighted audio and visual material is illegal. But is it unethical? The socio-legal debate surrounding the practice of file-sharing is whether consumers who try before buying are doing artists a disservice. Particularly concentrating on music, this chapter discovers why these files are downloaded and how music piracy is justified by those who do it. Significantly, it is seen as an effective way to discover new and rare music without paying exorbitant prices. By balancing the views of analysts, record company executives and fans, the costs and benefits, reasons and consequences of the ultimate mix can be determined.

Studies into the effects of file-sharing generally neglect the voices of actual users of these services.[4] Peer-to-peer (P2P) sharing has many different definitions, but is described by Michel's policy research project as:

> the common term used to describe internet file sharing services. The name derives from the underlying structure of the internet, in which various computers store information and other computers retrieve it through interconnected networks. With P2P, all computers sharing information over the internet are 'peers' because they both store and retrieve information.[5]

To use P2P services, a user downloads software that allows them to search other users' shared files and folders. Once the required file is found then it can then be copied directly from computer to computer. P2P software is not illegal as it was designed for the transfer of non-copyrighted digital files.[6] However, it is the unauthorised sharing of these files that has caused debate over the use of P2P services.

Illegal file-sharing creates an 'e-democracy'. It allows legal and illegal access to otherwise overpriced, copyrighted material. For many users, this availability creates a space where they can 'try before buying'. With regard to musical rarities, much of which have not been made available in an easily distributable format, consumers use P2P services to access what they cannot find in stores *or* for a reasonable price. I interviewed users of P2P software who all download music illegally. They offered a number of justifications for using P2P services, as described below:[7]

> Carley: Do you use these services as a way to build up your music library *or* to find rarities (albums and tracks only available on vinyl, whose production has been deleted or are difficult to find)?
>
> Daniel: Both. I copy it onto minidisc and I have a large collection.
>
> Abby: Both. Especially for rarities because some artists ... have back catalogues that are not readily available in ... Perth.
>
> Callum: Mostly to find rarities.
>
> Shay: Yes, live tracks especially.
>
> Oliver: A lot of the music I listen to can't be found in stores. It usually has to be ordered and in the past has taken up to three months to reach me.
>
> Trent: Since Australian music is quite difficult to find online, I generally find and download live bootlegs and tracks/albums that are never released on CD or vinyl.

Kym: I download lots of B-sides and covers that I can't find here.

Beck: I download a lot of Korean and Japanese pop and rock. Almost all of it is impossible to find in Australia and most has to be ordered online with inflated prices and postage. If I can't find it, I'll download it.

There are many arguments for and against P2P sharing. For some users, P2P is utilised to sample.[8] Most advocates believe P2P increases album sales,[9] whereas P2P critics argue that those who download music illegally would not have bought the music even if they had been given the opportunity.[10] Critics also suggest that consumers who try before they buy may dislike the music and not purchase full-length albums.[11] Some also find P2P an easy way to build up music libraries and acquire 'higher-quality'[12] free music, with the follow-on effect of lowering the price of music and attracting listeners who would not have otherwise purchased the material, increasing illegal music consumption.[13]

Carley: Do you have any qualms about 'robbing artists of money'? Do you see file-sharing as a way of 'trying before you buy'? Is P2P a way to bypass giving your money to large recording companies?

Daniel: Not really. I have a massive CD collection, and the live DJ sets [that I download] are usually from the radio, artists' websites or recorded live at venues. I'm just not keen on paying $25 for an album with only one or two decent songs on it ... Also, I download music I already have on CD so I can just listen to it on my laptop. Plus, I'm a student with little income to spend on music.

Abby: These new technologies offer the opportunity to expand my knowledge of music and listen to obscure artists that I would not already have access to (either due to economic factors or just availability).

Callum: Some yes, some no. But when the recording industry is making record profits and the artists are complaining they are losing money, exactly who is ripping them off the most? I wouldn't mind buying *a* song from the net for about $1.50, but $20 on an album I don't want seems way too excessive.

Stephen: If I find a rare song/track on CD or vinyl I'll usually buy it. I see my downloading habits as a kind of temporary robbery.

Shay: I do and I don't. A lot of the artists I listen to are independent. So, a lot of their music is only available via online forums, websites or within a circle of friends with similar interests.

Oliver: I think it's difficult enough for independent artists. I try to delete songs after I have a hard copy in my possession.

Trent: No, since I mainly download bootlegs of live sets, I don't see how I'm hurting the industry.

Kym: Yes I do. But I don't download as much as I used to ... Most of the bands I listen to are under very small labels. The more successful bands, whose singles I download, have such a huge fan base. I don't see how it affects them economically.

Beck: If the albums were made available in Australia, at a reasonable price, I would buy them. But seeing as many aren't and online ordering is usually a rip-off ... I have limited choices.

These downloaders are not only honest in the commentary on their behaviour, but clear in their justifications. The users of P2P services are broken down into two 'subpopulations' by Edward Felten in his comments on developing a unified theory of file-sharing.[14] He uses the terms 'freeriders' and 'samplers'.[15] Felten describes freeriders as generally young with few ethical qualms over the illegalities of file-sharing, who use P2P services as a way to build up their music libraries.[16] It should however be noted that younger users of these services have little to no disposable income. Many are students or are starting out in lowly-paid employment. These consumers have fewer moral qualms over using P2P as they tend to have fewer financial options than older or more affluent users.

Felten's 'samplers' are generally older and more 'risk averse'.[17] They engage more highly with consumable products and mostly use P2P to find rarities or music they do not value enough to purchase. For samplers, P2P services expose them to more music they enjoy and would be more likely to purchase[18] had they not sampled it illegally. Of my nine interviewees I consider (by Felten's definitions) only Daniel to be a freerider because of the variety of genres from which he downloads and the amount of music that he downloads. Even this labelling is debatable as he admits he has a 'massive CD collection' and mainly downloads electronic music that is difficult to find in stores or that belongs on a larger, more expensive compilation. Daniel would then be a borderline freerider/sampler, and the other eight interviewees are all, by Felten's definition, samplers.

Carley: What type of music do you download?

Daniel: Anything that tickles my fancy; but mainly live DJ sets and other electronic music ... acid jazz, house, techno, tech house and drum 'n' bass.

Abby: Mainly singles to albums that I don't want to buy. A lot of 'catchy' songs are on albums of mostly filler material.

Callum: Mostly dance that is hard to find in stores.

Stephen: Rare music that is either deleted and/or impossible to find and a lot of B-sides and remixes.

Shay: Drum 'n' bass, electronica, experimental.

Oliver: Mostly indie.

Trent: Mainly Australian rock; it's difficult to find online, though.

Kym: Punk when I can find it. Most of the bands I listen to are under very small labels.

Beck: A lot of Korean and Japanese rock and pop.

Half of the interviewees admit to downloading electronic dance music. This non-commercial genre (as opposed to popular dance singles) is widely unavailable in EP (single) format because it is mostly played and produced in long sets not suited to the CD single format. A vast array of dance music is only produced on vinyl, which is of little use to the listener unless they own a record turntable[19] or are using the vinyl for DJ-ing. Most P2P users 'sample' electronica which is not widely played on radio. Looking at the 'dance' music section in most CD stores, a consumer will find myriad subgenres within the dance category. Dance music now has an incredibly widespread distribution, even compared with ten years ago. The format of electronic dance music is different from traditional rock or pop albums. With particular reference to live sets and mixes, consumers can now find tracks that have not received radio airtime, sets by their favoured artists and generally much lengthier compilations. It is easy to sympathise with consumers not wanting to purchase a previously unheard set – again, they want to try before they buy. By Felten's definitions, this type of downloading is a sampler's habit.

Despite Felten's freerider and sampler categorisation, he does point out one important factor many surveys fail to highlight. Freeriders are more willing to admit to their downloading habits than samplers because they are less 'risk averse'. Freeriders are therefore generally overestimated in surveys and samplers underestimated. Survey-based research is inaccurate in its finding that file-sharing decreases CD sales.[20] Neither does survey-based research readily include comments from *actual* users. My interviewees have mostly adhered to the sampler model. They also answered my questions after I informed them they would be named through pseudonyms. For this reason, they have been open in admitting their illegal downloading habits and in expressing their opinions on P2P.

All my interview subjects were well aware of the ethical and legal issues involved in illegal file-sharing:

> Stephen: I see my downloading habits as a kind of temporary robbery.
>
> Owen: I think it's difficult enough for independent artists. I try to delete songs after I have a hard copy in my possession.
>
> Callum: [W]hen the recording industry is making record profits and the artists are complaining they are losing money, exactly who is ripping them off the most?

Any moral qualms these users have with illegally using P2P services originates from a guilt that artists, rather than record companies, may be suffering at P2P users' hands.

Theories of fans' subversive practices fold into this socio-legal debate. Audience studies[21] operate in and around the subversive behavioural spaces of 'the fan'. Music fandom is one of the more legitimated fandoms.[22] Dominant media hierarchies (the recording industry in this case) are supplying consumers with overpriced products and are not addressing consumers' concerns. Disabling P2P services will not halt illegal downloads. Many other services have appeared since the demise of Napster's free services.[23] Consumers are simply looking elsewhere for free and cheaper products. Just as fans poach 'raw' media material and reconstruct it for their own purposes, so do P2P users resist the hyper-capitalism of the music industry by acquiring illegal audio material. Consumers of illegal P2P services – the music fans themselves – are not damaging artists' careers. They are refusing to accept what the record companies produce. Fans are resisting and subverting the hyper-capitalist music industry.

The CD is an outmoded and expensive mode of musical consumption. To cull the theft of copyrighted material, music must be made less expensive and more attractive to consumers. As both legal and illegal P2P downloading escalates, the challenge for policy-makers and authorities does not lay in disabling illegal P2P activities but instead on marking down exorbitantly-priced music. The capitalist music industry has created its own resistance from within.

Notes

1. Quoted in Collins, S. (2005) 'Internet downloads spell death for the CD albums', *The West Australian*, 7 May, p. 3.
2. GWN (Golden West Network) broadcasts to regional areas in Western Australia that are not within satellite range to receive commercial television broadcasts.
3. The ABC's (Australian Broadcasting Corporation) television broadcasts can be received in most regions Australia-wide.
4. Although my research uncovered exhaustive studies, only one piece I sourced included opinions from file-share software users: Felten, E. (2004) 'A grand unified theory of filesharing', available at: *http://www.freedom-to-tinker.com/index.php?p=574* (accessed 12 October 2004).
5. Michel, N. (2004) 'Internet file sharing: the evidence so far and what it means for the future', available at: *http://www.heritage.org/Research/InternetandTechnology/bg1790.cfm* (accessed 10 October 2004).
6. Ibid.
7. All interviews conducted by e-mail in April 2005.
8. When asked if they viewed P2P as a way of trying before buying, all of my interviewees saw this method of acquiring music as a means of sampling an otherwise inaccessible or overpriced music catalogue.
9. See also: Collins, op. cit.; Felten, op. cit.; Lohmann, F. (2004) 'The Napster aftermath', available at: *http://www.legamedia.net/dy/articles/article_14636.php* (accessed 12 October 2004), Michel, op. cit.; Musicunited.org (year unknown) 'In one month 243 million files were illegally downloaded from P2P services', *http://musicunited.org* (accessed 12 October 2004); Oberholzer, F. and Strumpf, K. (2004) *The Effect of File Sharing on Record Sales: An Empirical Analysis*, Boston, MA and Chapel Hill, NC: Harvard Business School and University of North Carolina at Chapel Hill.
10. See: Buskirk, E. (2002) 'File sharing after Audiogalaxy', available at: *http://ecoustics-cnet.com.com/4520-6450_7-5021169-1.html?part=ecoustics-cnet* (accessed 12 October 2004; Collins, op. cit.; Felten, op. cit.; Michel, op. cit.; Oberholzer and Strumph, op. cit.
11. See: Collins, op. cit.; Felten, op. cit.; Lohmann, op. cit.; Michel, op. cit.; Musicunited.org, op. cit.; Oberholzer and Strumpf, op. cit.
12. Higher-quality than older forms of illegal copying, such as on cassette tapes.
13. See Collins, op. cit.; Felten, op. cit.; Lohmann, op. cit.; Michel, op. cit.; Musicunited.org, op. cit.; Oberholzer and Strumpf, op. cit.
14. Felten, op. cit.
15. These classifications are inspired by Oberholzer and Strumph's empirical analysis on file sharing habits.
16. Felten, op. cit.
17. Ibid.
18. Ibid.
19. Most domestic stereo systems no longer include a turntable.
20. Felten, op. cit.

21. See: Cranny Francis, A. (1994) *Popular Culture*, Geelong: Deakin UP; Hills, M. (2002) *Fan Cultures*, New York: Routledge; Jenkins, H. (1995) *Science Fiction Audiences*, London: Routledge; Jenkins, H. (1992) *Textual Poachers*, New York: Routledge; Lewis, L. (ed.) (1992) *The Adoring Audience*, London: Routledge; Penley, C. (1997) *NASA/Trek*, New York: Verso; Russ, J. (1995) *Magic Mommas, Trembling Sisters, Puritans and Perverts: Feminist Essays*, New York: Crossing Press; Tulloch, J. (2000) *Watching Television Audiences*, London: Arnold.
22. When compared with televisual or movie fandoms, for example, which are proliferated online and have a more negative stigma attached.
23. Napster was one of the first P2P networks to be closed down when authorities learned they were distributing copyrighted material. The service now runs for paying users only (see *http://www.napster.com/*). For a full listing of P2P software available for online download, see: After Napster – The Beat Goes On (*http://www.afternapster.com/*).

8

Record companies vs technology

Felicity Cull

The record industry is in trouble, but the music industry is not. (Chuck D)[1]

The recorded music industry makes money by selling sound to consumers. They market an intangible entity as an attractive package of plastic-covered fandom. Putting the voices, lyrics, beats and harmony of songs onto CDs and DVD, vinyl, eight-tracks, cassettes and other sonic platforms sells to consumers something that cannot be touched, seen or tasted. No matter the effort the artist puts into producing a song and the legalities of ownership and copyright law, the physical act of hearing sound is ephemeral. Walking down the street, thousands of familiar and unfamiliar sounds enter our sonic space. A car's engine revving, a child yelling, a magpie screeching and a train passing are sounds that reach our ears and then promptly die away. These sounds are transitory. They are not locked away for future use. They exist only in our memories. Recorded music is different from the ambient lived soundtrack of our lives. Songs are recorded and stored on a platform. Consumers, once they have paid for the privilege, can 'own' this sound and hold it for future use. CDs, cassette tapes and DVDs all allow sound to be stored by more than our memories. Record companies harness these technologies in order to sell the consumer an ephemeral product. When a technological platform allows fans to 'own' sound in a way that record companies cannot control, there is a backlash. Copyright lawyers are hired and fans are prosecuted for their listening practices.

The ephemeral nature of sound does not discount the artist's right to own their own music. The work an artist puts into the writing of music connotes an ownership and right to income. It is the record companies that have these artists under contract. They control how the consumer legally consumes music in an environment of iPods, true-tones for the mobile phone and downloadable music from the internet.

It is impossible to make money from ephemeral intellectual property if there is not some mechanism through which a consumer can buy it. Throughout their history, record companies have been threatened by technological advances that have caused shifts in how they market the music of their contracted artists – reel-to-reel home tape recorders, cassettes, DATs, VHS, BETA, listening booths, music videos, minidisc recorders[2] and even the radio[3] have all met with initial opposition from various parts of the music industry. They were attacked because they were uncontrollable sonic technologies at the time of their inception. Record labels and companies had not yet learnt how to control them in a way that could guarantee the continuation of a large profit margin. Most of the platforms were eventually controlled and used to the advantage of record companies and the artists signed to them. However, in our current environment where massive use of file-sharing services allows users to listen to music but not pay the record companies for a store-purchased CD, it is hard to see how control can be regained. Record companies and their marketing strategies have not kept up with this technology or harnessed it within their business plans. Through delay and denial, it may be impossible to restore the music industry into the money-making machine it once was. As addressed in Carley Smith's last chapter, new listening and purchasing habits have been created that are now difficult to unravel. File-sharing has changed the way people listen and buy music, and that change has threatened the profits of the record industry. While musicians can enjoy their music gaining worldwide exposure, record companies can no longer expect to profit from that exposure with such large margins unless they can legally control the file-sharing practices of music fans, or use file-sharing to their advantage. If they can achieve neither then record companies will be redundant. The Radiohead experiment will be watched by many.

The advent of new technology often heralds a shift in popular culture. When radio first became popular, it caused many movements in the way that music was listened to and how musicians could profit from their talents. In the mid-1920s,[4] critics 'waxed rhapsodic about the unprecedented access to information that people would have and about radio as an antidote to isolation and a flattener of hierarchy'.[5] Radio, like the internet, was initially seen as a revolution in communication rather than a means of gaining great profits. In America, Secretary Hoover announced that he found it 'inconceivable that we should allow so great a possibility for service to be drowned in advertising chatter'.[6] Like television and later the internet, educational and uplifting programming was the focus at radio's inception. However, what was initially seen as a means for a free flow of information soon became a means of entertainment. Radio was initially a platform for live performance. Singers or actors would come into radio studios and sing live or voice a play between the announcers' reports on weather and news. Frank Absher writes that in America, vaudeville performers found that this new technology was enabling them to gain another source of income and had the ability to gain them unforeseen popularity.[7] However, the practice of having live singers perform was soon superseded by the practice of playing records that the announcers and radio stations had purchased. This left the performers who had been recently so advantaged by radio in a similar position to artists renegotiating their rights and financial futures in modern music capitalism: their music is listened to and enjoyed, but they are not directly paid for their intellectual property. The singular profit from the price of the record was all that the musician received at the time of radio's burgeoning popularity, and yet thousands of people had access to their music.

If radio was to become a service that helped singers rather than hindered them, then this payment structure had to be remedied. James Caesar Petrillo, head of the American Musician's Union, applied pressure on radio stations to continue hiring in-house musicians. When the US Congress passed the Lea Act that made it illegal to 'threaten or compel a broadcaster to employ more persons than it needed and pay for services not performed'[8] some other strategy had to be employed to ensure that musicians did not lose their jobs. Petrillo developed an innovative solution: he convinced radio stations to hire former musicians as platter spinners – handling the technical end of record playing. Musicians who had formerly provided entertainment through live performance became the first disc jockeys. Radio was turned into an advantage for record companies through such innovations. As Con Frantzeskos writes:

> instead of seeing early radio technology as a positive opportunity for the music business, they refused stations the right to rebroadcast their recordings. It is with the same fear of the unknown that music companies are currently fighting the latest methods of distribution instead of developing new business models to utilize them.[9]

Eventually, rather than refuse radio stations the right to rebroadcast recordings, it was realised that the exposure radio granted the artists was positive in and for the music industry. The licensing of the radio stations, advertising and systems of payment, such as exist in Australia where radio stations pay APRA a small amount every time they play a track, has made radio integral to their marketing strategy.

Chuck D claims that he sees the internet as 'the new radio'.[10] With respect to sourcing new songs from a chosen genre or artist, a fan who file-shares has similarities with one who tunes into a particular radio programme. It is a way to hear new music that is being discussed in the music press, between friends or on internet fora. The difference between radio and file-sharing is that file-sharing enables the fan to 'own' the song they are looking for. Songs on the radio are like the ambient sounds we hear in our daily lives. A fan can enjoy them, take note of them, but without a recording technology such as a cassette recorder, cannot store them for future use. A consumer must spend money to own the sound. Downloading a file, however, gives the consumer ownership of the music without first paying for it.

The contentious issue is the consumer behaviour from this point. Without a doubt, file-sharing has changed the way in which fans consume music. Being able to personalise a playlist by picking and choosing which MP3s to include on an iPod or on a computer's music program has a certain ruthlessness to it. Gone are the filler tracks from albums. While records encouraged the kind of passive listening that was best done with large headphones while sitting on a beanbag, the CD allowed one to skip over the low points that were still included on the album, on to the highlights and the infamous 'secret song', often 'hidden' after the last track. With file-sharing, consumers do not even have to own the album, let alone listen to (or skip over) the tracks that are not to taste. On an iPod, the symbiotic platform for file-sharing, thousands of songs are available to play, none of which the user dislikes. The beanbag is no longer required. The single, the 120-second pop song which artists like Buddy Holly and Little Richard used to produce, is once again emerging. Albums are no longer necessary. As Chuck D states:

> Why do they have to come with an album if they are just a singles artist? Why don't they keep releasing singles and we buy them a single at a time. Why would I have to buy an album if they have one song that I like? Whereas, in Norah Jones' case or Outkast's case, I think they get an ... artistic diversity that would warrant

people buying an album. So I think now people will buy what they love and just won't be tricked into buying what they might like.[11]

The single may make a comeback and the single artist enjoy new popularity, but we will see whether fans will abandon buying the albums of their favourite artists on CD.

The evidence is contradictory. Record company Tower Records declared bankruptcy in February 2004,[12] citing illegal downloading as the cause. In Australia, ARIA-funded research found that 'more than 50 per cent of file-sharers tend not to buy music they have downloaded'.[13] However, research undertaken in America determined the opposite result:

> The most heavily downloaded songs showed no decrease in CD sales as a result of increasing downloads. In fact, albums that sold more than 600,000 copies during this period appeared to sell better when downloaded more heavily.[14]

In 2004, ARIA claimed their CD sales were in a slump. However, Steve Cannane the Triple J Broadcaster brings both history and logic back to this debate:

> Let's go back to 1998. The year before an 18-year old college dropout named Shawn Fanning wrote a file-sharing program called Napster, the software that kick-started the downloading boom. In that year Australian record companies sold 39.6 million CD albums. Five years later the figure had gone up to 50.5 million. That makes it hard to argue that downloading and CD copying is killing sales.[15]

With research into file-sharing being consistently at odds, it is hard to analyse how file-sharing has truly impacted both CD sales and fan behaviour. It is obvious that many people who download tracks from file-sharing services may never buy the album on which the song appears, but they may never have bought it after hearing the song on the radio either. The difference is that there are no regulations that force file-sharing services to pay for the songs they let people download. In order to profit from someone downloading a song from a file-sharing service, the consumer must then buy the CD. If they do not, the entire transaction has been without profit. Because of the nature of file-sharing, fans share the music they have downloaded with other fans.

This transaction can only benefit the fan or the musician, not the record company to which the musician is signed. If the fan has downloaded a song they would not have heard on the radio or been able to buy from their local music store, then not only has the fan benefited but so has the musician. However, the 'advertising' through file-sharing is at odds with the record companies' need for profit. Exposure for artists, songs and song-writing has no value if money cannot be gained from it.

File-sharing could have become a platform of exposure similar to that of radio. But record companies have not chosen that course of action. Record companies fought these breaches of copyright with legal prosecution. A lack of foresight created this situation. It took many years after the internet's inception for file-sharing to get to such a scale. John Schumann from the Australian band Redgum remembers his advice to Australian record executives:

> In the mid-1990s the internet was in the middle of a serious growth phase. I remember discussing the issue with a couple of senior record company executives and suggesting to them that the internet was about to rewrite the rules for the marketing and distribution of music ... I suggested that if they were smart they would seize this new technology and explore ways to get more music to more people more cheaply ... I remember suggesting to these executives that a label might well be able to put its entire catalogue online and have people download the songs they wanted on a fee-for-track basis ... In response I was solemnly informed that ARIA intended to resist the internet with all means at its disposal.[16]

The chance of curbing file-sharing by these means is small. Peer-to-peer file-sharing makes it hard, although obviously not impossible, to monitor and persecute users. It is impossible to sue everyone who uses file-sharing for copyright breach. Most people would never contemplate being sued for listening to a song without paying for it – even if the threat was real – so the warnings are futile. Ten years ago, a fee-for-track service may have offered a viable income stream and developed new literacies for listeners. Now there has to be another lure for the consumer and another way for the record companies to profit from what is now common customer behaviour. There are two ways to harness file-sharing for the good of both the consumer and the companies that put up the money for artists' music: platforms like the iPod and the possibilities in niche markets.

Every iPod that is sold to the consumer is sold with the knowledge that it is likely that a proportion of the songs on its hard drive will have been downloaded illegally. Apple Computers predicted the changes in the listening habits of music consumers and altered their strategy for generating profit accordingly. While many still predict that this 'will result in music companies signing fewer recording and publishing deals, lowering sales expectations and reducing staff as part of across-the-board cost cutting',[17] the success of the iPod actually proves that money can be made from file-sharing – but not in predictable ways. These profits are not derived from suing Joe Schmo for illegally downloading Metallica's 'Enter Sandman'. If the record companies' strategy for generating profit had been as innovative as that of Apple Computers then there would be no need to reduce the number of recording and publishing deals being signed.

Technology is not something that can be legislated to stay static. Marketing strategies that keep up with technological change, rather than remain nostalgic for an earlier age, will ensure that record companies do not need to sign fewer new artists. But instead of embracing this truth, record company executives like TVT's Steve Gottleib accuse Apple's CEO Steve Jobs of 'contributing to the problem'[18] with the iPod. Gottleib suggests that Jobs is 'using music to sell computers in a very calculated way'.[19] Any company that makes large profit out of recording artists is using music to sell 'a product' in a calculated way. That Apple Computers came up with a platform that allows the fan to listen to music differently from CDs does not make them any more calculated. It makes them more sensitive to the music consumer.

iPods have captured something new and innovative: their design is pleasing and the white headphones are an instant status symbol, a fashionable indicator of a jacked in and modern music fan. Their mobility is appealing and they allow the user to store everything from the new Britney to the rarest, most obscure recording of a little known artist. Few people would have the variety in their CD collections that they do in their iPods. Fans of more obscure music are rewarded in the current environment. While some intrepid collectors may lament their passing, the days of searching through bargain basement bins for a deleted album or braving the conceited employees at a 'cool' record shop looking for that new single by a band mentioned in a limited-run fanzine are now over. Back catalogues from old labels that never made the transition from vinyl are now accessible: 'Motown [is] emptying its archives into Apple's iTunes Music Store to mark its 45th anniversary'.[20] Whole libraries of music are becoming available through this platform. Services like KaZaA and Limewire provide access to obscure songs and rarities. Tracks unavailable in a music store can be found by the search engines: a live performance by the late Jeff Buckley covering 'Sweet Thing' by Van Morrison or Roy Orbison singing 'Danny Boy'. Often, prospective listeners would pay for these rarities if they could find them in store. But CD stores do not cater for niche markets in the way that file-sharing services do. While the newest U2 album is not hard to locate in a CD store, it is the less popular artists, who probably are not enjoying huge profits from the sale of their CDs, that can enjoy the exposure that file-sharing services provide.

This ability for niche markets to become more accessible through file-sharing helps artists who do not play by the rules. This new environment can foster their diversity and difference, and not just for new artists. For example, Billy Bragg, a performer who has never played by record companies' rules, released his song 'The Price of Oil' free to download from his website. Along with Bragg, Simply Red, Prince and David Bowie all use the new internet-based music culture as a platform for their continuing popularity now they have passed the age of usefulness for record companies. Their websites have allowed them to continue making music and selling it to fans. These artists need the exposure that downloads can give them. Billy Bragg stated in 2002:

> Napster was a bit like the radio – it's promotion! I'm relaxed about it as it's happening anyway… There's no point chucking your rattle out of the pram! The first music I ever owned was tapes of the chart rundown from the radio and that didn't stop me buying music.[21]

It is important to monitor how these artists are using diverse strategies both to maintain and build their fan base. It may be that the reign of cookie cutter pop and the predictable number one album are over. If we monitor the ways that music is being sold to and enjoyed by the consumer, music culture looks very different from the picture painted by the record companies and the chart listings.

It will be much more difficult to shape the buying practices of the consumer. Downloading may indeed spell the end for record companies in their current manifestation. As Chuck D states:

> I believe the record industry when they say downloading has cost them billions of dollars. But I also believe that the record companies have been beneficiaries of price hiking the CD where they've made so much of a surplus over the last 15 or 20 years that now finally it's evening out. You know [the record companies] are asking governments to protect something that might be outdated.[22]

An alternative music capitalism is the only way forward. Copyright lawyers can prosecute fans – but no matter how much the record companies pay them, they cannot make it 1985 again. Performers and consumers are being forced to pay for record companies' conservatism in handling the technological platforms of music. The music industry is now a multimedia industry. Controlling the way listeners use technology like copy-capable CDs, iPods and file-sharing services is not an option. Embracing the new music culture for the benefit of artists seems as unlikely for the record companies. If profits are the main reason for their operation, then this new environment may not suit them. Songwriter Janis Ian questions whether the new music culture is really costing artists anything:

> Costing *me* money? I don't pretend to be an expert on intellectual property law but I do know one thing. If a music industry executive claims I should agree with their agenda because it will make me more money, I put my hand on my wallet... and check it after they leave, just to make sure nothing is missing.[23]

What is of concern for record companies is not the intricacy of intellectual property laws, the rights of artists or the unlawfulness of fans' listening practices. Their interest is profit. The irony is that this change could have been managed to ensure profit, but their businesses and strategic plans remained conservative and wedded to analogue structures and audience practices. Through their errors and miscalculations, lawyers may find a way to reduce the flow of change, but the future has already happened. The artists and record companies who survive this shift in music technology will likely be those who follow an alternative path. As Chuck D says: 'Fight the power, but you know, be able to harness the power'.[24]

Notes

1. CBC News (2004) 'Download this! Interview with Chuck D', *CBC News: Disclosure*, broadcast 9 March, available at: *http://www.cbc.ca/disclosure/ archives/040309_swap/artists_chuckd_print.html* (accessed 21 April 2006).
2. Ian, J. (2002) 'The internet debacle – an alternative view', *Performing Songwriter Magazine*, May, available at: *http://www.janisian.com/article-internet_ debacle.html* (accessed 16 June 2007).
3. Frantzeskos, C. (2007) 'The dinosaurs of the recorded music industry must evolve or die', available at: *www.onlineopinion.com.au/view.asp?article= 861* (accessed 16 June 2007).

4. *US News and World Report* (1999) 'Ask radio historians about the internet – radio stock frenzy in 1920s' *US News and World Report* 126(3): 48.
5. Ibid.
6. Ibid.
7. Absher, F. (2005) 'Battle between broadcasters', *St. Louis Journalism Review* 35(274): 16.
8. Ibid.
9. Frantzeskos, op. cit.
10. CBC News, op. cit.
11. Ibid.
12. Koprowski G. (2004) 'The web: The effect of illegal downloading' *United Press International*, 18 February.
13. ARIA (2003) 'Impact of internet music file sharing and CD burning', available at: *http://www.aria.com.au/pages/CurrentIssueInternetMusicFileSharingCD Burning.htm* (accessed 12 June 2007).
14. Knight, W. (2004) 'Net piracy does not harm record sales', 30 March, available at: *http://www.newscientist.com/news/print.jsp?id=ns99994831* (accessed 12 June 2007).
15. Cannane, S. (2004) 'Music industry way off track with song and dance about falling sales', 29 March, available at: *http://www.smh.com.au/articles/ 2004/03/28/1080412234274.html* (accessed 1 April 2004).
16. Schumann, J. (2003) 'The music industry has only itself to blame for sales lost to the internet', *Online Opinion*, available at: *http://www.onlineopinion. com.au/asp?article=946* (accessed 19 July 2005).
17. Chang, S. (2004) 'Record companies must embrace the changing digital era', *Billboard* 116(10): 42.
18. Silverthome, S. (2004) 'Is iTunes the answer to music piracy?' HBS Working Knowledge, available at: *http://www.pwcglobal.com/Extweb/NewCoAtWork. nsf/docid/87a7BB6DE7449785256E58000CFB7C* (accessed 24 June 2004).
19. Ibid.
20. Lloyd, D. (2004) 'Mo Motown', available at: *http://www.ilounge.com/index. php/news/comments/mo-motown-comes-to-itunes/* (accessed 28 July 2005).
21. Mackintosh, H. (2002) 'Union Bragg: interview with Billy Bragg', *The Guardian*, 30 May, available at: *http://technology.guardian.co.uk/online/ story/0,3605,724212,00.html* (accessed 24 June 2004).
22. CBC News, op. cit.
23. Ian, op. cit.
24. CBC News, op. cit.

Part 3:
Uploading identity

Putting their life on(the)line: blogging and identity

Joanne Smith

In 2004, the blog erupted into the new fad in internet discourse, proliferating sources of information and entertainment.[1] Blogs, or online journals, are sites that enable internet users to record their thoughts and observations for a wide audience. The free buffet of blogging sites served alongside accessible and easy to use web tools provides an alternative venue outside traditional publishing sources for internet users to share their private thoughts and daily encounters. On the surface, such an enterprise and agenda appears a seamless and optimistically democratic usage of the internet. Yet the narrative of accessibility and diversity in blogging requires contextualisation within the changes infiltrating other media. The line between public and private lives is blurred in a world where the web-literate citizens collect their 15 minutes of fame by signing up for a place on a reality programme. With particular media poised to capture 'real' people – for news and entertainment – it is not surprising that the opportunity to reveal all about the minutiae of a daily life is becoming a popular pastime.

Such unquestioned complacency and contradiction between the right to privacy afforded to the individual and the increasing clamour for attention requires further scrutiny. Beyond the simplistic explanations rattled through tabloid journalism warning of online dangers, attention should be refocused upon the social and cultural practices that deem it acceptable to reveal our personal lives to an audience. This chapter examines blogging as a tool of free expression beyond the literary canon, yet questions whether this freedom exists at a cost to individual rights and privacy.

'Blogs' (an amalgamation of the term 'web logs') are websites available to individuals or groups to record their thoughts, feelings and observations for a World Wide Web audience. The increasing popularity of blog usage has culminated in its inclusion in the Merriam-Webster dictionary, which defines a blog as 'a website that contains an online personal journal with reflections, comments and often hyperlinks'.[2] Initially, blogging practices were maintained through personal web space but support technology and infrastructure has improved rapidly, allowing easy access and demanding minimal technical knowledge from the user. There are currently two dominant blogging technologies available. One example is Moveable Type – an open source program which allows the user to manipulate code and create a page to their personal specifications. Often the software must be bought but free packages with minimal features do exist. Open source programs allow the user to embed the blog into an existing webpage, granting uniformity within a site. These blogging tools are marketed as 'professional and business' publishing platforms (see, for example, *http://www.sixapart.com/*). Alternatively, numerous free sites exist, offering a blogging service but with limited capabilities. Free sites host the blogs themselves, such as Livejournal (*http://www.livejournal.com*), Blogger (*http://www.blogspot.com*) and Diaryland (*http://www.diaryland.com*). Often a fee can be paid to gain special membership privileges, such as greater freedom to manipulate page layout and the ability to embed into a personal webpage.[3] 'Free' site users can access and update their blog directly from a webpage or through a straightforward software program. These features enable bloggers who have minimal literacy in webpage construction to create and maintain their blog. These features create blogging as an accessible practice. The process requires no money or specialist knowledge and as a result, users flock to these sites to claim their slice of the blogging pie.

Young people in particular open and maintain blogs. What possible purpose could this have to them? Youth rarely possess a voice in mainstream media. News is presented about them rather than for them. Advertising is directed at them. Young people are silenced and spoken for, without an avenue to discuss or reply. They have limited options for presenting their vision of the world. Blogging is an alternative space. It is easy to access and can be read by a wide audience. The user feels as though they have gained control of a medium where their voice can potentially be heard by many. It exists as a dangerous exercise to previous generations who possess a strong hold on media power. It is their views that are disseminated to wide audience. As a result, blogging is often portrayed negatively.

The internet is frequently depicted as a medium fraught with dangers. Stories of the many dangers prevalent – particularly to children and young people – are publicised in various forms. One recent study had discovered that:

> Children as young as five are going online and virtually all pre-teens are using the internet for homework, entertainment and chatting to friends. But the study has found that almost 40 per cent of eight to 13 year olds have had an on-line experience of concern, such as stumbling upon pornography or being contacted by a stranger.[4]

These statistics came from the study kidsonline@home, conducted by the Australian Broadcasting Authority and NetAlert into children's internet usage. The report also stated that 99 per cent of parents believed the internet was beneficial to their child for educational and entertainment purposes.[5] Reporting online threats is predominantly depicted in the form of physical dangers. Internet chat rooms and online messaging are revealed as avenues for predators to strike, who pose a threat offline. A recent example is the story of Justin, who appeared on *Oprah*, describing how he was hired to become an internet pornography star after purchasing a webcam. The programme did not explain how Justin came to receive so much immediate attention. It simply claimed Justin joined a popular website and posted his profile and 'by hooking up his webcam, Justin unintentionally became a free face in a dark world where men prey on vulnerable teenagers and children'.[6] As a result of such fears, the Australian government introduced free downloadable software to prevent children being exposed to pornography. Little information is disseminated on the intricacies of internet usage such as cookies, pop-ups, spyware and adware. Blogging has become the new danger, particularly for children, where 'predatory adults could use an RSS feeder program – a syndication tool – to be instantly e-mailed any picture when it was added to a blogging site'.[7] Additional technologies such as third-generation mobile phones are also implicated in facilitating paedophilic activities. Alan Reid describes:

> The rise of 3G phones can make it easier for paedophiles across the globe to contact children to share images of children with other paedophiles, or encourage children to take and send images of themselves.[8]

Reid further identifies that the dangers posed to children through increased internet access should not be exaggerated and 'technical and legal responses to such risks must be appropriate, proportionate, effective and inclusive'.[9] While real risks exist and require attention and understanding in a media-specific context, it is the extreme cases which are emphasised through the news media and presented as frequent and common.

Negative news stories also focus upon issues such as weight and obesity. Inactivity and available leisure time spent online are labelled as causes for physical illnesses and an increase in both adult and childhood weight gain. In assessing the positive and negative impact of new technology upon the population, *The Gold Coast Bulletin* reported that 'there [also] are concerns about physical health in relation to the use of new technology, such as radiation and tumors, eye sight, obesity and other physical health illness'.[10]

The Sunday Telegraph claimed technology was seducing children at the expense of their health. It stated, 'Australian boys spend up to a third of their waking hours in front of a screen, putting them at greater risk of sleep disorders, behavioural problems and obesity'.[11] Such reporting generalises the correlation between interactivity with technologies such as computers, mobile phones and television and the extent of usage. According to a recent study of 129 high school girls' physical fitness by the European College of Sports Science:

> Physical fitness is unrelated to internet use time or television watching time. Furthermore, since these sedentary behaviors are unrelated to leisure-time physical activity, yet positively correlated with each other, it is suggested that time spent watching television or on the internet does not occur at the expense of leisure-time physical activity.[12]

People who invest significant amounts of time to online pursuits are labelled as 'addicts' and will suffer social problems as a result and 'concerns have been raised that children who form "electronic friendships" with computers instead of friendships with their peers lack the social competency and interpersonal skills, to deal with the real world'.[13] However, Michele Fleming and Debra Rickwood claim that research has shown that 'Most of the time, young people online are interacting with friends from their existing social networks'.[14] The internet and blogs have also been fingered as a new source for schoolyard bullying and harassment and 'any child with a mobile phone or web access can be a victim'.[15] Popular media examples[16] of cyber-bullying include the Columbine High School massacre, where killer Eric Harris constructed a website making death threats against other students, and 'Alex' who committed suicide after being harassed by instant messaging from other schoolchildren.[17] In particular, it is highlighted that Alex's parents and teachers were unaware of what was happening, emphasising the helplessness of parents in using and understanding new technologies. These extreme stories of internet-based misfortunes provide journalists with newsworthy criteria of generational conflict and fear.

News media and journalism are predominantly commercial enterprises, requiring a wide audience to sustain them. Advertising space and time is utilised to drain the most attention from an audience. Traditional news sources appeal to an older demographic while 'youth issues' are often relegated to supplements. The news media cater for a specific generation and as a result, journalistic representations of the internet and online journals are skewed towards appeasing this audience. The internet – similar to the introduction of television as a medium – is portrayed negatively, as an unknown entity and fraught with dangers. The intended audience for this information is assumed to possess minimal understanding of chat rooms, private messaging and online journals (blogs). Online threats are manifested as physical because this is a context and environment understood by analogue generations. Physical and personal safety is easy to understand because physical safety can be protected through laws and legislature. Physical threats and changes are also immediate and easily observable. Toby Miller highlights the physical nature of technological effects when he states, 'whether society and individuals will be fundamentally changed by technology is difficult to say, but so far all we have seen are physical changes, not psychological changes'.[18] By focusing on threats to personal safety or health and wellbeing, parents become armed with preventative measures rather than accumulating relevant knowledge of how the online world operates. Just as children and teenagers are simplistically positioned as vulnerable to new technology, parents are devalued as lacking knowledge and are positioned to view the internet defensively.

News journalism, established during the analogue age, is maintaining the criteria of its origins to assess the value and quality of a blog. Articles and media attention to online journals frequently dismiss them as inane and worthless. Any positive attention awarded to blogging is often focused upon what are considered 'good' blogs, such as those devoted to providing political comment and analysis. 2004 was considered 'the year of the blog' due to the proliferation of online journals discussing and analysing the US Presidential election.[19] Particular attention was also afforded to campaign blogs as an avenue for increased democratic participation in the public sphere.[20] These voices are important but they do not possess the exclusive and collective voice of bloggers. News media gatekeepers have acted to approve particular sections of media, which can be understood by their audience. The personal and private is devalued as a site of worthy knowledge. Online journals may be sanctioned areas of publishing, but they have been assessed and graded by what is considered worthy and what is 'rubbish'. An online medium is being assessed through a poor fit of previously institutionalised literary criteria.

People are rarely given credit for absorbing and learning online skills. These literacies are dismissed. It is online journals – or blogs – that enable an alternative voice in history to be provided. Sanctioned methods of recording history through books, archives and published works often omit the various voices that live that history. Online journals offer an alternative site for alternative histories, recording important artefacts of life and 'some predict that blogs will replace media comment sections entirely because many bloggers are far more knowledgeable about a subject than many of the paid pundits writing columns'.[21] Visiting a site such as Livejournal allows a visitor to explore a range of journals. Hopping from journal to journal enables a person to gain an insight into the microcosm of life. Many contain film reviews, photographs or general observations of the world which would otherwise not be heard in sanctioned publications of books and newspapers. It is through blogging that people outside traditional publishing realms are able to have a voice, to record their version of life which will later be tidied up and written over by the dominant, the powerful and the loud. They may be told about how to live their life. But for the moment, they can blog back.

While there are plenty of arguments affirming the democracy in action through blogs, it is also important to view such behaviour within a wider social and cultural context. There are circumstances which have not only inspired the surge of blog creations but have dictated that the practice is acceptable. Yet the news media concentrate upon physical threats resulting from internet usage, with a focus on online banking scams, where 'the sheer popularity of online banking is a magnet for crooks and con artists'.[22] Internet users are warned of the dangers of online banking. For example, in 2004 *The Irish Examiner* reported, 'conmen are stepping up an online banking scam in Britain, internet experts warned yesterday. They trick customers into giving away bank details with e-mails telling them to log on to a fake website for their account'.[23] Such information focuses on the immediate problems presented through storing personal data online. Attention afforded to individual responsibility and the personal sphere fails to address the responsibility of businesses in online protection. As reported in the *Sydney Morning Herald*:

> It is fast becoming apparent that, in their drive to encourage online banking, the banks could have done more to warn customers about the potential pitfalls and how to avoid them. The simple fact is that the e-mail scams have been able to proliferate, at least in part, due to the high level of unsolicited direct marketing consumers already receive from their banks.[24]

Such threats and fears are concurrent with the blogging-inspired divulging of personal information about the self.

Neoliberal political environments have naturalised the focus on individual choice and market decisions. The products we purchase become representative of the self. What we watch on television is compartmentalised and reduced into age and sex determinations, with advertising skewed so tightly toward demographics that it is difficult to move through precise sociological categories. In addition, there has been an increasing blur between media and audience. With programmes that now use 'real' people to depict 'reality', it appears possible for everyone to claim their moment within the spotlight. There is an increasing search within both the news and entertainment media to discover 'reality' and deliver it. Graeme Turner writes, 'public visibility per se is offered as an achievement to emulate and desire; little wonder that it is pursued with such tenacity and at some personal risk by a large number of people'.[25] Such a climate has emerged along with the rise of internet usage. Online access now allows people to distribute their views, ideas and general information to a large audience. The workplace has provided a place of access and computer hardware and web hosting are decreasing in cost, making the internet accessible to more people.[26] With a climate of media allowing 'real' people to share their lives and the opportunity to emulate this online, it is not surprising blogging has become so popular. It has become easier to maintain a blog for personal reasons at a time when it is becoming increasingly acceptable to share such personal information. Blogging places no restriction on what can be said about the self or others. Social norms are changing to permit this behaviour. If a person can audition for *Big Brother*, why not maintain an online journal? Turner writes that *Big Brother* offers 'the promise of media validation for just being who you are, every day'.[27] Blogging provides an online method for public validation and is simply another step in the infiltration of the internet in our lives. Chat rooms, e-mail, personal messaging, social networking sites like Facebook and webcams have enabled people to interact and share their information with others. Blogging is another stage in the evolving matrix of the digital self.

The counter-argument of 'choice' is frequently offered to excuse such behaviour. A blogger selects the amount of information they divulge. They possess the freedom to choose their friends and whether their journal can be viewed exclusively by these people, some of these people, everyone or only themselves. Bloggers control their topics and the frequency of entries. The availability of numerous options for the individual blogger presents them with the appearance of enjoying ultimate control over the flow of information. The individual is emphasised as the ultimate decision maker, masking the cultural practices of disseminating information about the self without question. With a media climate of increasing voyeurism and the prostituting of personality as politics, it appears simple and straightforward to write about the self freely and openly. The choice remains with the individual.[28] The increasing necessity of providing personal information to the shop assistant when purchasing clothing, or forced online banking due to fee increases at the local bank, suggests that the dissemination of information is harmless and normal.

Voyeurism is a larger threat than isolated instances of online bullying or obesity may suggest. The effects are not immediate or blatantly noticeable and are therefore easily ignored. However, such a practice is becoming normalised and it should be questioned. It is an unsettling thought to consider who may access our personal information, but it is more frightening to realise our compliance and complicity in such a violation. As *Business Week* reports of blog use:

> It's not just the prospect of predators and swindlers that has the social-network set alarmed. University officials and campus cops are scouring blogs and sites for tips on underage drinking and other student misbehavior. Corporations are investing in text-recognition software from vendors such as SAP and IBM to monitor blogs by employees and job candidates.[29]

With blogging skewed as a popular 'youth' pastime, the habit of providing personal information is learnt early and is a positive experience. The free dissemination of personal lives is rewarded through the accumulation of friends and social acceptance.

Blogging tracks the conditions of social change. It is presented as an avenue for personal expression outside the literary canon. But is championing the individual a worthwhile pursuit? Rather than an avenue for creative, literary expression, it is utilised as a tool for an individual to grasp the media spotlight at any costs, whether it is to champion the self or flaunt defamation laws. It is occurring at a moment in time when we are encouraged to give up personal rights – slowly and gradually. Methodical and planned social change rarely receives significant media attention as it fails the criteria of fast-paced news media that value immediacy and dramatic visuals. Blogging contains the power to become a valuable tool in online publishing and as an historical archive, but instead has created another avenue for media saturation of the self. Potentially it could become a worldwide forum for an e-democracy and dissent but has disappointed in this aspiration. Previous criticisms have centred on literary merit. Actually the greatest flaw of the blog discourse is the overinvestment in the self rather than an outward discussion of the world.

Notes

1. At the end of 2004, '7 per cent of the 120 million US adults who use the internet said they had created a blog or web-based diary. That represents more than 8 million people'. See Rainie, L. (2005) 'The state of blogging', PEW Internet and American Life, available at: *http://www.pewinternet.org/ pdfs/PIP_blogging_data.pdf* (accessed 28 June 2007).
2. BBC News (2004) 'Blog picked as word of the year', available at: *http://news.bbc.co.uk/go/pr/fr/-/2/technology/4059291.stm* (accessed 20 March 2005).
3. Unlike the Moveable Type interface, however, the web address still contains the hosts' name.
4. Barlow, K. (2005) 'Study confirms dangers facing children online', available at: *http://www.abc.net.au/pm/content/2005/s1351943.htm* (accessed 1 May 2007).
5. Australian Broadcasting Authority and NetAlert Ltd (2005) 'kidsonline @home: Internet use in Australian homes', Canberra: Australian Broadcasting Authority and NetAlert Ltd.
6. *Oprah*, 'The young boy lured into becoming an internet porn star', television programme, screened on Channel Ten Australia, 29 May 2006.
7. BBC Online (2005) 'Blogging "a paedophile's dream"', available at: *http://www.bbc.co.uk/go/pr/fr/-/1/hi/scotland/4209801.stm* (accessed 20 March 2005).
8. Reid, A. (2005) 'The rise of third generation phones: the implications for child protection', *Information and Communications Technology Law* 14(2): 89–113.

9. Ibid., p. 89.
10. Vernon, K. (2006) 'Always on: how technology is turning us into new people', *Gold Coast Bulletin*, 2 June.
11. Labi, S. (2006) 'Boys tuning out', *Sunday Telegraph*, 16 April.
12. Kerner, M., Kurrant A. and Kalinski, M. (2004) 'Leisure-time physical activity, sedentary behaviour and fitness of high school girls', *European Journal of Sports Science* 4(2): 1–17.
13. Vernon, op. cit.
14. Fleming and Rickwood also cite a PEW Internet and American Life Survey, which claims of the 73 per cent of American youths online, '43 per cent said that use of the Internet improved their relationships with friends; and 32 per cent reported that the Internet had helped them make new friends'. See Fleming, M. and Rickwood, D. (2004) 'Teens in cyberspace: do they encounter friend or foe?' *Youth Studies Australia* 23(3): 46–52.
15. Wilson, D. (2006) 'Texts and stones', *The Age*, 8 June.
16. These examples have been used to define 'cyber-bullying' in websites such as Wikipedia and Answers.com.
17. Meadows, B., Bergal, J., Helling, S., Odell, J., Piligian, E., Howard, C., Lopez, M., Atlas, D. and Hochberg, L. (2005) 'The web: the bully's new playground', *People Magazine*, 14 March.
18. Quoted in Vernon, op. cit.
19. The PEW Internet and American Life Project reported that between February 2004 and November 2004 blog readership increased 58 per cent in the USA. See Rainie L. and Horrigan, J. (2005) 'Internet: the mainstreaming of online life', available at: *http://www.pewinternet.org/pdfs/Internet_Status_2005.pdf* (accessed 26 June 2006).
20. For example, James Janack investigates the democratic nature of blogging through his analysis of Howard Dean's 'Blog for America'. See Janack, J. (2006) 'Mediated citizenship and digital discipline: a rhetoric of control in a campaign blog', *Social Semiotics* 16(2): 197–203.
21. BBC News (2003) 'A blog for everyone', available at: *http://news.bbc.co.uk/go/pr/fr/-/2/hi/technology/3078541.stm* (accessed 20 March 2005).
22. Sampson, A. (2004) 'Simple ways to avoid the crooks in online banking', *Sydney Morning Herald*, 24 January.
23. *The Irish Examiner* (2004) 'Consumers warned of online banking scam', *The Irish Examiner*, 9 December.
24. Sampson, op. cit.
25. Turner, G. (2004) *Understanding Celebrity*, London: Sage, p. 63.
27. Ibid.
28. Lifejournal's tagline is 'be a goat, not a sheep'. See, for example *http://news.livejournal.com/92448.html*.
29. Kharif, O. (2006) 'Big Brother is reading your blog', *Business Week Online*, 28 February, available at: *http://www.businessweek.com/technology/content/feb2006/tc20060228_241578.htm* (accessed 15 November 2007).

10

Is it all bad? Japan's internet suicide subculture

Joel Matthews

There's nothing bad about suicide ... It's always been a part of our culture. (Wataru Tsurumi)[1]

While Western iconography renders Japan as full of busy, scuttling, inner-Tokyo technology-savvy businessmen, the reality is distinct, complex and ambiguous. This chapter probes the relatively new and socially problematic area of *netto-shinjuu*[2] or internet suicide groups. Compared with English-speaking Western nations, the recent widespread uptake of the internet in Japan has led to a number of social issues dominating the Japanese press. Much academic work[3] has been published surrounding the issue of suicide in Japan. However, representations of Japanese suicide practices in Western media have long been associated with Japan's pugnacious wartime past and its *samurai* (warrior) heritage. Even though the circumstances paying influence to contemporary suicide practices have changed dramatically, representations in the West have remained largely the same. Therefore the fact that Japan's suicide rate still remains one of the highest in the world is worthy of meticulous academic attention.

The discipline of internet studies has a solid foundation in Western academia. However, there remains an academic void when researching the internet in Japan. Indeed, until recently, no credible research on the matter had been published in English. Moreover, the research conducted in Japanese tended to be empirical. Contrary to Western misconceptions, Japan's technological output throughout the 1980s and 1990s did not necessarily equate to a domestic market fluent in the use of this computer technology. The opening of the Japanese domestic market in 1992 saw American-made Compaq machines sell for half the price of the Japanese-made NEC machines.[4] The number of PCs grew rapidly once they became readily available. By 1997, the PC penetration rate was still only 20 per cent, behind countries like Australia (35 per cent) and the USA (40 per cent).[5] While the uptake of PCs continued to rise, the most remarkable new technology on the Japanese domestic market was the introduction of NTT DoCoMo's 'i-mode' in 1999. Just one year after being launched, DoCoMo had grown to become Japan's leading internet service provider. The i-mode technology meant that the mobile phone had the capability to connect to the internet and be used in similar ways to traditional desktop PCs without the restrictiveness of being confined to the home or office. This is of particular interest as it provided mobility to a whole raft of web-based communities. Individuals joined and participated in internet subcultural formations through the use of their mobile phone. This mobility has activated a discussion about the unfolding relationship between the internet and subcultures of – and concerning – suicide in Japan.

In 2004, the number of suicides in Japan reached over 30,000 for the seventh straight year. This was down from the record-breaking 34,427 people who took their own lives the previous year.[6] The growing fear within the domestic press is that the number is rising due to the ease with which individuals can now search anonymously for others who wish to take their own life. Many reports suggest that the troubled are too afraid or embarrassed to talk face-to-face about their personal problems and seek out other lonely people wanting to die. Numerous cases of internet-related group suicides occurred in increasingly rapid succession through 2006 and 2007.

Japanese suicide statistics can be analysed according to a number of different contributing factors. Chronic illness is believed to be the major cause of suicide among those aged over 60 in the suicide statistics. In 2004, 10,994 people over-60 committed suicide.[7] While euthanasia is not legal in Japan, there is neither the social nor religious outcry against such practices that is visible in the Christian West, and it is believed that medically-assisted deaths have become quite widespread. However, these deaths are not registered as suicides in governmental statistics. Another discernible realisation is that the number of men outnumbers women two to one.[8] Changing discourses surrounding masculinity and the responsibilities placed on Japanese men in both the public and private spheres has caused a dramatic increase in the number of men taking their own lives as a result of this seemingly unbearable pressure. Death by overwork (*karoshi*) and fatigue-induced suicide (*karo-jisatsu*) have also been on the rise since the burst of the Japanese economic bubble in the early 1990s. As Takashi Nakamura confirms, 'such suicide rates reflect the stress experienced by men under the now decade-long post-bubble recession'.[9] Economic factors may account for a significant proportion of suicides in Japan but most socially alarming, in terms of domestic press coverage, are the statistics for youth suicide.

An increasingly popular method of socialisation in Japan is being mediated by, what is referred to as *deai-kei* (type of encounter). It has become a form of social engagement where an individual places a so-called personal advertisement onto an electronic message board. Visitors to the message board can then read through a number of advertisements and decide to respond to these. Individuals will generally seek partners for either real-world face-to-face encounters or for *meru-tomo* (literally, 'e-mail-friend'). *Deai-kei* sites have come about predominantly due to the integration of internet technologies into the i-mode mobile phone platform. Holden and Tsuruki discuss *deai-kei* as being sociologically significant for three reasons:

> First, as a form of sociation, formal internet-based encounter sites have only been in Japan since the millennium. Second, as an internet subculture, *deai* is commonly considered to be among the murkiest ... A third, related point ... is that, although *deai* is a tool for sociation, it is also an important instrument for the mediation of identity, the exploration of the self, the management of emotions, the arbitration between the individual and the larger social world.[10]

So, while we can see that *deai* is an electronic cousin of Internet Relay Chat (IRC), the sociation process involved in *deai* can be seen more as a negotiation between the self and the society at large. One reason for this transgression could lay in the simple portability and ease with which *deai* can be accessed. It has become a 'staple of the faddish, mobile, mediated, gadget-centred, youth-oriented, licentious lifestyle of contemporary urbanised Japan'.[11] To this end, *deai* facilitates a virtual space with two important subcultural characteristics: trust and self-defence. The user has the ability to logon and logoff at any time, but also has the ability to carry it through to the end via online support and encouragement. Whenever there is a glimpse of doubt or apparent breach of trust, either party can escape without the real-world fear of 'losing face' or ensuing embarrassment.

Due to the nascent nature of *netto-shinjuu*, the limited amount of research material for this chapter was almost entirely found online. According to one particular website, contemporary Japanese youth have a 'weakness' when it comes to forming human relationships. The internet, they explain, 'has the ability to be anonymous and intimate at the same time'.[12] The shame of a normal face-to-face encounter is not felt. Thus, researchers can delve directly into a discussion about the contemplations of suicide without any real-world hesitations. Japanese internet message boards are littered with sites discussing the topic of suicide. The debate about whether to regulate the Japanese-language internet more thoroughly has also come under the media spotlight.[13] The imperative to stop this form of communication taking place is another perceived solution to the growing problem of group suicide. A node of debate is whether the problem and blame lays in Japanese social structures or the internet as a communicative tool.

The extreme rise in group suicides and media focus in general has heralded a whole new spate of suicide-related books and references in popular culture.[14] The most notable of these has been *The Complete Suicide Manual*,[15] the author of which claims:

> There's nothing bad about suicide. It's an individual's choice. It's not illegal, and we don't have any religion here in Japan telling us otherwise. So we're very broad minded about it. As for group suicides – before the internet, people would write letters or make phone calls. It's always been a part of our culture.[16]

It is true that there is a Buddhist connection to Japanese constructions of suicide and this has played a part in Japanese history. There is the belief in Buddhism that one can escape the pain of this life (*gense*) and carry on to the next life (*raise*). This historical continuity has been affirmed in the academic research concerning Japanese suicide practices; however, the problem that has arisen over the past few years is that those voices crying out for help are much younger and lonelier than in the past. This tends to suggest that the motivating factors, combined with the accessibility offered by net-based communication, are leading to unprecedented numbers of group suicides.

Is it theoretically viable to argue that a communicative tool such as the internet actually facilitates and promotes suicides that would not have happened had this tool been not so readily available? Or does the cause of this problem lie in the societal structures and economic, spiritual and religious circumstances surrounding those individuals who reach the conclusion that suicide is the only option for them? Primarily, many online commentators and the Japanese popular press[17] argue that, while people may have a desire to end their own life, they are too scared to actually go through with it by themselves and may talk to loved ones or friends who have the ability to discourage or persuade them to reconsider. The problem with the internet, they argue, is that 'a stranger's comments or advice online may have the reverse effect and act to provoke the situation hence hastening the process'.[18] A young telephone helpline worker claims: 'It's almost like a cult … these internet groups. When people are lonely and suicidal – but afraid of death – they find these websites which egg them on'.[19] Another individual who got caught up in the communal push towards suicide states that, 'there are some vicious sites which really encourage people to die. When you get in a group, there is a momentum which makes it hard to stop; people become irrational'.[20] Does this type of communal peer pressure equate to a problem with the medium and not the individuals involved? The issue remains for policymakers and theorists to determine if targeting the internet as the source and root of the *netto-shinjuu* phenomenon is a viable solution to this problem.

As Zygmunt Bauman has stated, '"Community" is nowadays another name for paradise lost – but one to which we dearly hope to return, and so we feverishly seek the roads that may bring us there'.[21] Community is evoked to make us feel that we are a part of something, that we belong. However, substantial theoretical work has been done on the ambiguity and superficiality of community-based relationships. Benedict Anderson's much-famed theory of the nation state as an 'imagined community' captures the ambivalent tether between geography and belonging structures. Anderson argues that 'Communities are to be distinguished, not by their falsity/genuineness, but by the style in which they are imagined'.[22] It is specifically the way in which Japanese suicide communities and identities are imagined that may offer a key to why these tragic events have been happening in such rapid succession. The community that these sites serve to form and uphold fulfils the needs of those participating in them. Individuals considering committing suicide are, in a sense, suffering from a crisis of community. As Bauman postulates:

> Identity sprouts on the graveyard of communities, but flourishes thanks to the resurrection of the dead. A life dedicated to the search for identity is full of sound and fury. 'Identity' means standing out: being different, and through that difference unique – and the search for identity cannot but divide and separate. And yet the vulnerability of individual identities and the precariousness of solitary identity-building prompt the identity-builders to seek pegs on which they can hang their individually experienced fears and anxieties, and having done that, perform the exorcism rites in the company of other similarly afraid and anxious individuals.[23]

Suicide groups work in the same way as other identity constructions. Suicide can be seen as a result of the failing of the nation-state, the workplace, social groups and the family as a stable community. Does the death of the societal community spell the rise of the new 'suicidal identity'? It not only places the individual at odds with the rest of society but also becomes the realisation of Bauman's theory. The suicidal individuals 'perform the exorcism rites'[24] in perfect precision by committing the act with simultaneous precision, thus fulfilling their final irrevocable obligation to the identity construction to which they aspire.

When questioned why they specifically chose to seek out others contemplating suicide online, many respondents expressed fear at fulfilling their desire to die alone. They spoke of how solitude and loneliness had driven them to want to take their own lives in the first place. A suicide website designer claims, 'it's hard to explain, but this [nation – Japan] is a very suffocating, restrictive society. You are supposed to fit in, and if you don't, it makes life really hard'.[25] Moreover, and in addition to the already stringent social expectations placed on individuals, the collapse of the Japanese economic bubble in the early 1990s also hit Japan like an ideological earthquake:

> A number of 'shocks' have buffeted Japan in the 1990s, including the collapse of the bubble economy, major currency fluctuations, a prolonged recession, the Great Hanshin (Kobe) Earthquake, scandals involving leading politicians, bureaucrats, and corporations, the Aum Shinrikyo cult gas attacks, and increased violence and drug-related crime. These have affected the very cohesion that helped Japan achieve economic success in the post war period, eroding self-confidence and leading to reflection on the state of society.[26]

Furthermore, continued frustration with the Japanese education system has caused psychological conditions such as *hikikomori*, which literally translated means 'retreat into the home', but has come to be associated with a psychological condition in children where they never leave the home, not even to go to school. Under the Japanese education system, a child's education and hence career has already been mapped out by the time he, or particularly she, leaves primary school. Under the relentless pressure to perform at school, some children appear to give up. In 2000, approximately 500,000 children were described as having conditions characterised as *hikikomori*: not interacting with the outside world and obsessive behaviour with respect to television and computer games.[27] Such behavioural characteristics, along with the growth in suicide statistics, may also point to a population that has taken literally Bauman's metaphoric death of community.

In spite of this evidence, many Japanese and Western cultural theorists claim that Japan is a 'group-oriented' society, as opposed to the individualised 'West'. It is claimed:

> Most Japanese consider it an important virtue to adhere to the values of the groups to which they belong. This loyalty to the group produces a feeling of solidarity, and the underlying concept of group-consciousness is seen in diverse aspects of Japanese life.[28]

In light of Japanese social conceptions of group consciousness and group consensus, how does *netto-shinjuu* fit theoretically? Group suicides, while occurring collectively, appear to fly in the face of notions of group consciousness. The suicidal subject feels alone or trapped. While discourses of Japaneseness are inclusive, suicide remains an ideological scar that will not disappear. The internet holds a gateway role: to bring together the people who have slipped through the cracks, to take one final look at the group before clocking out one last time.

In light of the current research, the *netto-shinjuu* phenomenon is a contemporary response to the ideological intersection of the mass-mediated internet and the failings of the nation-state and other traditional communal formations to provide a stable community. The collapse of Bauman's community reinforces the notion that 'identity is invented'[29] and thus a plethora of new identity formations become apparent. The internet, in the case of 'suicidal identities', facilitates the bringing together of these individuals suffering 'community crisis' on a macro level. The somewhat ironic twist with internet suicide groups is the perceived desire to turn back to the group once again for a final round of 'group consensus' before saying goodbye.

Notes

1. BBC translation, quoted in Harding, A. (2004) 'Japan's internet "suicide clubs"', *Newsnight*, broadcast 7 December, available at: *http://news.bbc.co.uk/2/hi/programmes/newsnight/4071805.stm* (accessed 27 July 2005).
2. Unless otherwise stated, all translations are the author's own.
3. Robertson, J. (2003) 'Dying to tell: sexuality and suicide in Imperial Japan', in R. Corber and S. Valocchi (eds.) *Queer Studies: An Interdisciplinary Reader*, Malden, MA: Blackwell; Axell, A. (2002) *Japan's Suicide Gods*, London: Pearson Education; Wolfe, A. (1990) *Suicidal Narrative in Modern*

Japan: The Case of Dazai Osamu, Princeton NJ: Princeton University Press; Iga, M. (1986) *The Thorn and the Chrysanthemum: Suicide and Economic Success in Modern Japan*, Berkeley, CA: University of California Press.

4. Gottlieb, N. and McLelland, M. (2003) 'Introduction', in N. Gottlieb and M. McLelland, M. (eds.) *Japanese Cybercultures*, New York: Routledge, pp. 1–16.
5. Ibid.
6. UPI NewsTrack (2005) 'Japan suicide rate tops 30,000', 2 June.
7. Ibid.
8. Ibid.
9. Nakamura, T. (2003) 'Domestic violence and men's movements', in J. Robertson and N. Suzuki, (eds.) *Men and Masculinities in Contemporary Japan: Dislocating the salaryman doxa*, London: RoutledgeCurzon, pp. 150–66
10. Todd, J., Holden, M. and Tsuruki, T. (2003) '*Deai-kei*: Japan's new culture of encounter', in N. Gottlieb and M. McLelland (eds.) *Japanese Cybercultures*, New York: Routledge, pp. 34–49.
11. Ibid., p. 34
12. Niigata Seiryo University (2005) '*Netto shudan jisatsu no shinri* [Internet group-suicide psychology]', available at: *http://www.n-seiryo.ac.jp/~usui/news/jisatu/2005/netsyuudan.html* (accessed 1 June 2005).
13. Niigata University (2003) '*Netto jisatsu kenkyu HP* [Internet suicide research home page]', available at: *http://www2.cc.niigata-u.ac.jp/~c40804/dzemi98/dzemi2003/ia0100.html* (accessed 27 July 2005).
14. Tsurumi W. (ed.) (1994) *Bokutachi no 'kanzen jisatsu manyuaru'* [Our Opinions about 'The Complete Manual of Suicide'], Tokyo: Ota Publishing.
15. Tsurumi, W. (1993) *Kanzen jisatsu manyuaru* [The Complete Manual of Suicide], Tokyo: Ota Publishing.
16. Harding, op. cit.
17. Toshinao, S. (2005) 'Introduction', available at: *http://homepage3. nifty.com/sasakitoshinao/pcexplorer_5.html* (accessed 29 July 2005); Niigata Seiryo University, op. cit.
18. Niigata University, op. cit.
19. Comment by Yukiko Nishihara, quoted in Harding, op. cit.
20. Ibid.
21. Bauman, Z. (2001) *Community*, Cambridge: Polity, p. 3.
22. B. Anderson quoted in Brabazon, T. (2001) 'How imagined are virtual communities?', *Mots Pluriels* 18 (August), available at: *http://www.arts. uwa.edu.au/MotsPluriels/MP1801tb2.htm* (accessed 15 November 2007).
23. Bauman, *Community*, p. 16.
24. Ibid.
25. Comment by Amaterasu, quoted in Harding, op. cit.
26. East Asia Analytical Unit (1997) *A New Japan: Change in Asia's Megamarket*, Canberra: National Library of Australia, p. 15.
27. Kikkawa, T. (2001) *Hikikomori wo kangaeru: Sodate ron no shiten kara* [Thinking about *hikikomori*: From a childrearing perspective], Tokyo: NHK Books.
28. Davies, R.and Ikeno, O. (eds.) (2002) *The Japanese Mind: Understanding Contemporary Japanese Culture*, Boston, MA: Tuttle Publishing.
29. Bauman, op. cit, p. 15.

11

When home is away: re-thinking the travel weblog

Rebecca Bennett

> The problem is we all have the same idea. We all travel hundreds
> of miles just to watch television and check into somewhere with all
> the comforts of home. You gotta ask yourself: What is the point of
> that? (*The Beach*)[1]

The protagonist of *The Beach*, played by Leonardo Di Caprio in the
filmic version of the famous backpacking novel, exemplifies a recurring
question in tourism discourse and theory. The relevance of this question
increases as globalisation emerges as a defining trope of late modern,
'new' capitalist times. Global technologies such as television and sonic
media platforms – from radio and stereos through to digitised sound
media – are available in all but the most remote of tourist locations.
Watching a familiar television show or listening to a favourite song can
evoke a sense of 'home' while 'away'. Such technologies allow tourists to
feel safer and more comfortable in unfamiliar surroundings, alleviating
some of the fear of the unknown. Internet cafés are appearing in less
developed areas to cater for tourists. This marriage between tourism and
technology affirms the dominance of global capitalism and the
emergence of globalisation as a defining discourse. Critically probing the
merger between tourism and technology in the form of the travel weblog
prompts a critique of globalisation as an easy answer to difficult
questions.

In the context of globalisation – a discourse that is as complex,
convoluted, fragmented and unfinished as Wikipedia – readings of the
private-come-public explosion of online journals in popular weblog

formats reveal powerful and politically dangerous links between tourism, the internet and economic rationalisation. My primary concern is that the increasing interdependence between tourism and technology fuels a global (post)colonisation of local spaces. To be able to take a global slice of home on travels across territorial borders means that tourists can spend less time engaging with the localised face-to-face communal travel spaces. Spending increasing amounts of time in cyberspace while travelling is concerning. Consider the results of a recent United Press International (UPI) publication:

> in globalized countries, people lived longer, healthier lives, and women enjoyed the most social freedom, educational and economic opportunities. One troubling aspect of the survey was that 50 per cent of the world's population lives in the 10 least globalized countries: Brazil, Kenya, Turkey, Bangladesh, China, Venezuela, Indonesia, Egypt, India and Iran.[2]

People in globalised countries have a greater access to internet and travel literacies, as well as better health and economic opportunity. To participate in global tourist networks and information flows, individuals have to be *globalised*. This research was published under the title, 'Globalization survives through tourism and tech'.[3] The UPI study sets up internet users and travellers as being the saviours of the globalisation discourse. The global marriage between tourism and technology is consummated in the travel weblog. Critical readings of travel weblogs reveal politically exclusive and problematic narratives about who is being saved and who is being systematically ignored in exclusive, online, 'public' collections of individualising, subjective visions of a so-called 'global' worldview.

Weblogs are digitised spaces that allow techno-literate individuals and groups to reveal their opinions for public viewing on the internet. Internet users can experience a seemingly borderless, inclusive, free-flowing international communications network. Cyberspace is a metonym for globalisation because it celebrates a consumer-driven space where freedom of movement, agency and choice dominate in the construction of identity. 20six.co.uk states:

> a Weblog is a contemporary form of communication, just like your mobile, e-mail or instant messenger. No one 'needs' a Weblog – yet. But they are becoming more widespread and more essential

because of the way they give you a constant presence on the internet.[4]

Through weblog construction, users mark cyberspace and stake a claim in global information territory. A constant presence on the internet is deemed necessary in the race to keep up with changing global literacies and technologies. Webloggers do not have to be refereed, published or edited to put a site online. The internet allows once private thoughts and 'unpublished' writings to become public discourse. With imagined and known audiences made up of strangers and friends, bloggers are able to feel that their thoughts matter because they are allowed in a public form. A search on Google lists weblogs alongside 'official' publications and corporate websites. This blogger confidence and agency is only available to those who have access to internet technology and literacy. Blogging is an exclusive freedom, considering there are more people offline than 'on'.

To create a weblog is to exercise global power. Offline voices and opinions are not validated in the same way. In offline environments, a strict selection process and criteria are required for published writings, photographs exhibited or films viewed in public formats. Buffoni states that 'a reduced set of capabilities due to age, material resources and technological illiteracy makes life in globalised conditions even more difficult'.[5] Technological illiteracy makes life in global cyberspaces disconnected and hyper-local. The power of writing a weblog narration is barred to those who do not have – to use Mike Kent's model from earlier in this book – cultware. It is much more difficult for offline identities to narrate, speak or conduct dialogue and thus 'own' a slice of global discourse in the same way.

Travel offers corporeal experience of global power. It embodies the power of mobility which is articulated in Zygmunt Bauman's discussions of globalisation. He states that in the global arena:

> mobility climbs to the rank of the uppermost of coveted values – and the freedom to move; perpetually a scarce and unequally distributed commodity fast becomes the main stratifying factor of our late modern or postmodern times.[6]

Travellers obviously exercise the power of mobility. They move with relative ease across many political and economic borders that divide and define macro visions of the 'world'. A problem with making globally familiar spaces such as travel weblogs, readily available in local destinations is that they allow travellers to temporarily disengage from local voices, practices and limitations that form the backdrop to tourist imagining. Bauman states that:

> [a] new hierarchy is operated by a strategy of disengagement which in its turn depends on the ease and speed with which the new global powers are able to move, cutting themselves off from their local commitments at will and without notice and leaving to the 'locals' and all those left behind the awesome task of cleaning up the debris.[7]

The use of local, communal spaces to signify travel movement, while accessing experiences of familiar global comforts, diverts attention away from the *discomforts* that occur when mobile techno-literate 'globals' meet immobile offline 'locals' face-to-face. To be able to disengage from locality by entering cyberspace means that moving on can be achieved by logging on. Many hosts in tourist interactions do not have access to such 'buttons', leading to double marginalisation because they cannot afford a plane ticket to another 'locality'. Nor do they have access to a 'global' ticket into cyberspace.

Cyberspace allows travel-space to become more malleable, flexible and pliable. Weblogged tourist conversations with imagined cyber-audiences provide a more comfortable and less challenging experience of difference. This is because weblogs invoke the power of narration. Online travellers paint subjective pictures of tourist encounters. Mobile webloggers are free to mould the shape of their local hosts and fellow travellers into whichever forms suit their narrative. Travellers can blog their alternative voice into the 'global' picture if they have access to internet technology but offline locals and tourists cannot. Looking at a weblog entry from a tourist in Mumbai, it is evident how local poverty is rationalised from being devastating to deviant in the cyber travel manifesto of a global elite. It reads:

> Heart breaking – at first. They follow you around, tugging at your sleeve/trousers & after the 50th time in 10 mins it gets annoying. And, although these kids can speak English well enough there are certain words they don't understand; principally 'NO!' & any word usually associated with '...OFF!' We also got the impression that they'd soon as spit on you & rob you. Paul caught a girl who couldn't have been more than 5 years old attempting to pick pocket him [sic].[8]

This narrative exemplifies a global worldview that contextualises and assesses cultural and economic difference, speaking directly about a 'global' experience of 'locals' in a safe digi-space. In this context, surface poverty is heartbreaking and endearing when it frames 'new' experience and signifies an arbitrary move away from the 'known'. Once local pleas become repetitive, demanding and uncomfortable, they transform from 'heartbreaking' to 'annoying'. Repetition of similar local encounters means poverty loses its appeal as it becomes a problem (for the tourist), and thus a political reality. Bauman states that:

> In the soft, pliable, shapeless world of the global business and culture industry elite, in which everything can be done and redone while nothing stays tough and solid for long, there is no room for obstinate and stiff realities like poverty, or for that matter the indignity of being left behind and the humiliations attached to the inability to join the consumer game.[9]

Tourism is a source of income and relegated to the necessary status of work, not leisure. Locals, for whom the responsibility of producing a tourist experience for consumption falls because of their 'local' presence, do not necessarily frame tourist experiences as pleasurable. This alternative perspective has potential to dampen the tourist-consumer's holiday pleasure and is not validated in this weblog narrative. As soon as the experience of global-local relations becomes an obstinate repetitive reality, the blog narrative quickly moves on. Relegated to criminal status, the locals in the Mumbai narrative do not play the global consumer game well enough for this tourist to buy into their demands. The tourist, through their blog, gets the final say.

As this blogger travels to Goa, the 'local' morphs into a more pleasing shape. Locals here are framed as friendly and humble. The blog continues:

> Kerry has made best friends with sarong/jewellery/henna selling sari women & they sit around our sun beds chatting away, interspersed with us buying them drinks & fruit for their kids. Paul is best friends with the bar man Joseph who is hilarious. Calls Paul 'Paul Sir' & nothing is too much trouble for him [sic].[10]

Good, happy and chatty locals are rewarded with drinks and fruit. For locals to serve, respect and go out of their way to please their global 'hosts' means they adhere to the pleasure principle of the tourist consumer game. Pleasant, welcoming and willing local servants paint a digestible picture of 'local' life. A pleasurable appearance masks local poverty and discontent with saris and laughter. In this submissive local scenario, the tourists write themselves as generous and inclusive by recounting a philanthropic display of charity. Using the power of narration in the translation of travels into a weblog format, the tourists are able to make up for their damning account of the local beggars in Mumbai. This narrative turn is predicted by Bauman who states that in late modern global discourse 'the moral ugliness of deprivation is miraculously reincarnated as the aesthetic beauty of cultural variety'.[11] By creating a comfortable tourist atmosphere free from obvious poverty and discontent, 'happy' Goan local characters are embraced and praised. Conversely, 'unfriendly' and 'unhappy' local characters in Mumbai are dismissed, rather than representing desperate situations that require change. Local/global discomforts and conflicts cannot be so easily written off if the unequal global hierarchy is to change. Travel weblogs are politically dangerous spaces for travel narration because local voices and perspectives are easily brushed aside in the powerful postcolonial experience of writing local others into a strange pleasure-driven submissive/deviant binary.

In Mumbai, locals are framed as corrupt because they tried to pick Paul's pocket, thus breaking a well established global tourist 'law'. When Paul and Kerry's local Goan 'best friends' break local law, however, the bloggers seen unperturbed:

> Big Scandal on Saturday. The fuzz turned up and arrested 4 of the sari women for illegally trading on the beach. Funny to watch the women pegging it down the beach, a whirl of bright blue, red & yellow saris throwing their sarongs as they went or stuffing bags under sunbeds. The sad bit is that the women were locked up for the night & then a 'fine' of buying back their confiscated goods & paying more backsheesh [sic].[12]

The image of colourful locals fleeing from the law is re-told as a slightly humorous and anecdotal travel tale. The narrator feels a little 'sad' for the locals but because her body, possessions and pleasure are not threatened, the narration has an objective neutral tone. This weblog narrative aligns itself again with Bauman's theory. He suggests that:

> Closely intertwined with the uneven development of economy, politics and culture once coordinated in the framework of the nation state is the separation of power from politics: power as embodied in the worldwide capital and information, becomes exterritorial; while the extant political institutions stay, as before local.[13]

This weblogger does not intervene in 'local' laws and customs when they do not interrupt the ease with which she can move between the realms of active local participant (corporeal tourist) and global social commentator (weblogger). 'Best friends' are left to fend for themselves when the local 'fuzz' arrives, yet enemies are made when 'in your face' begging and discontented pleas interrupt tourist mobility. This is the power of the 'global': to be able to engage, disengage and pass judgment on localised conflicts at will. Local people do not often have the same authority or ability to alter their role (and the role of mobile others) in tourist contexts at will.

Disengagement from local culture and politics is allowable in the weblog format. Weblogs are mediated, disembodied accounts of travel experience calling upon an unaccountable style of biographical authorship. Neither 'fact' nor 'fiction', travel weblogs are framed as individualised truths, representing a travel *reality* rather than a story. This format means biases in the text are easily absorbed by audiences who have an interest in the tourist destinations and the cultures being discussed. However, the malleable texture of the weblog shirks political responsibility for generalisation and labelling in its content because it represents individual opinion. Online travel journals are de-politicised through their personal, anecdotal tone, yet accounts of the cultures and people written about are readily absorbed as representing a form of non-fictive tourist truth.

Pleasure travel and online travel journals are not bounded movements or discourses. Online literacy means bloggers can say what they like about their travel experiences without immediate retribution or rebuttal. Travel weblogs fuse technology and tourism in a powerful global arena. Missing in these spaces, are the voices of the techno-illiterate, immobile 'locals' whose everyday lives and homes are being analysed, defined and discussed online. As Bauman states:

> what [the travel weblog] lifestyle celebrates is the irrelevance of place, a condition most conspicuously beyond the reach of ordinary folks, of the natives tied fast to the ground and (in case they try to disregard their shackles) likely to meet in the 'big wide world out there' sullen and unfriendly immigration officers rather than invitingly smiling hotel receptionists.[14]

Mobility means travellers can move on or go home if they tire of their surroundings. Online literacy affords them another escape into a familiar global territory to vent about – or forget – the stiff realities of their local, embodied context on the other side of the computer screen. In this malleable, global (ex)territory travel, bloggers can write themselves into the travel picture as any character they wish. This kind of identity formation and free writing style is not necessarily damaging in the private formats of face-to-face or phone conversations, letters home or private travel journals. It is the public presentation of personal philosophies, thoughts and rants that empowers individualism, exclusivity and narrative power. Travel weblogs create a 'global' discourse that bars many 'locals' from contribution, although they play an integral part in the tourist industry and travel-blog subject matter. Bloggers are afforded the power to narrate without the usual self-reflexivity and cultural sensitivity necessary in other forms of non-fictive public discourse.

The problem with being allowed to escape from locality, difference and the unfamiliar by logging on or moving on means that the necessary difficult conversations about gross economic and political differences evident beneath an invisible and precarious 'global' banner are not being had. A quick search using Google reveals that all ten countries on the UPI's 'least globalised' list[15] have travel weblogs written about them. This suggests that the travel weblog is not assisting the historically less-developed and less-globalised access the benefits, powers and pleasures found in writing global tourist discourse. Less globalised nations, localities and individuals are analogue, two-dimensional cardboard subalterns when they are translated into the cyber-speak of a globalised elite.

My answer to Leo's cinematic questioning of the point of desiring 'home' comforts while 'away' is to continue critiquing and pushing dominant global technological and tourist discourses to include conflicts and *dis*comforts in leisure-visions of the world. If the exclusivity of global pleasure pursuits is not questioned, the spaces between the 'global' and the 'local', the 'mobile' and the 'immobile', the 'online' and the 'offline', and the 'wealthy' and the 'poor' will digitally disappear.

Notes

1. *The Beach*, directed by Daniel Boyle (Twentieth Century Fox, 1999).
2. Haddix, D. (2004) 'Globalisation survives by tourism and tech', United Press International, 24 February, InfoTrak Web, full-text academic database, article no: A113576608.
3. Ibid.

4. Anonymous (2005) 'Touring', available at: *http://www.20six.co.uk/services/weblog.htm* (accessed 10 April 2005).

5. Buffoni, L. (2003) 'Shifting the boundaries of poverty in the global city', in J. Beynon and D. Dunkerly (eds.) *Globalization: The Reader*, London: The Athelone Press, p. 70.

6. Bauman, Z. (1998) *Globalization: The Human Consequences*, Cambridge: Polity Press, p. 2.

7. Bauman, Z. (2001) *Community: Seeking Safety in an Insecure World*, Cambridge: Polity Press, p. 105.

8. Anonymous (2005) 'The honeymooners', available at: *http://www.travelpod.com/cgi-bin/guest.pl?web_UID=wordsworths&tweb_tripID=honeymooners&tweb_entryID=1101043080&tweb_PID=tpod#ENTRY_START* (accessed 10 April 2005).

9. Bauman (1998), op. cit., p. 62.

10. Anonymous (2005) 'The honeymooners', available at: *http://www.travelpod.com/cgi-bin/guest.pl?tweb_tripID=honeymooners&web_UID=wordsworths&tweb_entryID=1101771000&tweb_guest_password=tweb_PID=tpod* (accessed 10 April 2005).

11. Bauman (1998), op. cit., p. 62.

12. Anonymous (2005) 'The honeymooners', available at: *http://www.travelpod.com/cgi-bin/guest.pl?tweb_tripID=honeymooners&web_UID=wordsworths&tweb_entryID=1101771000&tweb_guest_password=tweb_PID=tpod* (accessed 10 April 2005).

13. Bauman (1998), op. cit., p. 97.

14. Ibid., p. 56.

15. Haddix, op. cit.

eBay: marketing the real body in the virtual world

Angela Thomas-Jones

> The shaping of technology is not just down to government and business, but also to the rest of us – we can *adapt* technology as well as *adopt* it; the best description of this remains novelist William Gibson's observation that 'the streets finds its own uses for things'. We might think, for instance, of hip-hop's adaptation of the turntable, turning an instrument of reproduction into one of new production. Or of early house music producers' use of the Roland 303, taking what was designed as a home practice aid for guitarists and turning it into the creative centre of an entirely new style of music. (Graham Meikle)[1]

The internet surrounds myriad aspects of our lives – work, education, communication, leisure and shopping. The World Wide Web allows users to purchase products such as food, gifts, books, furniture and clothing. The majority of virtual stores sell new or hard-to-get articles, and while eBay started in a similar vein, it is now a trading site which permits web-active shoppers to buy and sell almost anything. In 1995 Pierre Omidyar founded eBay in the USA, starting out as AuctionWeb and then later developing the eBay name from his personal company, EchoBay. There have been attempts to sell everything from baby naming rights to ET look-a-like cereal grains, but for varying legal reasons eBay often cancels dubious auctions. It has been used to raise money for charity through auctioning *Big Brother* paraphernalia, a car for 'Youth off the Streets', and couture dresses for AIDS organisations. There are now 26 eBay sites worldwide, and the trading experience has been transformed from a garage sale to a shopping smorgasbord; it is indeed, as it proclaims to be, 'The World's Online Marketplace'.

To trade on eBay requires a literacy beyond that of being technologically-savvy. This chapter examines the rationale, form and consequences of the consumerist literacy of eBay. As this domain is so large, I focus this chapter on the subcategory of women's clothing on eBay. I begin with a brief description of the function of the women's clothing finder. By looking at the language used within this subcategory I discuss the fashion and body literacies needed to navigate the area of women's clothing. I also observe how eBay is changing the shape of clothes shopping, metaphorically and literally.

To understand shopping requires an applied literacy, linking consumerism and context. Henry Giroux confirms that:

> a master dialectician, Gramsci viewed literacy as both a concept and a social practice that must be linked historically to configurations of knowledge and power, on the one hand, and the political and cultural struggle over language and experience on the other. For Gramsci, literacy was a double-edged sword; it could be wielded for the purpose of self and social empowerment or for the perpetuation of relations of repression and domination.[2]

Internet literacy is no different. Knowledge of web language and technology can allow the user to attain information and navigate through the online world. This same knowledge can also exclude those who have not been trained or do not have access to the web. Individual websites have particular structures, rules and regulations that must be learned. Visitors to eBay are exposed to a cultural site hailing diverse and varied literacies. Users must know how to navigate the web generally, the eBay site more specifically, and then move through the individual categories.

When an eBay newcomer enters the site, they are faced with the option to buy, sell, check 'My eBay', or search for an item or category. Browsing the homepage at this level necessitates basic web literacy, requiring the ability to read and follow hyperlinks, and use a search engine. Buying and selling requires a higher literacy, which the site specifies and teaches. The user must learn the eBay vocabulary, including phrases such as 'Buy It Now', 'Fixed Price', 'Bank Deposit' and 'PayPal', and, finally, they must understand the feedback system:

> Feedback is your reputation on eBay. Each time you buy and sell successfully your trading partner can leave you positive, neutral or negative feedback with a comment on how you conducted yourself during the transaction. Feedback is also the way you let other

members know how you feel about your dealings with a particular member.

Every eBay member has a feedback profile, it includes a rating number in brackets, as well as comments from other members you've bought from and sold to.[3]

The feedback system is integral to the eBay literacy, and it is the mechanism that allows eBay to function successfully. Feedback not only allows judgment of the trustworthiness of a trader, it also affects the way items are explained. Items have to be clearly described, including all flaws. The women's clothing category is an example of the function and value of this presentational modality.

The 'women's clothing finder' allows the user to browse the category. Using this search engine is based on a series of assumptions about femininity, shopping and fashion. A basic clothing literacy is required as differences between dresses, jeans, knitwear, outerwear, sportswear and sleepwear must all be noted and understood. Alternatively, there is a categorical search function that splits clothes into specific groups. This also requires a literacy of women's clothing in order for the correct categorical placement (items are often in multiple or incorrect categories) and discovery of the article. In order to search this site quickly, the buyer or seller must know the difference between a tailored jacket and a coat/jacket outerwear, plus-sizes and petites, or lingerie and sleepwear. The size of an online marketplace like eBay necessitates this increasing specificity. The user must have a basic knowledge of types of women's clothing in order to search the site.

A look at the 'Buying Guide', teaches the user about the language the category uses:

> To further narrow your search, include the following acronyms commonly used on eBay.
>
> NWT: New With Tags
>
> NWOT: New Without Tags
>
> NIB: New In Box
>
> NBW: Never Been Worn
>
> SZ: Size
>
> DB: Double Breasted
>
> SB: Single Breasted
>
> AUTH: Authentic
>
> NR: No Reserve[4]

This section of the site teaches the user how to browse the particular category's portals, defines the shopping experience and provides details on how to accurately measure the body. In regards to women's bodies, eBay provides measuring information as:

> Bust: With your arms at your side, place the tape measure around the fullest part of your chest, under your arms. Make sure that the tape measure remains parallel to the floor.

> Waist: While standing, wrap the tape measure around your natural waistline. Keep the tape comfortably loose.

> Hips: While standing with your feet together, wrap the tape measure around the fullest part of your body between your waist and your knees. This is approximately 20 centimetres below your waist. Make sure that the tape measure remains parallel to the floor.

The site provides a basic level of eBay clothes shopping information through the use of the acronyms and body literacy – how to measure bust, waist and hips. The auctions on the site are evidence that literacies beyond those of acronyms and basic body measurements are needed in order to shop within this category.

Women's auctions summon complex vocabularies relating to high fashion and specific body literacies. The fashion literacy that is required within this category necessitates knowledge beyond simply knowing the difference between a tank top and a singlet. It calls for the user to be informed on the difference between brands, designers, fabrics and cuts. The user must know what fashion is, and how it functions in the relationship between women and shopping. Tara Brabazon writes:

> all fashion is consciously irrational, maintaining a knowingness about its own performance. Most purchases make sense at the time. Only in retrospect, when glancing through old family photo albums, do we ask, 'what was I thinking?'[5]

Fashion literacy requires knowing this performance. The relationship between the women's clothing category and fashion is to provide a space for the 'bargain' purchase.

High fashion literacy is required in order to be able to pay below retail price. The shopper must also be literate in recent offline sales.

For example, prominent designers like Sass and Bide seasonally hold warehouse sales, in which seconds and end-of-season stock are sold at heavily reduced prices. To prevent store returns of these sale items, the tags are slashed in a particular, recognisable manner. Items within these sales are often sold on eBay for equal or more than the sale price. A fashion literate eBayer can determine whether the stock is a sale item, or second, by checking the label. Knowledge of how a genuine designer item appears is also required. For example, certain branded bags, such as Balenciaga and Louis Vuitton, are sold with authenticity tags and numbers. Prada items also come with similar validity labels. This literacy can be learnt within the eBay forums, where discussions on how to tell the difference between genuine and fake articles are conducted. Discussion threads include:

> * * Designer Label AUTHENTICATION Thread * * * (*parkavenueprincess*)
>
> Fake Tiffany & Co Vs Fake Louis Vuitton – Ebay police (lambopoulos)
>
> Stealing pictures of authentic Chanel, Louis Vuitton listings to sell FAKES (oswirly1)
>
> DIESEL JEANS – HOW TO KNOW IF AUTHENTIC. (mariah70)[6]

The traders/shoppers police the site as they demand and teach a model of fashion literacy. This links to a basic knowledge of eBay rules, which is that the system is built on trust and feedback. If a seller betrays this trust then they are given negative feedback and sometimes removed from trading.

High fashion literacy is also required as items are often linked to style trends and celebrities such as models, pop and movie stars. A browse of the whole site reveals the use of phrases such as 'boho', 'vintage' 'urban' and 'glamour'. These phrases are used alongside phrases such as 'Sienna' or 'Kate Hudson' when describing a piece of clothing, for example: 'KHAKI GREEN w/LACE SINGLET Sz M Boho Hippy Kate Sienna'. Such a statement implies that the item is of a Sienna Miller and Kate Hudson 'style'. A high fashion literacy that encompasses knowledge of international dress, such as the Japanese 'fruits', and celebrity styles, is required in order to understand this category. Having this literacy enables the seller to market and sell their goods quickly. As a marketing tool this can be deceptive, for example a worn t-shirt can be marketed as 'retro-chic and so

Sienna Miller', but as long as any flaws in the item are described correctly the seller is not at fault. Therefore, understanding fashion and marketing is needed in order to refrain from being 'cheated'. The marketing of fashion items is therefore linked directly to the feedback mechanism. Failing to understand the specific literacy of the feedback system will potentially result in a failure to list an item for sale in an acceptable manner. Feedback necessitates that sellers are honest when marketing their items. This can be demonstrated clearly in the terminology used when describing size.

A specific body literacy is also needed in order to navigate the women's clothing category. Within the Buying Guide, eBay provides the basic women's body measurements and discloses that the sizes of clothing can vary.[7] The item descriptions present the need for a specific body literacy. They portray exact measurements of the item such as inseam, outseam, rise, thigh and width of leg. A question/answer dialogue is often presented at the bottom of the page between seller and potential buyer. An example of such is at the bottom of the following advertisement for a pair of Sass and Bide jeans:

> Q: hi, whats the rise on these jeans? also, you said that the blue jeans are a bit more roomy than the other colours. if the pale grey fits me in a 26, will i fit these or will they be too tight?? thanks =)
>
> 01-Oct-05
>
> A: Hi the length of these jeans from the waist to the crotch are 7 inches. From the waist to the zip is 5 inches. These will probably not be that tight on you if you are a 26 in the grey jeans. The blue wash also gives more than the grey.
>
> Q: What is the length of the jeans? In the inner seam? and in the outer seam?
>
> 28-Sep-05
>
> A: Hi note these jeans have a bit of stretch. These are the measurements: Waist: 28.5in or 72.5cm Length: 40in or 101.5cm Inner leg length: 33in or 84cm Rise: 7in or 17.5cm
>
> Q: Hi, What size is on the tag – 25 or 27?
>
> 27-Sep-05
>
> A: Hi these jeans are tagged 25, which is an Australian size 7. However they measure as 28" at the waist.[8]

The inconsistencies in garment sizing are circumvented by the use of actual measurements. The tag sizing on the garments are nullified in lieu of a literacy of the body. In order to buy garments, shoppers must know the length and width of their bodies, rather than the number on the labels. Even where the tags supply a specific measurement, such as the 25-inch waist highlighted above, these are invalidated by the seller's hand measurements. Therefore the seller must be accurate within the literacy of the body when measuring clothing dimensions and the buyer must know the exact size of their body. This prevents the buyer from purchasing an incorrect size and the seller from receiving negative feedback.

The feedback system demands that items are described as specifically as possible. This in turn affects the way that clothing within this section is marketed and enforces the literacies required to navigate the category. There is an interdependent relationship between eBay, feedback, fashion and body sizing. Literacies such as fashion and body, which are often dissonant outside the online world, are forced to work harmoniously, because of the nature of feedback. The customer, rather than the retailer, markets the items. This in turn forces women to change the relationship they have with their own bodies. In relation to Wendy Chapkis, Sarah Grogan writes:

> She argues that women are entrapped in the beauty system, but that there are possibilities for change if women are willing to accept themselves and their bodies as they really are. This would involve a close examination of 'beauty secrets' (the rituals that most women undertake to try to conform to the cultural ideal) and a rejection of these in favour of a celebration of the 'natural' body.[9]

While eBay, a website based wholly on consumption, does not reject the cultural ideals of women's bodies, it does, by accident or design, enforce a specific body literacy. The user must know the measurements of their natural body and make it fit within the variables of the clothing industry.

The knowledge required within the subcategory of women's clothing relates to the basic eBay buying/selling literacy, which operates on the feedback system. Along with eBay's clothing buying guide, high-level fashion and specific body literacies are required in order to sell and buy articles accurately and with ease. Knowledge of the world of fashion, sales, designers, fakes and celebrity styles, must be demonstrated. The subcategories present multiple literacies that must market a product and adhere to the rules of eBay. The women's clothing category allows the browser to purchase a multitude of items in an environment, which although using fashion marketing, is ordered to be honest regarding body size. The fora and feedback system monitors buyers and sellers and ensure that the majority of items are displayed legally, correctly and honestly. While some literacies may be required in order to navigate this site with ease, eBay has changed internet shopping. It has brought the garage sale, trash and treasure and weekend markets to the 24-hour online world. It is an arena that necessitates new literacies and subverts corporate consumption practices. There is no changing room on eBay, and this shopping system offers hope to the clothing consumer ordinarily disenfranchised by retail practices.

Notes

1. Meikle, G. (2005) 'Open publishing. Open technologies' in J. Hartley (ed.) *Creative Industries*, London: Blackwell Publishing, pp. 70–82.
2. Giroux, H. (1987) 'Literacy and the pedagogy of political empowerment', in P. Freire and D. Nacedo (eds.) *Literacy: Reading the Word and the World*, South Hadeley, MA: Bergin, pp. 1–25.
3. eBay (2007) 'eBay explained: feedback', available at: *http://pages.ebay.com.au/ebayexplained/feedback.html* (accessed 6 November 2007).
4. eBay (2007) 'eBay Australia's clothing & accessories buying guide', available at: *http://pages.ebay.com.au/buy/guides/apparel-accessories-buying-guide/?ssPage Name=BUYGD:CAT:11450:LISTINGS:1* (accessed 6 November 2007).
5. Brabazon, T. (2002) *Ladies Who Lunge*, Sydney: UNSW Press, p. 39.
6. eBay (2007) 'eBay forums: clothing, home & lifestyle', available at: *http://forums.ebay.com.au/forum.jspa?forumID=22* (accessed 6 November 2007).
7. eBay (2007) 'eBay Australia's clothing & accessories buying guide', op. cit.
8. eBay (2005) Auction listing for Sade and Bide jeans, available at: *http://contact.ebay.com.au/ws/eBayISAPI.dll?ShowAllQuestions&requested= bootifool12&iid=5428557454&frm=284&redirect=0&ShowASQAlways=1 &SSPageName=PageAskSellerQuestion_VI.*
9. Grogan, S. (1999) *Body Image*, London: Routledge, p. 55.

13

Cyber sluts: the new Victorians

Melinda Young

In 1727, Helen Morrison, a lonely spinster, became the first woman to place a Lonely Hearts advertisement. It appeared in the Manchester Weekly Journal. The mayor promptly committed her to a lunatic asylum for four weeks.[1]

Helen Morrison was a pioneer in trying to establish a non-corporeal/virtual relationship. Placed in an historical context, the reaction to her unorthodox initiative at companionship still receives stigma. Virtual relationships provoke tittering, laughter and disbelief. While contemporary women do not share the corsets, delicate sensibilities, love of embroidery, abundance of time or fainting spells of heroines like Helen or those concocted by Jane Austen and Louisa May Alcott, the courting rituals employed in their quest for love, friendship and casual sex are comparable. Advances in technology mean that there are no agonising weeks or days waiting for correspondence via snail mail. Now we eagerly await instantaneous messages and e-mails from friends, lovers and significant others. This emotionally and geographically safe communication is reminiscent of the disengaged, distant form of intimacy found flowing from Elizabeth Bennet's humble homestead to Mr Darcy's palatial estate.[2] The rules of virtual intimacy and courtship appear to have come full circle. One obvious difference is that rejections, fantasies and acceptances arrive faster. The similarities with Victorian sensibilities are less about the retardation of romantic and sexual interaction, and more about personal safety. In an online survey[3] conducted in the USA, '77 per cent of total respondents said they spend more time dating online since September 11'.[4] Does virtual interaction make dating more democratic? Can anyone play? In the current sceptical, cautious climate of terrorism, is this just a safer route to a root?

This chapter answers these questions using responses to a questionnaire distributed online. Overwhelmingly, my respondents admitted to using e-mail, MSN Messenger and chat rooms. Some engaged in online fora to share personal interests such as music, cultural and political issues. This chapter, while mentioning these wider online interests, highlights matters concerning online relationships that are established and maintained on common, all-purpose virtual communication platforms such as e-mail and non-specific chat rooms. Venues available for the express intention of dating and romantic interaction such as Lavalife, Adult Matchmaker and RSVP, often where (paid) membership and subscription are required, are beyond the scope of this discussion. My interest lies in the development and preservation of relationships using e-mail and generalised chat rooms and how the dynamic of these virtual acquaintances is reminiscent of the courting rituals and constrained correspondence of the Victorian era.[5]

Virtual correspondence and interaction

Virtual interaction and correspondence transcends identity, space and time. Geography and appearance are not issues when generating or perpetuating contact. For those who are internet literate, virtual vehicles such as e-mail and chat rooms provide a simple means of rapid communication. This was the consensus from a selection of respondents to my e-survey.[6]

MeMe: 'It is quick, cheap and effective.'

Dylan: 'You can be anyone you want to be. Disguise and reinvention are extremely appealing online *or* off.'

Terri: 'I'm better at answering e-mails than snail mail. Gives you a rapid response. Like sending funnies, which is a lazy way to keep in contact.'

Kimber: 'I like e-mailing friends who live inter-state and my sisters because they are at work all day and it's difficult to call them.'

Beth: 'It is quick and easy ... Great for travelling because it is a one step process, sit down, type and send. Doesn't have the hassle of snail mail, finding stamps, post boxes etc.'

Kate: 'I use it sometimes as an alternative to formal letter writing (e.g. with uni or work) for its speed and ease. I also find it less personal and intrusive than phoning someone. I also use it to keep in contact with friends and family that live overseas. It's cheaper than phoning and easier/faster than letter writing.'

Sally: 'You have the chance to talk and learn about people all over the world.'

Bruce: 'The dislocation in time and space that lets you maintain relationships, even though you may not share a time zone, let alone a location.'

Ada: 'Quick form of communication, cheap form of communication for overseas friends, plus I can type faster then I can write and my writing is terrible.'

Sue: 'Given my time constraints it is great to be able to communicate *when it is convenient to me*. The downside is you do not know *if the message got through*.'

Virtuality has a liberating quality. The boundaries of the body can be pushed and exceeded. Those not physically confident in communication can use chat lines and e-mail more comfortably because of their corporeal displacement. However, as Jude describes, noncorporeal communication acts 'as both an agent of freedom as well as a protective device'. The choice to ignore those whose company is not desirable is only a mouse-click away. Respondents had diverse motivations in commencing virtual conversation or interaction.

Annabelle: 'I'm not very good with social interactions and I'm a bit shy so talking to people online is a good way to interact with someone. I can think about my answer before I reply and it's easier to contribute to a conversation in a forum because you're not a focus of the group or competing to have your voice heard. I'm not very good at that.'

Courtney: 'It is a way of being social even when I'm relaxing at home in my own time. I began doing it (using chatrooms) when I didn't have a job and felt a little isolated. I've made some great friends online and like to keep in touch with them.'

Jude: 'I find not having to talk to people in person very appealing. I also find it easier to converse textually as it allows me the time to write/say precisely and concisely. The ability to be able to send an e-mail, or even a message in a chat room, off into the ether lets me be more open and I feel I can say exactly what I feel like without necessarily having to read the response.'

> James: '[I] find it appealing due to the wider range of viewpoints and arguments available in comparison to a usually more limited real life social opportunities. Also I'm free to participate whenever I feel like it and respond at will.'

The most prominent advantages for my respondents are a freedom of time and space. Online communication becomes preferable and viable where, to use Ada's description, 'space and time are being compacted'. Increased demands placed on time and blurring of work and leisure realms means interactions usually done in public are now performed in private. As Courtney explains, chat rooms and e-mail allow a 'bridge between the inner world and the external world'. Access is granted to interact anywhere, anytime, with the possession of a modem, personal computer and a phone line or wireless connection. Technological, cultural and political mores have transformed. But modes of communication and courting have not. They remain very Victorian.

Virtually sexy

Supposedly, only the ugly and insecure date virtually. In popular culture there has traditionally been a stigma linked to the desperate and dateless that employ the internet as a courtship tool. However, this tool is becoming fashionable. Annabelle explains that internet dating is a 'good way for people who are too shy to meet other people'. It is also increasingly popular. I was listening to a radio station[7] on the way to the gym and the 'breakfast show' DJs were asking listeners to phone in and give their comments or experiences related to internet dating. Numerous stories revealed interactions with potential/current lovers. Some were successful. Others were not. There is no longer a fear of confessing to being a closet internet dater. My respondents also had stories to tell:

> Annabelle: 'I don't know if it can be called 'dating'. I mean we were online at the same time and spent time talking to each other but it was more like hanging out together. It was an interesting experience. While there were definitely feelings involved, there was a barrier as to how far things could go and that was frustrating. There was always an expectation that 'dating' online would lead to a real life meeting. I don't really believe it's possible to have

a relationship with someone that is purely virtual. It's different talking to someone face to face than online. It feels like you know the other person really well but once you meet them, you realize there's a lot you can't know online. You can know the surface things like their age, their job or what pets they have but you don't know the finer details, like how they react to a stressful situation or whether they bathe on a regular basis ... This guy I met online seemed nice enough but after spending time with him, my opinion was rapidly changed. He was rude, arrogant, a habitual liar, messy and didn't appear to understand the concept of 'soap'. You can't know these things just through online 'dating'.

I think online 'dating' is a longer ritual. It's harder to get to know someone and you have to make sure this person is who they say they are. From my experience, the guy didn't lie but it was very different being in the same room than talking online. It was easier to see flaws, which aren't always revealed through just talking online. If they're in a bad mood, they don't log on but if you're dating someone in real life, you still see that person, bad moods and all.'

Sue: 'Perhaps it is easier to get on a footing of intimacy with virtual dating? This may make it awkward if there is no real attraction when you meet. The tangibles such as looks, smell, sound of voice and plain old physical attraction are all missing from virtual dating.'

James: 'I expect they (internet relationships), will be largely artificial relationships on many different level, due to the lack of face-to-face contact.'

Annabelle and Sue comment on the selective nature of virtual interaction. Presenting only the positive attributes or the non-physical aspects of identity creates an inauthentic experience of dating and companionship. The falsification of identity and behaviour leads James to be wary of internet relationships.

A subset of respondents also remembered negative internet dating experiences and conveyed reservations.

Sally: 'Met on mIRC, chatted for a while, then decided to meet. Ended in disaster.'

Jude: 'I have met a number of friends virtually. One of my friends, who I have never met, lives in England. One of my good friends, who also met him on the internet, actually ended up moving to England to be with him and live with him. She lived with him for two years. She then met another guy on the internet who lived in L.A. She flew over to meet him and they married last year. I am married now, but if I was single I think I would be too scared of meeting an axe wielding maniac.'

Dylan: 'I have twenty or so close online friends, but I've never dated anyone online. I have considered it though and have had a lot of both genuine and seedy offers! If I was more adventurous I'd probably try it.'

Kimber: 'It is more dangerous in many ways. How can you tell from the way that someone types if they are a good person? I know it's not easier in a bar, but in a bar you can bring a friend. On the internet, you are alone.'

Jude, Dylan and Kimber express concern over online dating. There is an assumption that bodily interaction allows a firmer grasp of identity and behaviour. Hiding or disguising identity is easier virtually. To escape an uncomfortable situation is just as simple. Getting away from unwanted physical interactions requires more complex actions than clicking a mouse. Yet two respondents revealed positive experiences with online dating.

Ada: 'I know of two couples who met over the net. One person was in her 30s and met a person in the Netherlands who was 19. They met on a Lord of the Rings site. They have been in a relationship for over two years now. The other was married. Her marriage busted up and the person came to Australia from the US and they have been in a relationship for over two years.'

Courtney: 'I've used internet dating sites quite a bit over the past two years since the end of a relationship that lasted over seven years. It began when I was 19, so it was difficult for me to adjust to single life in my late 20s for the first time. All in all, I think I've met up with around 10 men from dating sites, and chatted online with more. I had an 8 month relationship with one man, a month fling with another before he suddenly moved away to Melbourne and a 3 month relationship with another.

Apart from that, I have some friends in Sydney who I met on a web forum, and every time I go over there to see my family I make some time to catch up with those friends as well. Last Christmas

(2004) I stayed with one of them in a flat he was minding for some people, and we caught up with the others a few times over the two weeks.

I have been very emotionally intimate with one person online, who I chatted with every day for around 18 months. He was quite a bit younger than me and living in Florida. I developed strong feelings about him at a time when my long term relationship had some big problems and I wasn't dealing with it very well. In a way it was an emotional affair, but it wasn't really reciprocated.'

My fellow cyber sluts know the complex customs involved in online courting and creating a corporeal contact:

> Dylan: '[N]o matter how much anyone denies it, corporeal dating is dependent upon physical attraction. Virtual attraction is dependent upon personality. If you find them witty, intelligent and/or funny, you want more virtual and possibly corporeal contact.'

Proposing to meet too early in the courtship can scare an online partner. The meeting should always take place in public.

I have some understanding of these issues. I also dated someone I met over the internet. I was 17 and very insecure about my appearance. A school friend introduced me to mIRC and we frequently met up in a chat room to discuss the gossip from the day at school. We became virtual friends with the other users of the chat room. My school friend invited a few of our virtual friends to a party at her house. After physically meeting one of the men from the chat room, we decided to catch up again. We met in a public place at a predetermined time. We started dating and it was good while it lasted. After a time I was using a chat room again, and started conversing with a man who seemed personable. There were some more extensive chats, e-mails and phone calls. Then we decided to meet in real space. This time we both brought a friend to the public meeting place. We dated for nine months but grew apart. The next man I met I found in the more conventional environment of the local pub. We both arrived with a big group of friends then separated from the crowd. After three weeks of getting to know each other, we started dating. While this was not an internet romance, it did have the disengaged, dislocated characteristics. He went to work in Dunsborough[8] in Western Australia for three months, driving home for the weekends. During the week we would accumulate expensive phone bills because the house he was staying at did not have a television let alone an internet connection. Although we got to see each other on the weekends, our communication was constrained. We got engaged after dating for four months. We have been together for eight years and married for four.

There is much scepticism of a solely virtual romantic relationship. Jude expressed concerns 'with any kind of dating that does not have at least some physical contact'. Sally envisaged problems because 'you don't have the intimate touch of your partner'. Virtual relationships were regarded as inferior, a poor substitute for largely corporeal companionship. As described by Courtney, however, using e-mail and chat rooms to facilitate courting was 'just a way of getting into contact with people you would like to date corporeally'. Clearly, for some, e-mail and chat rooms are a virtual route to a corporeal root. For Dylan, they reveal 'a smorgasbord of try before you buy options ... longer working days give people less time to socialise and more of an excuse not to leave the home after a long day at work'. Technology has permitted the regression of courting rituals to the disengaged correspondence common before the sexual revolution. For Beth, virtual interaction was a safe and detached environment where she was able to work through her sexuality and then translate it to a corporeal space.

> Beth: 'When I returned to Perth from living abroad for 2 years I chatted to a girl for a few months. I came back having "come out" in the UK, and I found it difficult to meet other gay girls, seeing as all of my friends were straight and predominantly male. I also didn't look like the dyke stereotype so I got ignored or written off as a "fag hag" in gay spaces. I started chatting to a girl. We exchanged e-mails and spoke on the phone once. We weren't "dating" or anything. Our conversations were fairly inane ... She told me about her infidelity; I told her about my lesbian "no life". We decided to meet face-to-face, but then she met a nurse and our conversations dried up. We e-mailed daily at first, but interest on both sides waned. I found it all a bit too "distant" and boring. When the chance of us meeting face-to-face looked less and less likely and I met corporeal lesbians, I found the cyber-chat unsatisfying because there was too much room for bullshit, exaggeration and embellishment.'

Beth used a virtual environment to practice and perform her sexuality. When she became adept at these interactions, she grew tired and sought corporeal companionship. Courtney comments on the transition from virtual courting to corporeal dating:

> Courtney: 'In the end, knowing people as just words on a screen has the same effect as getting to know a character in a book. You fill in all the details of that person from your imagination. Meeting then in real life can sometimes be a complete surprise, as you tend to react to each other as strangers at first. Over time though, you will recognize the familiar kernel of that person's character that you've gotten to know over weeks, months or even years. I'm sure this is something people have dealt with for centuries, as long as letter writing has existed.'

The virtual is a stepping stone or temporary alternative to corporeal dating but never a substitute for it. What makes Courtney's commentary evocative is not only her recognition of the historical continuities but the surprises of courtship between the analogue and digital eras. Even with the physical 'surprises', there is a kernel of character captured through words and ideas.

Virtual rehearsal: practising for the corporeal real

An integral characteristic of any relationship with friend, lover or significant other, is intimacy. Technological advances have changed the meaning of intimacy. Traditionally, intimacy was dependent on corporeality. This is not to suggest that correspondence cannot be intimate but intimacy is viewed more as an act or performance. Many respondents revealed they were able to be more intimate online because of the detachment of virtual interaction. Chat rooms and e-mail are virtual alcohol, acting as social lubricant. Distance was equated with inhibition. Courtney stated that internet intimacy 'helped me ... as I am now a lot more comfortable with courtship in the corporeal world than I was'. Three respondents did not provide their opinions regarding online intimacy, but the rest were concerned with the limits of interaction.

> Annabelle: 'I think there's something intimate about talking to someone online, especially in private messaging. You're both alone and focusing all your attention on the other person. It's sort of

similar to corporeal intimacy, but without the touching ;) I guess it's intimate to an extent because it's only talking. You can't interact any other way.'

Annabelle highlights an intimate quality of virtual conversation. Interaction is mediated by words. All focus is directed toward the words and what they mean from the virtual companion. There are no extraneous interruptions and the interaction is purposeful. Both users are in this space with the specific purpose of conveying their thoughts and feelings. Desire and intimacy are created through the typed word. However, these words can also be used to create fantasy and an artificial performance of the self.

Courtney: 'Sexual intimacy online is more difficult for me, because I don't have the talent for role playing that it seems to require. From my experience, it seems to be like two people collaborating on a piece of erotic fiction. The closest I've gotten to that is describing sexual likes and dislikes, experience and fantasies with someone. None of this is very different from real life, but people are less inhibited when they are interacting with just words on a screen. It's also easier to exaggerate and embellish things when you're writing them down.'

Dylan: 'I think it's [online intimacy] very similar to corporeal intimacy; both in relationships and friendships. If you're interested you see/type/send more. But again, disguise and reinvention are extremely appealing. You can be anyone you want to be if you haven't met in person. I suppose it is titillating in that respect.'

Terri: 'Online intimacy is a fantasy. Totally make-believe. But then real life intimacy can be a large proportion of make believe too. You don't have to worry about herpes or aids if it is online. You can create different fantasies and play them through ... You can go same-sex, different-sex, and transgender with much more ease online. Just a click or two of the key. How well you maintain that persona is up to the degree of interest. Online "intimacy/fantasy" can lead to offline confusion. Someone I know into BDSM had conversed online with a female who said she enjoyed high levels of pain & then arranged to meet. I think he used a cane on her arse and she screamed blue murder because she had only done it via the internet before.'

Kimber: 'I think you can become quite intimate with someone online. It's because they are outside your "real" world, they don't know you in that sense so you can confide in them, and it will never get back to your "real" friends and family.'

The appeal of the non-real is conducive to fantasy and deceit. While some respondents saw this as a positive aspect of virtual interaction, others thought it bred unreality and mendaciousness. Respondents' opinions of online dating were split on this issue. For some, the corporeal must be present to make an interaction real.

Jude: 'I do believe that you can have some kind of online intimacy as the textual nature of the net allows boundaries to be broken down, enabling people to express themselves more easily. E-mail and net chatting is contemporary letter writing and talking over the phone. But I do not believe an online *only* relationship could have the same intimacy as a corporeal relationship.' [author's italics]

Beth: 'I do not feel intimate in an "online" environment unless I am intimate with that person "offline" first. I know some people feel they can let go of inhibitions when they are in cyber-space and find like-minded people without being judged by the outside world. I do not find this intimacy, partially due to my cyber-illiteracy and the awkwardness I feel when attempting to use internet/computer technology ... I do not feel I have the right skills to communicate intimate feelings and I lack the trust in the technology as well as the non-corporeality of cyber-encounters. If, however, I am already intimate with someone corporeally (not necessarily in the sexy sense), e-mails and (MSN) Messenger do enhance intimacy, especially over long distances. The distance and semi-detachment of cyber-communications also provides a safer space to articulate feelings without immediate retribution. When you don't have to deal with the consequences corporeally right away, it is easier to say things you might be hesitant to address in a face-to-face encounter.'

Kate: 'I've never used the internet to achieve intimacy. In fact I find it *less* intimate than phoning or face to face contact ... I find it far less personal and thus don't believe "online intimacy" exists ... I don't think it [online dating] will become more popular. The intimacy achieved in a corporeal relationship cannot be compared with or replaced by e-mails. While I think e-mails, chat rooms may change the way in which couples and singles communicate, intimacy is ultimately reliant on the corporeal.'

Bruce: 'With my somewhat limited experience, I have found that online intimacy can be used to maintain intimate relationships when physically separated from that person.'

With the exception of Kate, my respondents were optimistic toward online intimacy. Boundaries are more easily traversed because of the 'fantasy' or non-real-world character of digital environment. The ability to maintain a corporeal relationship virtually was also popular. The geographically distant and emotional dislocation themes are also linked to safety. Online intimacy acts as an emotional buffer; as Courtney describes, 'it allows you to filter potential dates really well so you only meet up with people you are likely to be comfortable with'. E-mail and chat rooms can be employed as rehearsal spaces for corporeal interaction. Jude states that the benefit 'to virtual dating is that probably gain for confidence in expressing your feelings more quickly due to the nature of the internet'. My respondents felt safe in revealing their sentiments in e-mails and chat rooms because of the implication that these venues and the people interacted with were not of the 'real world'. Non-corporeality is not authentic; the consequences such as rejection and humiliation are lessened because there is no 'face-to-face' connection. Virtuality is associated with security:

> Courtney: '[T]he benefit, I suppose, is that you can both get to know each other while you're still in your own comfort zones, sitting in your home, maybe in your pyjamas, chatting with someone every now and again for a few weeks.'

The concern is what happens when this dislocated, detached 'comfort zone' is violated.

Bypassing boundaries: a corporeal collision

Boundaries have been mentioned extensively by my respondents. The ability to permeate boundaries non-corporeally that would not be permissible corporeally is viewed as a virtue of the digital platforms of e-mail and chat rooms. When virtual boundaries are transgressed and the corporeal is brought too close to the virtual, many respondents experienced discomfort. When interactions are virtual, they have a sense of inauthenticity. When the virtual invades the corporeal and the boundaries between both realms are blurred, uneasiness emerges. The following respondents describe their virtual to corporeal clash:

Annabelle: 'The worst was being cyberstalked by an ex boyfriend (who I met online). He was from the UK and returned there after the relationship was over. He e-mailed me regularly, usually once a day, sometimes more. Usually it was to inform me he was coming back and he wanted to be friends and I have to be his friend. Sometimes it was sneaky, like a casual question that I would answer so he could reply with some obsessive dribble about how I had to be his friend. What made it worse was that he was lying to his friends, telling them I was being nasty to him and had cheated on him, which was untrue. He also told them he wanted to come back to Australia to "travel" so they encouraged this and he used this as evidence that his friends supported his harassment of me. Occasionally I would get e-mails from his friends abusing me, telling me I had to talk to him or trying to counsel me in the right thing to do (despite the fact I'd never met these people!) He also managed to get into my e-mail account and distributed an e-mail to other people I knew online. It was a frank discussion I was having with someone about what I thought of his behaviour. He also, when he was here, read my personal written diary and distributed the contents to the same people. This harassment (although he or anybody else failed to see it as such) continued for about 6 months. He eventually stopped after, I suspect, an intervention by his parents who discovered what was going on.'

Jude: 'I remember I was in an IRC chat room when I was sixteen [and] this guy sent me a picture of him (or so he said) naked. That freaked me out. Especially when he said he lived in my neighbourhood and if I gave him my address he would come over. I hadn't given him my address but I still disconnected from the net and shut all the lights off in my house. I thought some how he might be able to trace my computer or something.'

Kimber: 'In Yahoo Chat you always get the filthy PMs [private messages] etc, but it never usually bothered me. The only time it ever did was when a guy asked me my a/s/l and I told him and he was also from WA and he got all creepy. It only bothered me because once I knew he lived close, he wasn't just some virtual dickhead.'

Courtney: 'One man I knew online for a little while confessed to me that he was a paedophile, in that he was attracted to children, but he hadn't molested any and didn't intend to. I think he confessed that to quite a few people because he was having difficulty dealing with it. I found that uncomfortable because I wasn't sure whether to keep his secret or inform the police where he lives.

A couple of times I have been chatting with people when they were extremely depressed and threatened suicide. One of these times some other people who were in the chat room, at the same time tried to get in contact with the emergency services in the person's area, but we weren't sure of his real name or address, so we were very worried.'

The proximity of the virtual to the corporeal is of concern to many respondents. This is epitomised by unwelcome sexual interaction. The problems and issues associated with corporeal sexuality are translated to the virtual. Like unwanted physical sexual advances, virtual communication is littered with sexually explicit content. As the internet is not policed, this content invades personal spaces and causes offence or distress. When asked if they had experienced anything virtually that caused discomfort, it is no surprise that sexual content and contact were commonly reported:

MeMe: 'I entered one chat room and everyone was talking about black breasts.'

Dylan: 'Nothing has fazed me too much ... I've had a lot of leftfield encounters. I'll share a few tame ones ... I was chatting to a friend's friend once and halfway through the conversation he informed me that he had a "gigantic erection". I didn't realize that my whingeing about my job was that stimulating. When he gets drunk he calls me and sends sexually explicit text messages. If I don't answer my phone he starts e-mailing his thoughts instead.'

Terri: 'I'm getting e-mail spam such as the following:

2005 year: Greatest hardest f@cked kinders (kidz) vids and photos!

Only hardcore illegal content. G42hf1

All models 2 – 14 y.o. We produce high quality video and photo archives.

24h support, Forum for our users (you can exchange your collections with another [sic] members)

twOVrrT Hard KindersEx

http://www.kindersuprize.biz

o39PiedoLand Mostly [sic] recommended! Thanks.ue

I've kept this as I sent it to my internet provider in the hopes that they can track it down. Apart from that, I pretty much ignore the penis extensions, Viagra wonders and cum sluts that occasionally (well, daily really) make their way into my e-mail inbox. My service provider does tend to weed them out but a few do get through.'

Sally: 'You get the occasional person asking about "cybersex" and other things but because you are online, you can choose to ignore them.'

I was using a local IRC chat room when I was privately messaged by another user. I engaged in conversation with him and found out he was in the US Navy. I was sixteen and he was in his early twenties. I was interested in his naval experiences because my grandfather was on the HMAS Trenchant, a submarine, in World War Two. This also piqued his interest. The conversation was harmless. We exchanged e-mails for a few weeks and he seemed friendly enough. I was using the same chat room when he privately messaged me again. He told me that his ship would be docking at Fremantle in a week and suggested that we meet up. He proposed that I meet him at his hotel room one evening and he would take me out to tea. Red flags went up and I decided the best course of action was to play naïve. I replied that my parents would not let me out alone in the city, after dark. I said that we should meet up at the movies, have lunch and I would bring a friend. He was insistent that I should come to his hotel room alone, and during the day. I stated that my friend would be disappointed because she was thinking of joining the services after graduation. This banter went back and forth; him trying to get into my pants and me pretending to be totally oblivious to it. He eventually tired of my game and terminated the conversation. I never heard from him again.

I was able to control this boundary intrusion because I was not directly – physically – confronted with his indecent proposal. I had confidence in the knowledge that our interaction was dislocated through space and time. Distance provides safety, which is of paramount importance in the current political and social climate. It is easier to invade and possess a corporeal body. Transgression is harder when there is nothing tangible to grasp. This informs the parallels drawn between contemporary cyber sluts and traditional Victorians. For the latter, corporeality was removed from conversation and courtship to ensure social propriety. The virtual interaction of cyber sluts permits physical safety; the issue for Victorians was social safety. The traversing of boundaries, space and time allows users of e-mail and chat rooms to feel protected in virtual communing. This is evidenced by my respondents' assertions of uninhibited personal disclosures. There are few consequences to revelations conducted in a virtual arena. Through such a realisation, chat rooms and e-mails are virtual rehearsal and training rooms for corporeal performance.

Notes

1. 'The People's Almanac' (2005), available at: *http://www.date.com/dateinfo/infotopic_89.html* (accessed 15 November 2006).
2. Austen, J. (1996) [1813] *Pride and Prejudice*, London: Penguin Books.
3. This survey was conducted by online dating service 'Date.com' between 30 December 2001 and 3 January 2002. There were 11,927 respondents.
4. The percentage cited was 'virtually identical for male and female respondents', from 'Date.com News Room' (2005), available at: *http://info.date.com/infotopic_89.html* (accessed 15 November 2006).
5. In constructing this chapter, I note the thought-provoking monograph by Denfeld, R. (1995) *The New Victorians: A Young Woman's Challenge to the Old Feminist Order*, Sydney: Allen and Unwin.
6. All interviews conducted via e-mail between 17 February and 16 April 2005.
7. Nova is 93.7 FM; I heard this specific programme at 9 am on Saturday 30 April, 2005.
8. Dunsborough is about 3.5 hours' drive south of Perth.

14

The I in community: it's all about ME in gaydar's global gay diaspora

Luke Jacques

I first put my profile on gaydar.com.au this year, at the not so tender age of 31. I am a little old to be a gaydar newbie. At 31, I am a little old in the gay community – period. However, within a few short weeks this online dating virgin has blossomed into cyber slurry. I simply do not know how I functioned as a gay man without it. At 31, I have always been uncomfortable around computers – they regularly refuse to do what they are supposed to when I am around. They often will not turn on, will not open anything once they are on, and then refuse to shut down once I am finished pleading with and screaming into the stoically inert monitor. Working as an English teacher in Bangkok, this jinxing power became readily apparent when I would somehow manage to effect a cascade reaction that shut down every terminal whenever I risked a visit to my local internet café. With the staff running around accusing me of all kinds of techno-terrorism and told in no uncertain terms to sit down and wait for the manager, I executed a hasty retreat the second their backs were turned, vowing never to return.

Barely comfortable with sending an e-mail, I revelled in the stigma online dating and chat sites had accrued by the late 1990s.[1] Masking my computing ineptitude with a certain smug satisfaction that I was *not* one of those online cyber desperados unable to score a man in the 'real' world, I continued the time-honoured tradition of getting plastered in gay bars across the world and taking home the best piece of trade available to me that night. Then something happened. Three years into university, the game had seemingly changed. The gay 'scene' had become increasingly stale. Same faces, same places, and same conversations over the same cowboys to the same gay-me-up anthem beat. While I had certainly made more gay friends at university than I ever had anywhere else, it became apparent *they* were no longer meeting each other in the same manner to which I was accustomed. Somehow, quietly and completely unnoticed by me, online dating and socialising was no longer the refuge of the damned. It was not only cool. It was downright successful. Almost every new couple I met had chatted online *and they were happy*. Suddenly, everyone was meeting their boyfriends and friends online. Nobody actually *met* at the bars anymore; they simply socialised with their new online buddies there.

Feeling somewhat of an anomaly within a scene I thought I knew so well, I finally succumbed when a technically-proficient friend offered to create my profile. He assured me it was fast and – most importantly – it was free. This consisted of taking photos of me as we drank red wine in his apartment, scanning them in, and attaching them to my profile. Next came the hard part. I had not only to describe what I was looking for (what *was* I looking for?), but describe myself (what *am* I like?). With the profile name of 'discobboy', I wound up looking like a glassy-eyed alcoholic endowed with all the charm and masculinity of Liberace minus the bling. In short, I was *fah-laming*. Boys line up!

Dreading what kind of reaction was in store for me from the hitherto unknown cyber gay world, I was stunned when I received two messages within five minutes of posting my profile. It seemed that even on gaydar there is a demand for *fah-laming* nellies. Within hours, everything had changed, not only was there a veritable sea of new men all waiting to be explored but I was getting attention, making dates and 'chatting' to men I would never have had the courage to speak to in the 'real' world. With everyone claiming to be either gay, bi or at the very least bi-curious and available at the deftest left click of the mouse, I felt like Carson's platinum American Express card in an Armani boutique. Baby I was ready to charge.

Similarities between an individual's online profile and 'real-life' identities are often tenuous at best. Melinda Young's respondents' experiences in heterosexual encounters are matched in the queer sphere. Some people's idea of 'defined', 'muscular', and 'under forty' are abstract in the extreme. However, the fact that one must create and post a profile before they can view others provides at least some (albeit limited) assurances against people not being somewhat related to who they say they are, that is, male and same-sex attracted. There are easier sites where cyber homophobes can harass gay men.

Gaydar allowed me to indulge my every narcissistic tendency; its lure became rapidly addictive. My ego simply could not let a day pass without checking my messages, seeing who had viewed my profile and at least a cursory glance at who was online. Apparently, I am not alone.

In his project, 'Fully Exposed', De Wit Steyn[2] asked a number of Sydney gay men about the addictive lure of gaydar:

> Gaydar at times is very addictive. I find it is a place where you can meet genuine guys off the scene.

> It is addictive but better than television most of the time.

> I do think gaydar is addictive. The hunt is addictive and gaydar is a means by which we can oh so easily slip into that mode.

> I wouldn't say I am addicted but I check my messages nearly everyday.

> I go online to find a root. I have to say though, this is Sydney, a boy can get a root anywhere in this town.

Gaydar allowed me to cut through much of the dating 'red tape'. Looking at men's profiles allowed me to ascertain whether they were up for a chat, a coffee, sex, or all three. Here lies the recurring charm of gaydar; not only is it actually possible to find 'what you want when you want it' but, with the ability to view profiles from almost anywhere in the world, users feel part of something larger, a small link in a chain of global gayness. Individuals are connected not by history, ethnicity, or nation but by mutual sex, sexual attraction and sexuality. For even if a gay man restricts his participation to his immediate local area, eschewing all beyond it, he cannot help but be aware that at any given moment men just like him all over the world are logged in, chatting and meeting.

My use of 'global gayness' is not to be confused with 'globalised gayness'. Within the context of this chapter, the two are distinctly formed and separate. 'Globalised gayness' connotes the active colonisation of a singular 'Western-derived' gay identity onto the 'subaltern', non-Western same-sex attracted 'other'. Indeed, there is considerable academic conjecture regarding the internet's role in the erosion of global cultural diversity. For example, Roy fears that:

> the very speed of dissemination that the internet [may] create a borderless world where the American concept of a gay movement can spread like a virus and infect all cultures. Countries with fledgling GLBT movements risk losing the process of building a movement that is about them and their needs [by] assimilating into Western models because they are more accessible.[3]

Berry, Martin and Yue posit how 'Western gayness' has been described as an 'unstoppable virus that permeates the porous membranes' of the non-Western 'other'.[4] However, viewing profiles posted by non-Western gay men in non-Western countries reveals this is not always the case. The sheer diversity of bodies, languages, wants, desires and identities posted on gaydar confirms that there is no such thing as a typical gay male. Nor was I able to establish an essentialised globalised gay identity. 'Gay' as a global identity remains semiotic: it continues to hold different meanings to different people at different times. Thus 'global gayness' refers to different identities linking together and relating to one another within a localised space such as gaydar.

With over 60,000 registered members in the Sydney area alone[5] as well as thousands of subscribers from over 170 countries and regions, gaydar is not simply an online community but an indicator of a gay diaspora. Websites such as gaydar signify the extent to which discourses of identity and community continue to evolve. Traditional notions of diaspora suggest movement, populations physically emigrating from one national/regional space to another.[6] Their identities must encompass their relationship with their adoptive homeland as well as that of the 'motherland'. Geographical locales such as 'nation' intrinsically underpin identity formation, yet are imagined.[7] Subsequently, belonging to a national space or participating in a national community is as imaginary as belonging to or participating in a virtual space or community. By simply clicking on the 'travel' link, my profile can be posted and viewed in Argentina, Cambodia or the Maldives without me ever leaving my home.

While Davidson, as cited in Monteagundo,[8] and Hawkins[9] confirm the existence of a 'real-world' gay diaspora, their definitions remain dependent on the physical movement of gay populations. In *One Mykonos*:

> Davidson takes time out from his historical rambles to analyze some of the other foreigners on the island, 'representative[s] from every part of the gay diaspora': Italians, Spaniards, Dutch and Germans who 'have moustaches and look like dying Gauls' (the statute), and even 'modern Greeks from Athens huddling together in a corner on their own'. There are even Americans, whose 'gym-built bodies and loud voices seem to take up much more space than a similar number of Europeans.'[10]

Conversely, Hawkins observes the correlation between New York's 'shy-rocketing LES [Lower East Side] rents and the gay diaspora's Brooklyn trajectory'.[11] Whether or not the gay diaspora is on the move, its formation is mobilised through sexuality, transcending race or ethnicity.

While I do not agree with Davidson's suggestion that only Europeans and Americans populate the gay diaspora, his argument regarding the existence of gay tourism is of significant interest. Davidson implies diasporic movement may be impermanent, ongoing and transitory in nature. Tourists move but by their very definition return to their point of origin. In this sense, gaydar becomes a site of negotiation between point of origin and 'travel' destination for the online global gay community. Just as Davidson's gay diaspora visits Mykonos in the real world, gay men are free to 'visit' the local, regional, national and international sphere while logged on to gaydar, immediately returning to their point of origin in the real world the moment they logoff. Their journey may be virtual but members of the gay diaspora do 'move' on gaydar.

While gaydar represents what a global gay diaspora may look like, it is far from ideal. Gaydar by its digitised nature behaves as a diaspora only when an individual is logged in and immediately disappears in the transition from the virtual to the real world. Unlike ethnic diasporas that simultaneously exist online while retaining a tangible, visible and filial presence in the real world, when a gay man logs off gaydar he abruptly disengages himself from the digi-gaydar community. Like gay bars and clubs, gaydar offers gay and same-sex attracted men a fleeting community, for unless one resides in one of the real world's few gay diasporic centres such as central Sydney or the Castro district in San Francisco, individuals cannot exist online or in a nightclub forever.

Gay men often express their 'addiction' to gaydar. We feel addicted because there are too few virtual or real-world spaces like it, where we are free (however briefly) from the dictates of the heteronormative gaze. Yet gaydar itself is not inherently political. Despite giving gay, bisexual and bi-curious men what we want when we want it, gaydar seemingly has no other agenda to push. Researching this chapter has (naturally) entailed spending extended periods on gaydar, viewing profiles and affording me an appreciation (however limited) of just who uses gaydar and to what degree. White men are over-represented within 'Western' and indeed many 'non-Western' countries including Afghanistan, Cuba and Cambodia as well as many kingdoms and nations within the considerably more affluent Middle East region. This suggests that other gay identities and voices are not always heard solely due to socioeconomic and/or infrastructural limitations but may instead be silenced by hegemonic power structures, even with the relative freedom of the internet. Mike Kent's concept of cultware also has an application in homosocial environments. It may also suggest that different men from different regions remain happy having sex and forming relationships with other men offline; they may not identify themselves as gay, and may feel uncomfortable with gaydar and its limited profile setup options. This would seemingly lend credence to Roy's fears of the aggressive neocolonising power of 'Western derived/globalized gay identity'.[12] However, it should be remembered that gaydar may simply offer a glimpse of what is to come, a space where 'gay' history and identities, in all their global cultural diversity, may extend.

While gaydar appears to possess the potential to hybridise and dehomogenise the local as well as global gay 'community', this may only be feasible at a superficial level. This is due in part to the fact that any access gaydar may provide to the 'global' is sharply undercut by its overt focus on the individual. I *chose* to join gaydar. I was not born into it. My family has no longstanding tradition of belonging to gaydar. While I certainly did not choose to be gay, as a white Australian I do not have to 'wear' my otherness. In this sense, sexual identities are fluid. They can be overt, celebrated, sublimated, disavowed or closeted. As a gay man, I have decidedly more agency with which to choose. As a minority (but not an ethnic minority) I can largely choose to whom I reveal my sexual 'otherness' and from whom I wish to keep it hidden. I *chose* to post a profile on gaydar because I kept hearing my friends and acquaintances talking about their profiles, their exploits and the people they had encountered along the way. Gaydar gradually became something more than just a geeky activity to do online to pass the time; it became framed as a part of the gay community, part of my community from which I was excluded. For the most part, gaydar seemed to work. There was a direct translation between the virtual and the real world, I would 'meet' people online and then meet in a club, bar or coffee shop.

However, shortly after posting my profile, any thoughts of a utopic online gay community began to dissipate. With profiles from all over the world just a mouse-click away, I felt wonderfully connected to something bigger, knowing there were men just like me messaging and hooking up in over a hundred countries at any given time. My wonderful world of gayness had just become wonderfully bigger. Yet this feeling would disappear the second I logged off. I was no longer part of this global community. I was alone looking at a suddenly blank computer monitor. Within two weeks of joining, I realised something. For all my newfound global communication potential, all I ever used gaydar for was to message and view profiles from my home city of Perth in Western Australia. As a gaydar 'guest' (that is, someone who elects to not pay the monthly membership fees), I am allocated a strict limit to the number of profiles I can view and messages I can send per day. I simply could not see the point in wasting my daily 'ration' on anyone I was not likely to ever meet in the real world. Virtual 'global gayness' is all well and good but only if it helps me in my real world of Perth.

The individualistic nature of gaydar is reflected in the profile creation process. A gaydar profile consists of two text boxes in which you describe who you are, what you do, as well as what you are looking for. Other details are listed by selecting keywords against set criteria such as this random profile cut and pasted from gaydar.com.au:

- I am a: Single Gay Man
- Interested in meeting: Single Man, Gay Male Couple, Group
- For: 1-on-1 Sex, Group Sex
- Between: 18 & 45 years old
- Profession: Watch Tech and Plant lover:
- Height: 5' 9" (175 cm)
- Body Type: Defined
- Ethnic Origins: Caucasian
- Hair: Blond
- Eyes: Blue
- Scene: Casual
- Out: Yes
- Dick Size: Large
- Cut/Uncut: Uncut
- Body Hair: None/Little
- Orientation: Gay
- Role: Bottom/Versatile
- Safer Sex: Always
- Smoke: Socially
- Drink: Occasionally
- Drugs: Socially

None of the above criteria are compulsory. Any detail can be left out if one so chooses. However, with so much of the self invested in the creation and posting of a profile, distinct parallels can be drawn between participating in gaydar's online 'community' to going to a real-world gay nightclub or bar. Gaydar becomes another means of 'selling' oneself.

That is, the same rules are just as applicable in the virtual as they are in the real world: men can judge and bypass your profile just as easily as they can avoid your eye contact in a bar. I soon realised that I had not joined a warm and comforting global gay community. I was simply one individual profile posted among myriad others. Thus gaydar does not and cannot generate a sense of community, not only because it dissipates as soon as one logs off but because it is inhabited by disparate and separate individuals. That is, unlike even gay spaces such as real-world nightclubs, there is no space for groups, group identities, or collectives to form or mobilise themselves within the virtual world of gaydar.

If gaydar so divisively pits the individual against the communal, why has it become such a global (again, not universal) phenomenon? I believe gay men are attracted to gaydar not because of its delivery or even the promise of the delivery of community but because gaydar offers the *illusion* of community, just as television's *Queer as Folk* creates:

> [the] mythical world of [the nightclub] Babylon. Mythical because it is a dream, an ideal. We all know no such place really exists – except in our fantasies. It's a collective desire and, to be honest, a self deception. Because in that fantasy everyone is young, everyone is beautiful.[13]

Gaydar creates the illusion of a collective, communal space where everyone is gay, free from the socially and politically dominant heteronormative gaze. This communal, collective desire to be gay within a totally gay space remains illusionary because it cannot translate into the real world once you logoff. Gaydar provides gay men with the illusion that there is at least one space in which they are not only dominant but also the sole inhabitants.

Gaydar's popularity can further be explained through the collective desire to belong. That is, gaydar represents the paradox between security and freedom, identity and community[14] where:

> identity means standing out: being different and through that difference unique – and so the search for identity cannot but divide and separate. And yet the vulnerability of individual identities and the precariousness of solitary identity-building prompt the identity-builders to seek pegs on which they can together hang their individually experienced fears and anxieties, and having done that, perform the exorcism rites in the company of other similarly afraid and anxious individuals.[15]

By thrusting disparate individuals into the global gay diaspora, gaydar exemplifies Bauman's 'peg' community. Individual gay men choose to join gaydar because of the desire to belong. Yet gaydar's profile creation process does not facilitate the individual's transition into the communal. Identity becomes encapsulated by and isolated within each individual profile. Identity means standing out; when posting your profile on gaydar, you really hope it (you) stands out.

If gaydar and its ilk are the home of the global gay diaspora, they are a problematic home indeed. Heller, as cited in Morley, confirms:

> to live in a home, be it one's nation ... ethnic community or family ... is ... an activity ... with formal requirements ... [in which] one participates in a language game. X can say 'this is my home'; but if others (members of the family or religious community) do not co-sign the sentence, he will not be home there. In a home, one needs to be accepted, welcomed or, at least, tolerated. [16]

Within the digitised realm of gaydar a member can only feel they belong if they are not ignored. It is only through gaining the attention of and subsequent contact with other gaydar subscribers that a person can be said to be 'participating' in the online home of the gay diaspora. Sexuality may be a foot in the door yet only other people can keep a participant in the (cyber chat) room, as so clearly demonstrated by a profile I recently encountered. The following excerpt, taken verbatim from an actual active profile, seems to confirm my argument:

> My profile has been viewed over 60500 times and Ive yet to see a single online message, pvt, a track e.g. flame, or a single nomination/vote in the sex factor.Ive been on Gaydar a while now and Im still without m8s with a face pic on my profile I think its really unfair. This site is getting worse not better. Not much point on having my pic on this site.[17]

When describing what he was looking for he simply wanted a 'chat, maybe meet for a pint/coffee but no one seems interested these days'.[18] With gaydar's focus on the individual at the expense of the communal, gaydar places the onus of participation squarely on the shoulders of the individual subscriber. Gaydar is designed to facilitate an individual interacting with (an)other individual(s). This design subsequently renders the individual solely responsible for the quantity of interaction in which they participate. It is *their* fault if their profile does not resonate with or attract anyone. Bereft of interaction, individuals are essentially on their own. With few avenues of support, the home of the global gay diaspora can be a cold and lonely place.

Having spent so much time online researching this chapter, my interest and participation in gaydar has waned. I rarely logon or look at other profiles anymore. Subsequently, I no longer receive as many 'hits' on my profile and I rarely receive messages. Just like Perth's real-world gay clubs and bars, gaydar has become a little stale. The same profiles are online everyday and having exactly the same small-talk conversations I had the day before has become tedious. Just as I chose to join gaydar, I now seem to be choosing to part from it. This has led me to re-evaluate the problematic nature of the digital gay diaspora. By deciding not to logon, can I be said to be still participating in the global gay community? Is the mere existence of my inactive profile participation enough? The agency to choose when I participate and when I withdraw from the global gay diaspora obliges me to ponder how the birth of the cyber gay community will translate into macro-political empowerment in the real world. Cyberspace offers unprecedented opportunities for global transculturation and hybridisation among gay men. We can communicate and learn from each other like never before, yet when I logoff, my virtual presence or participation in the global gay diaspora does not translate with me into the real world.

Despite our reluctance to forego individualism, gaydar exists because gay men *need* to see and feel part of a global gay community. However, this leads into questions of access. Who is in and who is left behind? Internet access is not limited just by economy and infrastructure, but also by macro-political censorship and online entrapment that make online participation in the gay environment for some extremely dangerous. While gaydar provides gay men with the mobility to 'travel' throughout the *virtual* world, gaydar's ability to transcend *actual* national borders in the real world is superficial and illusory at best. The prohibition or censoring of some gay identities in turn allows others to flourish and/or become dominant. Neither gaydar nor the internet is politically neutral. Yet they are also not the saviour or the destroyer of minority identities in the twenty-first century.

Notes

1. De Wit Steyn, S. (2003) 'Fully exposed: the gaydar boys of Sydney', *DNA* 44 (September), pp. 28–9.

2. Ibid., p. 32.
3. Roy, S. (2003) 'From Khush List to Gay Bombay: virtual webs of real people', in C. Berry, F. Martin, and A. Yue (eds.) *Mobile Cultures: New Media in Queer Asia*, London: Duke University Press, pp. 180–200.
4. Berry, C. Martin, F. and Yue, A. (2003) 'Introduction: beep – click – link', in C. Berry, F. Martin, and A. Yue (eds.) *Mobile Cultures: New Media in Queer Asia*, London: Duke University Press, pp. 1–18.
5. De Wit Steyn, op. cit., p. 28.
6. Safran, W. (1991) 'Diasporas in modern societies: myths of homeland and return' *Diaspora* 1 (Spring): 83–99.
7. Anderson, B. (1992) *Imagined Communities: Reflections on the Origin and Spread of Nationalism*, London: Verso, p. 15.
8. Monteagudo, J. (2002) 'One Mykonos: Being Ancient, Being Islands, Being Giants, Being Gay by James Davidson', available at: *http://gaytoday. badpuppy.com/garchive/reviews/021901re.htm* (accessed 1 May 2007).
9. Hawkins, K. (2005) 'Girlsroom', in 'January Bar Buzz' available at: *http:// newyorkmetro.com/nymetro/nightlife/barbuzz/10792/* (accessed 1 May 2007).
10. Monteagudo, op. cit.
11. Hawkins, op. cit.
12. Roy, op. cit. p. 181.
13. Cowen, R. and Lipman, D. (2003) 'QAF. Season Three. And the beat still goes on!', in *Queer as Folk: The Third Season Music from the Showtime Original Series*, CD liner notes, Tommy Boy Entertainment, p. 1.
14. Bauman, Z. (2003) *Community*, Cambridge: Polity, p. 4.
15. Ibid., p. 17.
16. Morley, D. (2002) *Dreams of Home*, London: Routledge, p. 17.
17. This profile was retrieved from gaydar.com.au on 26 June 2006; for obvious reasons the profile/username is not given here.
18. Ibid.

Part 4
Packet switching resistance and terrorism

Information at the speed of thought

Valentin E. Fyrst

Cyberspace is created and sustained by the world's computer and communication lines, in which the global traffic of knowledge, secrets, measurements, indicators and entertainment takes shape.[1] Cyberspace initiates a constant desire for progress, movement and discovery. It is also limited by barriers of creativity, law and imagination. From such a framework, cyberspace becomes more than a global traffic network. It collapses the borders and boundaries of the physical world, giving access to a new mode of transport in an environment where information and content are the currency. It has democratic potential, but as revealed through this book, it brings risks and injustices.

When the gates of cyberspace opened, a seemingly expansive flux of data framed and transformed the determinations of the real and the imagined. Cyberspace is a living matrix feeding off data, sustaining growth. The question is how long this growth can be sustained, and how these limits will be discovered and managed. Cyberspace is a virtual expanse of nothing, yet it immerses into social practice and behaviour. Empowered citizens are using cyberspace to collapse space and time in the search for information and knowledge. Political maps are an evocative representation of the world from a pre-cyberspace perspective. They include a static pattern of borders and geographical boundaries that represent hurdles in the ability to access the wealth of information it holds. The pre-digitised era imposed limitations of a physical nature, making access to information a potentially difficult and time-consuming proposition. The digital 'revolution' reconfigured political maps, erasing their familiar pattern of borders and boundaries. It also abolished the need for official documentation when physically travelling across digital borders, as information became electronically and globally available. The cyberspace 'revolution' increased accessibility of information for a few, while considerably reducing the time factor associated with previous methods of information retrieval. The cyberspace 'revolution' enabled empowered individuals to browse data beyond local and national borders. As disclosed by Mike Kent, the prerequisites for information access in the information age are hardware and software, along with the literacies to use them. It is the technological fluency level of each individual that determines the extent of their ability to explore cyberspace. In developing the skills required to navigate the digital environment, citizens configure alternative models of identity. We are witnessing the advent of the cybernaut.

We carry memories of a time when data were not stored electronically and browsing drawers filled with endless rows of reference cards constituted the most efficient way to access information. The development of electronic data storage facilities has dramatically impacted on the time spent on information discovery, retrieval and interpretation. Decreasing the amount of effort necessary to track down and obtain information has given inspired minds more time to focus on the thought processes rather than data gathering. The intervention of digitisation increases the amount of information available through the search. The speed at which information is made accessible has increased to a point where data can be available almost within the time it takes to formulate the key words and synonyms. As information retrieval has increased in speed, it may impact on the amount of interpretation that takes place. The importance of source validation is paramount to information access. A conclusion or hypothesis only has a level of soundness proportional to the validity of the data on which it is based. The importance of assessing the value of information sources cannot be overlooked. The slower research methods commonly used during the proto-digitised era presents advantages over the wide-ranging and fast-paced avenues of information access available to cybernauts.

The validation of information sources was easier during the analogue era, as they frequently involved referenced publications circulated through a network of libraries and publishing houses. These publications owed their presence and status to a system of refereeing, where scholars validated the quality of source material. This systematic method of evaluation enabled researchers to gather information with a high level of relevance from which they could draw to fuel their own work with a reasonable degree of intellectual credibility. Through the ease of search engines like Google, there is a reduced lag between the search and acquisition of information. Searches generate results ranging from high to low relevance, moving from a refereed academic article to ranting bloggers. As a consequence, the literacy required to assess online sources has become indispensable. This considered authentication process allows searchers to sift out cyber-junk and ensure that their search preserves all references worth their weight in gold or more.

The digital environment provides an escape for web-literate searchers away from their analogue context. Yet it is a transitory evasion. Cybernauts accessing cyberspace are accessible via cyberspace. This means that any information stored on computers is available for browsing and usage by other cybernauts if the appropriate level of protection is not installed. Protection is an operative and critical concept online, as it has become a platform for perversion and abuse. The potential marketability of this sensitive information is coveted by cyber-thieves, who consider it as a highly liquid asset.

Creating awareness of the potentials and risks associated with cyberspace and the storage of personal, confidential or restricted information within the boundaries of organisational, corporate or private cyber-estate may seem evident to the technologically-savvy cybernaut. The ability to make known the unknown, or uncover the intentionally undisclosed, is set to become an increasingly marketable and powerful skill. Emphasis needs to be made on teaching others the literacies of evaluation and interpretation. If citizenship is to exist in and through digitisation, then it must include rights and responsibilities. As we move through the final chapters of this book, downloading is tempered by 'revolution' of disquiet and discord.

Note

1. Benedikt, M. (1991) *Cyberspace: First Steps*, Cambridge, MA: MIT Press.

16

Keeping an eye on Big Brother

Garan Lewis

The internet is potentially a forum where ideas and information can be freely disseminated. As discussed in the previous chapter, for the cybernaut there is enormous potential to view a variety of ideas from diverse sources and political perspectives. This diversity contrasts sharply with our traditional mainstream media where the framework of these institutions results in the absence of critical and alternative thoughts and provides a view of the world compatible with dominant interests. In news and current affairs, political viewpoints are limited to a restricted spectrum of opinion. News stories are fragmented, viewed from a narrow perspective and not placed in any overall, meaningful context. The CEO of Clear Channel, the company that dominates the US airwaves, confirms these highly mediated media when he acknowledges that 'we're not in the business of providing news and information ...we're simply in the business of selling our customers products'.[1] The customers in this relationship are the corporate advertisers and the product being sold is the audience. Similarly, public television has also been shown to be subservient to political-economic power. A Glasgow Media Group study showed that the supposedly impartial BBC was actually the most pro-war channel in the UK at the time of the 2003 Iraq invasion, even though the war was strongly opposed by many British citizens.[2] The British government did attack the BBC later for war bias, but ironically the critique was for being anti-war. The impression given by this 'debate' was that 'we' still have a vibrant democracy. However, the boundaries of debate only extended from the BBC arguing it was neutral towards the British government against the government's charge that it was anti-war. Dissent was excluded from the discourse. However not everyone is relying on the traditional media outlets as their main source of news. A PEW survey found that when the 9/11 terrorist attack occurred in New York,

3 per cent of people used the internet as their primary source of information. The Iraq conflict saw this increase to 17 per cent.[3] On a cautionary note though, only 17 per cent from a national population found alternative opinions. Although people are looking to the internet for perspectives different from those of the traditional media, it seems only the more resolute, determined and online literate researchers are finding them. Media watchdogs have appeared which critique the mainstream media effectively. Take, for example, the UK media watchdog Media Lens (*www.medialens.org*), which sends out 'media alert' e-mails to tens of thousands of subscribers on a regular basis. They attempt to evaluate how factors such as media ownership, advertising, lobbying and sourcing combine to shape the news product. They encourage their readers to write to news organisations and challenge the news product served to them. There are imaginative and creative ways citizens have used the internet to increase the public sphere of debate.

While the Australian media and academia largely ignored the genocide in East Timor for over 15 years,[4] reports of the atrocities were being broadcast on US community radio and via web streams. Amy Goodman, the presenter of the 'Democracy Now' daily broadcast, was smuggling compact discs of compressed video programming into Australia and then transferring the data from an internet café to New York.[5] Award-winning journalism from 'Democracy Now' and other investigative journalism websites such as The Center for Public Integrity (*www.publicintegrity.org*) gave people the kind of incisive commentary that is excluded from the traditional media. The Center for Public Integrity encompasses 92 investigative reporters and editors from 48 countries. The tiny, politically progressive magazine Z, run initially by only two people, refuses advertising in order to retain its independence, and has moved onto the internet with a remarkable impact. The ZNet website (*www.zmag.org*) is a huge resource of alternative perspectives that are not available through mainstream media. It is regularly updated and attracts thousands of visitors on daily basis. Concurrently, and as discussed by Joanne Smith and Rebecca Bennett in this book, weblogs have risen rapidly in popularity as they allow internet users an opportunity to get feedback from others on various subject matters. This recent phenomenon became more widely recognised when a blogger calling himself Zeyad was widely followed for news on occupied Iraq. Readers were visiting his site first before clicking to the BBC and CNN, to compare the versions of events.[6] The investigative journalist John Pilger pointed out that when people wanted to know what was happening when the first attack on the city of Fallujah occurred, many relied on the human rights blogger Jo Wilding, as there were no actual journalists in the city.[7] Critics of blogs have pointed out that they are not reliable sources of information. This may be so, but the issue of ownership of mainstream media demands that the latter's reliability be similarly questioned. The Australian public relations scholar Alex Carey noted the extensive use of public relations material in the media as if it were accredited journalism. Estimates from surveys have shown anywhere between 40–70 per cent of what appears as news is actually a PR product.[8] Similarly, universities are increasingly corporatised institutions selling education to the highest bidder[9] and simply do not have the independence to assist citizens in their decision making. This is the function that Bertrand Russell argued universities should hold.[10] The Media Education Foundation (*www.mediaed.org*) has been set up on the internet to provide educational materials to help students and educators to reclaim what independent space is left in academia. The list of advisers for the foundation include political and cultural critics such as Noam Chomsky, Henry Giroux, Stuart Hall and Naomi Klein. The goal of the foundation is also to provide tools for the general public and activists to enhance democracy by challenging the corporate domination of society. These projects are a welcome sign that democracy is still alive and functioning. In addition, many popular file-sharing websites have appeared on the internet, most notably Napster, which was sued by the music industry for breaching copyright. These file-sharing facilities allow people to download software enabling them to sample and use music, video and text files from other members of the file-sharing community.[11] It is not only Hollywood movies and popular music that are being widely disseminated. Searches on most of the popular file-sharing applications show many audio and documentary files of people such as the US intellectual dissident Noam Chomsky are being widely downloaded and heard. In an effort to silence him, his views have been largely ignored in both media and academia.[12] The internet has become a communications tool for citizens who wish to hear, watch and read alternative views and perspectives that have been marginalised from the popular information sources. How often do we see or hear any challenges to the supposed 'free trade agreements' on television, radio or the print media? The internet has made the research, transmission and dissemination of new ideas much easier. Global advocates for democracy have been significantly empowered as this public information sphere has expanded on the internet.

Remarkably, one of the main inspirations for internet activism came from the rebellion of the poor indigenous people from the depths of

Lacandona jungle, in Chiapas, Mexico. On 1 January 1994, from seemingly out of nowhere, people all around the world received in their in-boxes 'The 1st Declaration of Lacandona Jungle' from the indigenous Zapatista movement, notifying the world of their stand.[13] The indigenous people from the poverty-stricken region of Chiapas who barely had access to their local media never mind the national media, had informed the world of their predicament. With the aid of internet activist groups, they were able to counter the 'official' version of events proclaimed by Mexican authorities. Later the same year, a leaked Chase Manhattan Bank memo calling for the elimination of the Zapatistas, was rapidly disseminated on the internet. The news spread so widely that the mainstream media picked up the story, which resulted in such negative publicity that Chase Manhattan distanced themselves from the memo and its author.[14] David Ronfeldt, a Rand Corporation analyst, was particularly concerned about the rise of democratic media, speaking about 'netwar' and related governing problems in Mexico due to an uncontrollable medium. Vested corporate interests have realised that democratic access to the internet can interfere with the establishment's ability to conduct aggression and manufacture the consent of its respective populaces.[15] Even though the majority of people do not have internet access in the region, only a few internet links were necessary to get the information out to the world. The speed of this medium of communication allowed activists sympathetic to their cause to spread their message. This type of electronic resistance gives powerful, private interests food for thought.

In sharp contrast to Chiapas, South Korea – which has one of the most advanced, high-speed internet communication networks in the world – demonstrated its new found electronic freedom. OhmyNews was established in 1999 to provide alternative news coverage from the highly concentrated, conservative, corporate-owned mainstream news. The site encourages citizens who previously felt they had no voice to become citizen reporters. Over 26,000 people contribute stories and approximately 70 per cent of daily stories submitted are published. In 2002, its power was demonstrated when it reported the story of two schoolgirls accidentally killed by a US military vehicle.[16] The story, which was widely ignored by the mainstream press, resulted in widespread outrage. OhmyNews, now attracting millions of readers, was also believed to be largely responsible for election of the relatively unknown candidate Roh Moo Hyn as President. Significantly, he granted his first presidential interview to OhmyNews, ignoring the three major newspapers.[17] Before the internet, unless a person had a large amount of money to invest, there was little marginalised citizens could do to have a significant voice. Those with internet access have an opportunity to communicate globally.

Various social movements in recent times have recognised that they have many common interests with each other, even though they do not focus on the same issue. As neoliberal globalisation has accelerated, the gap between the rich and the poor has increased. Movements advocating democratic alternatives have started networking and working in unison. The internet has helped facilitate this global community networking by providing rapid communications which are widely accessible in many countries. The first major victory for these social networks communicating via the internet was their contribution to the defeat of the Multilateral Agreement on Investment (MAI). The MAI essentially meant that corporations and investors could sue governments for decisions that they viewed as a restraint to 'free trade'. The potential effect of such an agreement can be demonstrated by considering the North Atlantic Free Trade Agreement, where a corporation in a test case sued the Canadian government for banning a toxic fuel additive, arguing that the ban was a barrier to free trade.[18] Over 600 organisations collaborated to form a global campaign to stop this agreement. As there was no hierarchal leadership, it was comparable to a modern anarchist-style organisation. The police at various massive anti-capitalism demonstrations have repeatedly asked the activists 'who are your leaders?' They simply could not comprehend how such a highly-organised event could be possible without a hierarchy. Anarchist political philosophy was absent from the police training curriculum. Rudolf Rocker describes anarchism as, 'a federation of communities which shall be bound together by their common economic and social interests and shall arrange their affairs by mutual agreement and free contract'.[19] Canadian intelligence also seemed to agree and was impressed by the way the internet had been used as an organisational tool. Their official report noted, 'the internet has breathed new life into the anarchist philosophy, permitting communication and coordination without the need for a central source of command, and facilitating coordinated actions with minimal resources and bureaucracy'.[20] The success of this alternative organisational style may help explain why the famous anarchist Emma Goldman, a hugely prominent social activist in the early twentieth century, is absent from our history textbooks. Anyone studying modern political theory at university will also find anarchism bypassed in their courses.

In November 1999, in the buildup to the World Trade Organization (WTO) protests in Seattle, activists saw the need of an alternative perspective to the mainstream media coverage of the events. They decided on creating an internet website that allowed anyone to upload text, audio and video reports, incorporating the values of the open source movement. The free software called 'active' that ran the original Indymedia website, enabled automated, multimedia open publishing and was written in Sydney by Community Activist Technology, in the first half of 1999.[21] The Seattle protests were one of the first times that those engaged in the protests were able to directly reach a worldwide audience, thereby bypassing the unsympathetic corporate media. Text news reports, video footage and radio broadcasts were uploaded to the site. CNN, citing official sources, stated that no rubber bullets had been fired in Seattle. Hit rates on the Indymedia site soared as people wanted to know what was actually going on in the streets. They were shown video footage of police officers firing plastic bullets into crowds.[22] CNN was bombarded by e-mails from outraged viewers and was forced to retract the story. While computer technicians worked frantically to keep the site up in Seattle, activists in Sydney were providing support for installations and upgrades. Indymedia attracted over a million hits during the Seattle WTO protests, which rose to 10 million hits for the anti-G8 protests in Genoa two years later.[23] Indymedia is an industrious example of how people have bypassed the mainstream media and organised, distributed and published information online. It aims to encourage the distribution of information on social justice issues and promote a grassroots democracy. Today Indymedia websites dot the globe and are found in places as diverse as the Philippines and Peru.

Citizens are organising and networking the internet through sites such as Indymedia. Only recently the search engine Google announced the removal of Indymedia from its listings, citing its 'concerns' over the absence of any 'centralized editorial control'.[24] If citizens want to stop freedoms and democracy from being further eroded – if there is a chance the revolution can be downloaded – then they have no choice but to organise and make a stand to defend such exclusions. In a post-Google web, citizens must move out of a list ranked on 'popularity' and seek alternative ideas and arguments to further not only social change, but political debate.

Notes

1. Cave, D. (2002) 'Inside Clear Channel', *Rolling Stone Magazine*, available at: *http://www.rollingstone.com/news/story/_/id/6432174?rnd=111606666 2218&has-player=true&version* (accessed 28 June 2007).

2. Edwards, D. (2003) 'Beating up the cheerleader', available at: *http://www .medialens.org/alerts/03/030724_Beating_Cheerleader.html* (accessed 28 June 2007).
3. Allan, S. and Zelizer, B. (2004) *Reporting War*, New York, Routledge, p. 351.
4. Pilger, J. (2004) 'Power, propaganda and conscience in the War on Terror', UWA Extension Summer School Lecture, Winthrop Hall, The University of Western Australia, 12 January, available at: *http://www.lewrockwell.com/ orig4/pilger3.html* (accessed 6 November 2007).
5. Gillmor, D. (2004) *We the Media*, North Sebastopo, CA: O'Reilly Media, p. 146.
6. Ibid.
7. Pilger, J. (2004) 'Books and writing', available at: *http://www.abc.net .au/rn/arts/bwriting/stories/s1253799.htm* (accessed 30 June 2006).
8. Borjesson, K. (2002) *Into the Buzzsaw*, New York: Prometheus Books, p. 368.
9. Chomsky, N. (1997) 'What makes the mainstream media mainstream', available at: *http://www.medialens.org/articles/the_articles/articles_2001/nc_ mainstream_media.html* (accessed 6 November 2007).
10. Chomsky, N. (1994) 'Democracy and education', Mellon Lecture, Loyola University, Chicago, 19 October, available at: *http://www.zmag.org/ chomsky/talks/9410-education.html* (accessed 6 November 2007)
11. Gillmor, op. cit. p. 38.
12. Herring, E. and Robinson, P. (2003) 'Too polemical or too critical?' *Review of International Studies* 29, available at: *http://uk.geocities.com/dstokes14/ Eric/chomsky.htm* (accessed 16 November 2007).
13. Jordan T. and Taylor, P. (2004) *Hacktivism and Cyberwars: Rebels with a Cause?* New York: Routledge, p. 87.
14. Ibid., p. 134.
15. Herman, E. (1995) *Triumph of the Market*, Boston, MA: South End Press, p. 227.
16. Gillmor, op. cit. p. 127.
17. Gillmor, op. cit. p. 126.
18. Cromwell, D. (2001) *Private Planet*, Charlbury: Jon Carpenter Publishing, p. 11.
19. Rocker, R. (1989) *Anarcho-Syndicalism*, London: Pluto, p. 9.
20. Van De Donk, W., Loader, B. D., Nixon, P. G. and Rucht, D. (2004) *Cyberprotest: New Media, Citizens and Social Movements*, London: Routledge, p. 101.
21. Schuler D. and Day P. (2003) *Shaping the Network Society*, London: MIT Press, p. 329.
22. Barsamian, D. (2002) *The Decline and Fall of Public Broadcasting*, Cambridge, MA: South End Press, p. 68.
23. Schuler and Day, op. cit., p. 330.
24. Gillmor, op. cit., p. 145.

17

Dot-com, dot-bomb: (cyber)terror on the internet

Christina Lee

Tomorrow's terrorist may be able to do more damage with a keyboard than with a bomb. (National Research Council)[1]

The footage is heavily pixellated and the handiwork of an amateur videographer. Five masked and armed members of a terrorist organisation stand against a bare wall, resembling a primitive firing line. A lone hostage kneels before them with his hands bound together. He is dressed in the now recognisable orange jumpsuit of the foreign (read 'Western') enemy. A statement is read by one of the captors before the hostage is forced into a supine position on the floor. The camera zooms in at various points to provide a blurry, intimate close-up for dramatic effect. It clumsily navigates around the terrorists who have gathered around the detainee and are engaged in a flurry of activity. Amid the din, piercing screams are audible. The scene is stomach-wrenching and uncomfortably compelling. After less than one minute, the terrible finale arrives. The decapitated head of the victim is raised to showcase and confirm the successful execution. The final frame freezes.

The actions of the terrorists evoke repulsion and despair, but also incensed frustration. I remain unconvinced that the invasion and subsequent occupation of Iraq by the Coalition of the Willing was a rationally conceived plan. The footage of the decapitation makes doubtful the alleged victories of the Coalition in bringing about progressive and welcomed change. In the attempt to 'free Iraq', this world war has also created its own injustices and brutalities. While military bravado continues to be saluted and patriotism is seen as fashionable, scepticism stirs beneath the façade of political correctness.

For each smiling face that pro-war news stories boast, other incidents attest that there are a commensurate number of citizens (if not more) protesting against the violation of what they consider *their* civil rights. The distinction between good and evil has ceased to be clearly demarcated. Mission accomplished?

The video of the beheading of American civilian contractor Nick Berg by Islamic militants in Iraq on 11 May 2004 was posted on the internet. An example of psychological operations, it served as an unfortunate reminder of how the media and technology can be appropriated in terrorist campaigns. Recent decades have witnessed television magnify isolated events and transform them into international platforms for the dissemination of radical ideologies of rogue states, religious factions and political activists. While 9/11 and the Jemaah Islamiah-inspired bombing in Bali in 2002 will be remembered as black stains in recent history, with their coverage in the news unprecedented, the manipulation of media and technology by terrorist organisations to gain free publicity is derived from an already established tradition. An earlier example was the televised events that occurred at the Olympic Games held in Munich, Germany in September 1972. Terrorists from Black September, a faction of the Palestine Liberation Organization, infiltrated the Athlete's Village, directing their violence towards the Israeli sporting contingency. Their plan was to capitalise upon the international exposure of the Games to mount pressure for the release of over 200 known terrorists detained in Israeli prisons. Before the day's end, a final standoff culminated in a bloody massacre. One German police officer died. Five of the terrorists were fatally shot and the remaining three arrested. None of the Israelis survived. The September massacre was not unique, although where it took place was. Hijackings and hostage situations are tactics commonly employed in terrorist attacks as bargaining tools.[2] The reports emanating from Iraq of foreign nationals being taken captive exemplify this point. What was so shocking about the Munich Games was the media's intervention in the unravelling of events and its own exploitation by the terrorists. This was lucidly captured in Kevin Macdonald's documentary *One Day in September* (2000). During the hostage situation, news crews swiftly descended upon the scene. The event was aired live on local television networks, implicating the media as a significant actor in the dramatic unfolding of the narrative. As with home viewers, the terrorists were able to assume the panoptic perspective of Big Brother. Police efforts were countered by the terrorists using the technology that attempted to expose them – live broadcasts.

This protracted example not only underscores the integral function of media sensationalism in terror campaigns and the lurid transformation of crises into marketable headlines for the tabloids,[3] but furthermore segues into the equally pressing issue of the impact of the technology and information revolution upon methods of terrorism. The rapid transfer of information through print media, television, radio and the internet has formed a more knowledgeable global audience that is accustomed to the accelerated speed at which current affairs are relayed. Adversely, it has contributed to a shared culture of fear that not only makes us sensitive to the slightest suggestion of panic and emergency, but also primes us to expect it. In conjunction with major advances in computer and telecommunication capabilities, the social, political and economic changes of '[t]he much vaunted globalization, new liberalization in formerly autocratic states, increasing privatization of state functions' have generated new concerns over national and international security.[4] Specifically, cyberterrorism has featured as a primary source of anxiety. In a climate where 'the war against terrorism' has become the much bandied axiom of politicians, military figureheads and nationalist partisans, and a universal enemy has been named, the possible threat of terrorist acts waged in cyberspace has agitated the imagination of a public already fed on a steady news diet of impending danger and apocalyptic scenarios as depicted in popular cinema and the much cited theorisations of prominent scientists, security strategists and analysts.

While the mass media has made the perils of terrorism a constant presence in the everyday consciousness of the public, the personal computer has become the entry point for a unique strain of home invasion. From the benign irritations of unsolicited e-mails to the more severe ramifications of online theft from personal bank accounts and the costly damage to databases and software from destructive Trojan horses, worms and viral outbreaks, the low-key medium of the PC and dialup access to the internet have transformed the liberties of virtual roaming into a potential site for cybercrime and attack from an often unidentified assailant. Cyberspace has become a simulated extension of the home(land). As its imagined boundaries are more nebulous than those of the sovereign state, the regulation of its borders is arguably even more imperative to the maintenance of identity and sense of entitlement. As the tool for neocolonisation of virtual territories that are the equivalent of international waters, the internet holds the promise of claiming, commanding and conquering a space, or at the very least corrupting it.

The minor grievances of personal cyberattacks are symptomatic of the wider problems that face critical national infrastructures such as defence, air and land transport systems. As modern societies become increasingly digitised and reliant upon networked computer and telecommunication systems, the more vulnerable they become.[5] Although there is no substitute for military might, a popular line of reasoning has emerged arguing that offensive information warfare has become a viable 'weapon of mass disruption' in the terrorist's arsenal.[6] These asymmetric threats do not strictly adhere to the 'break things, kill people' (BTKP) principle of terrorist activities. Instead, they provide non-traditional tactics that take advantage of the weaknesses of the adversary where physical strength is not a requirement for victory.[7] This is encapsulated in a dramatic statement by François Debrix, '[i]n a sense, yesterday's hapless victims of gunfire and bomb attacks have become today's digital casualties of cyberterrorist data swarming and ping assaults'.[8] Debrix's proposition echoes the concern to safeguard the most important of currencies in today's political economy – information – from outside threat, but it also perpetuates a misconception of the intentions and capabilities of terrorist operations waged in cyberspace. Fuelled by equal amounts of wariness and imagination, Debrix's argument exemplifies the problems surrounding present discussions of cyberterrorism. This chapter begins to clarify the concept of cyberterrorism to recalibrate its feasibility as a weapon of mass destruction/disruption.

Cyberterrorism has been liberally extended to all manner of scenarios involving violation of information systems. This has included acts of recreational hacking, ping attacks (swarming) by network groups who flood a website to temporarily paralyse it, defacement of websites and the stealing of classified information from computer databases. This has problematically conflated cyberterrorism with cyberwar, cybercrime, netwar and strategic information warfare. All have their own distinct attributes and are not necessarily synonymous with cyberterrorism. For instance, John Arquilla and David Ronfeldt define netwar and cyberwar as various approaches to conflict – the former referring largely to social conflict and the latter to military operations – in which the *organisation* of information and technology is paramount, and where there is a shift from inflexible hierarchies to more dispersed networks of power.[9] Gabriel Weimann argues that cybercrime and cyberterrorism are not coterminous as cybercrimes often do not evoke fear in the victims and tend to lack political motivation.[10] The result has been a generalised term shadowing the prevailing state of alert against foreign agents. The more ambiguous the parameters of cyberterrorism, the greater the threat it appears.

Dorothy Denning provides a concise and practical definition of cyberterrorism that will be referred to throughout the chapter. She writes:

> Cyberterrorism is the convergence of terrorism and cyberspace. It is generally understood to mean unlawful attacks and threats of attacks against computers, networks, and the information stored therein when done to intimidate or coerce a government or its people in furtherance of political or social objectives. Further, to qualify as cyberterrorism, an attack should result in violence against persons or property, or at least cause enough harm to generate fear. Attacks that lead to death or bodily injury, explosions, plane crashes, water contamination, or severe economic loss would be examples. Serious attacks against critical infrastructures could be acts of cyberterrorism, depending on their impact. Attacks that disrupt nonessential services or that are mainly a costly nuisance would not.[11]

This working definition isolates the ideological, technological, psychological and physical determinants of cyberterrorism, filtering out acts of mass disruption from mass destruction. While it must be acknowledged that cyberterrorism is a volatile creature that adapts to emergent technology and the altering sociopolitical environment, there is a need for distinction between attacks in cyberspace which cause inconvenience as opposed to grievous bodily harm and serious threats to national security. As the vogue in current literature has concentrated upon the intentions of cyberterrorists, it is a worthwhile project to consider the likelihood of success of terrorist acts carried out in cyberspace.

As television and radio have functioned as highly effective media for terrorists in gaining international visibility and spreading fear in the past, the exploitable potential of new technologies such as the internet has naturally become suspect. The image of the malevolent cyberterrorist, feverishly tapping away at the keyboard, extends the iconography of the guerrilla soldier. Thousands of kilometres away, an anonymous group riled by political and religious injustice will hack into various mainframes governing a country's critical infrastructures. They will disrupt road traffic signals and interfere with national air traffic systems. The result will be chaos and death. National security and defence systems will be rendered vulnerable. The rogue team will then shut down power grids so that private and business operations without backup generators will be disabled. Likely casualties will be the aged, the poor and the sick that have been turned away by hospitals barely coping with the strains upon their limited resources. Control centres for major water repositories will be tampered with. Contaminated drinking supplies will trigger a health epidemic. The finance sector will be immobilised, inducing the most catastrophic stock market crash of our times and subsequent economic depression. The corporate sector will collapse and suicide will be on the rise.

These scenarios are plausible, but also speculative. As fact becomes increasingly difficult to distinguish from fiction in the current milieu of misinformation and trigger-happy suspicion, numerous studies have been carried out to gauge the probability of such events and their anticipated corollaries. In a paper presented at the Center for Strategic and International Studies in Washington, DC in 2002, James Lewis reviewed the risks of cyberterrorism, cyberwar and other cyber-threats upon critical national infrastructures in the USA.[12] Factoring in routine system failures and automatic responses to an event, the level of human intervention, control and monitoring in critical operations, the accessibility to critical functions from public networks and the design of seemingly interconnected systems (which are often diverse, distributed and may utilise dated equipment), the author found little evidence for the aforementioned claims. Lewis argues:

> Terrorists or foreign militaries may well launch cyber attacks, but they are likely to be disappointed in the effect. Nations are more robust than the early analysts of cyber-terrorism and cyber-warfare give them credit for, and cyber attacks are less damaging than physical attacks. Digital Pearl Harbors are unlikely. Infrastructure systems, because they have to deal with failure on a routine basis, are also more flexible and responsive in restoring service than early analysts realized. Cyber attacks, unless accompanied by a simultaneous physical attack that achieves physical damage, are short lived and ineffective.[13]

Cyberterrorist attacks yielding significant 'collateral damage' and large-scale destruction are not as easily achievable as had previously been thought. Furthermore, there appears to be no conclusive evidence to date that computer network operations, offensive and defensive digital acts that include the handiwork of cyberterrorists, hacktivists and cyboteurs, have created the type of physical damage envisaged by the public, the media and doomsday theoreticians, or that they are even capable of doing so.[14] While cyberterrorism has certain appeal for the terrorist, for instance operations can be conducted from a remote location, cyberspace offers relative anonymity to the perpetrators and there is potential to affect a large populace as opposed to those in the immediate vicinity,[15] a study by Giampiero Giacomello suggests that the costs far exceed the remunerations. After analysing the logistical complexities of coordinating a sustained assault upon vital infrastructure systems (in a hypothetical scenario), the monetary investment in training cyberterrorists and the time required to execute such operations, the author concludes that 'for the time being, investing resources in cyberterrorism *alone* would entail high actual as well as opportunity costs and meager returns'.[16] This comment reiterates Lewis's observation that should cyberterrorism become a more popular method for wreaking havoc, the weapons of choice would have to involve both the bomb *and* the keyboard. Kevin O'Brien's proposition that 'the use of cyber-means to enhance, distract from, or otherwise support a real-world attack is becoming of increasing possibility and relevance to terrorist aims in today's world' supports the importance of cyberterrorism as an adjunct to more conventional BTKP modus operandi in the future.[17] Plunging an online community into a digital void may hold romanticised, symbolic connotations for the terrorist crusader, but it is the body count that ultimately matters. The grotesque spectacle of a plane hurtling into a skyscraper, or the charred human remains caused by explosives detonated on a crowded commuter train has far more intense and enduring emotional resonance than 'impersonal' attacks upon computer systems. There is a reason why television specials will still commemorate 9/11 years after the event, and why the ILUVYOU virus was a passing blip in the mediascape despite estimates that the cost in lost revenue and damaged networked systems worldwide had run into the billions.[18]

While cyberterrorism still remains a danger 'in theory' with the actual capabilities of the aggressors lagging behind those imagined in sci-fi urban legends and ill-conceived news reports, terrorists have found other ways of implementing the internet to champion their causes. Most commonly, it has been utilised to facilitate terrorist activities and agendas. These softer options include fund-raising, intra-group communication, recruitment, holding forums for debate and for public relations purposes that technically do not fall within the topography of cyberterrorism.[19] Organisations are able to capitalise upon the relative freedom of speech that is offered in cyberspace. Al-Qaeda, the Zapatista National Liberation Army, the Kurdish Workers Party, the Irish Republican Army and the Japanese 'Supreme Truth' (Aum Shinrikyo) sect are among the many terrorist syndicates that have established their own websites, profiling the groups' histories, actions and political motives.[20] The goal is to inform (as well as misinform), promote and educate. The fact that many of these sites are offered in the English language is indicative of the broad audience base that is sought and the multiple objectives of the sites. Here, information is used as a strategic resource that 'may prove as valuable and influential in the post-industrial era as capital and labor have been in the industrial age'.[21] Its dissemination is reminiscent of earlier and more rudimentary forms of employing technology for psychological campaigns. The subversiveness of public relations, propaganda and psychological operations is their ability to sway and unsettle public opinion. In this case of 'information operations' and 'perception management', it is impossible to disregard the part played by the media.[22] Returning to the earlier example of the beheading of Nick Berg, the posting of the video on the internet served several purposes. It conjured dread and disgust, but also raised questions of the deplorable sacrifice of life, both civilian and military, in the current conflict in the Middle East. Is anyone really winning this war? Exposure to horrific events through audiovisual and print media further compresses space and geography. Detachment from the problematic world affairs of the Other is transmuted into a matter of international, humanitarian concern. The terrorist operating in cyberspace is able to tap into this collective consciousness. A sense of social responsibility and conscience is an inadvertent side-effect of witnessing atrocities from the comforts of our own home as we surf the internet or peruse the evening news. In relation to television broadcasts of Americans held hostage in Iraq, Jean Baudrillard states:

> Along with the spectacle of these prisoners or these hostages, the screens offer us the spectacle of our own powerlessness. In a case such as this, information exactly fulfils its role which is to convince us of our own abjection by the obscenity of what is seen. The forced perversion of the look amounts to the avowal of our own dishonour, and makes repentants of us as well.[23]

Implicated in the barrage of scenes of violence is the audience's own submission to 'forced voyeurism in response to the forced exhibitionism of the images'.[24] Through access to footage of war crimes that are occurring in real time, or the ability to freeze-frame and replay recorded events in delayed time, there is recognition of the heavy mediation of the images and contrived scenarios – the stilted declarations of terrorist leaders, the gritty settings and the customary props of automatic rifles, balaclavas and orange jumpsuits. It is as if we have seen it all before. The real event has become a surreal viewing experience like a shared waking nightmare. This does not render its impact less intense or disturbing, but fortifies it. Internet broadcastings of beheadings and executions via firing squad not only make it difficult to refute the actuality and atrocities of terrorist acts and war, but impossible to ignore.

As developed nations become progressively more networked and dependent upon digital technology, the tangible threat posed by cyberterrorism will undoubtedly alter. As fears of attacks both on the homeland and in cyberspace intensify, there is a need for vigilance and awareness but not wanton paranoia. The greatest threat may not be the menace of the scheming cyberterrorist, but our own lack of understanding and knowledge. Arquilla and Ronfeldt have ardently maintained how the conduct of war has changed as a result of the information revolution, but they also counsel that it is the organisation – as opposed to the impressive gadgetry per se – of information and communications technologies that will ultimately determine the outcomes of conflict.[25] Whether it is corporeal or cyber-warfare, there will be unnecessary casualties and more losers than winners. Whether tomorrow's terrorist will inflict more devastation with a keyboard than a bomb may also become a moot point of debate in the future. While critical infrastructures may be destabilised, buildings may crumble and lives may be lost, it must not be discounted that the decimated confidence and support of a nation's citizens for its political leaders and involvement in international affairs is just as damaging.

Notes

1. National Research Council (1991) *Computers at Risk: Safe Computing in the Information Age*, Washington, DC: National Academy Press, p. 7.
2. Crenshaw, M. (1992) 'How terrorists think: What psychology can contribute to understanding terrorism', in L. Howard (ed.) *Terrorism: Roots, Impacts, Responses*, New York: Praeger Publishers, pp. 71–80.
3. One of the more recent examples of this media sensationalism was the reportage of the hostage situation and eventual rescue of Australian-born Douglas Wood in Iraq. The event unfolded on the daily news like a carefully constructed screenplay. It was complete with a countdown to the prisoner's execution (the ultimate climax) which was averted and recognisable archetypes of the courageous 'Aussie battler', the Middle-Eastern aggressors and the Australian Muslim cleric, Sheikh Taj Aldin Alhilali, who functioned as the virtuous counterpart of the foreign Other. Upon Wood's liberation, Australian television and print media scrambled to secure exclusive rights to his story and trumpeted the victory with a virtual welcome home to this national hero (although Wood actually resides in the USA).

4. O'Brien, K. (2003) 'Information age, terrorism and warfare', *Small Wars and Insurgencies* 14(1): 183–206.
5. Ibid., pp. 185, 193.
6. Ibid., p. 185.
7. Ibid., p. 186.
8. Debrix, F. (2001) 'Cyberterror and media-induced fears: the production of emergency culture', *Strategies* 14(1): 149–68.
9. Arquilla J. and Ronfeldt, D. (1999) 'The advent of netwar: analytic background', *Studies in Conflict and Terrorism* 22(3): 193–206.
10. Weimann, G. (2005) 'Cyberterrorism: The sum of all fears', *Studies in Conflict and Terrorism* 28(2): 129–49.
11. Denning, D. (2000) 'Cyberterrorism', Testimony before the Special Oversight Panel on Terrorism Committee on Armed Services, US House of Representatives, 23 May, available at: *http://www.cs.georgetown.edu/~denning/ infosec/cyberterror.html* (accessed 6 November 2007).
12. Lewis, J. (2002) 'Assessing the risks of cyber terrorism, cyber war and other cyber threats', paper presented at the Center for Strategic and International Studies, Washington, December, available at: *http://www.csis.org/media/csis/pubs/021101_risks_of_cyberterror.pdf* (accessed 6 November 2007).
13. Ibid.
14. Giacomello, G. (2004) 'Bangs for the buck: A cost-benefit analysis of cyberterrorism', *Studies in Conflict and Terrorism* 27(5): 387–408. Giacomello distinguishes between cyberterrorism and computer network operations, a subset of information operations. The author associates the former with insurgent micro-groups and the latter with legitimate organisations, such as the military, which operate under the command of a sovereign government.
15. Weimann, op. cit., p. 137.
16. Giacomello, op. cit., p. 401.
17. O'Brien, op. cit., p. 184.
18. Festa, P. and Wilcox, J. (2000) 'Experts estimate damages in the billions for bug', CNET News.com, 5 May, available at: *http://news.com.com/2100-1001-240112.html?legacy=cnet* (accessed 6 November 2007)
19. Lewis, op. cit., p. 8.
20. See Tsfati Y. and Weimann, G. (2002) 'www.terrorism.com: terror on the internet', *Studies in Conflict and Terrorism* 25(5): 317–32.
21. Arquilla J. and Ronfeldt, D. (1997) 'Cyberwar is coming!' in J. Arquilla and D. Ronfeldt (eds.) *In Athena's Camp: Preparing for Conflict in the Information Age*, Santa Monica, CA: RAND Corporation, pp. 23–60.
22. Arquilla and Ronfeldt (1999), op. cit., p. 194.
23. Baudrillard, J. (1995) *The Gulf War Did Not Take Place*, translated by Paul Patton, Sydney: Power Publications, p. 39. While *The Gulf War Did Not Take Place* may seem an unlikely inclusion in this chapter, Jean Baudrillard's salient observations of the major shifts in the operation, design and representation of the postmodern war provide a relevant point of reference to the present argument.
24. Ibid.
25. Arquilla and Ronfeldt (1997), op. cit., p. 25.

18

Conclusion: What do you do with the other one in a duo?

Tara Brabazon

> We anchor our identities in delicately constructed webs of friendships and families, localities and workplaces that are easily disrupted by global economic forces which demand that jobs be cut, production reorganized, firms go out of business, occupations disappear. The gap between the intimate way most of us make sense of our world and the global forces which can disrupt it is one of the main sources of our unease. (Charles Leadbeater)[1]

> What do you do with the other one in a duo? (Chris Lowe)[2]

This book commenced with Chris Lowe's fear of not gaining entry to a club. He offered a piquant example of the difficulties in negotiating entry to spaces of desire and possibility. It seems appropriate to conclude with another of his fears: constructing an identity as the less visible, less verbal member of a duo. Neil Tennant and Chris Lowe are the godfathers of dance music. Having survived as long as Madonna but without the Botox, rollerskates or leotards, they have crafted more subtle strategies for pop success. Neil Tennant is the singer, verbally loquacious, intelligent and personable. Chris Lowe has spent much of his public life in the last 20 years behind sunglasses and under a hat. He only speaks when badgered. Once more, he provides a model for this book's project. Those who are not web literate, who do not consume and behave in the patterns proscribed by record companies or eBay ratings hold no secure place in the information age. Their revolution – their calls for change – will not be downloaded. These analogue 'avoiders' or 'dissenters' are unnecessary anchors to post-industrial progress and the knowledge economy. Yet by placing attention on these 'other ones', there are alternative views and truths to reveal.

Daniel Pink, in his book *A Whole New Mind,* offers a considered interpretation of our digital future. Instead of moving from the agricultural to the industrial and – finally – the information age, Pink argues that we are already moving to the next stage, the conceptual age. In such an epoch, not only creators but empathisers are the citizens of value:

> To survive in this age, individuals and organizations must examine what they're doing to earn a living and ask themselves three questions:
>
> - Can someone overseas do it cheaper?
> - Can a computer do it faster?
> - Is what I'm offering in demand in an age of abundance?
>
> If your answer to question 1 or 2 is yes, or if your answer to question 3 is no, you're in deep trouble. Mere survival today depends on being able to do something that overseas knowledge workers can't do cheaper, that powerful computers can't do faster, and that satisfies one of the nonmaterial, transcendent desires of an abundant age.[3]

The Revolution Will Not Be Downloaded has not only presented the voice of the excluded from the age of information, but how this exclusion will present a bill in the conceptual age. Investing in hardware and software is a short-term strategy. There will always be a(nother) designer to develop a faster processor, a larger hard drive or a more efficient accounting package. Training a workforce to complete mindless and repetitive tasks with spreadsheets, forms and mail merge will destroy not only the skill base of the individual worker, but an entire economy. Selling more clothes, DVDs or plasma screen televisions will – very quickly – reach a point of satiation. Those who think and live differently will not only create the economic development of the future, but a more complex and intricate social organisation of citizenship.

Through the filters of avatars, cyberspace and virtuality, there is a concurrent desire for authenticity, to move beyond the brand, and a yearning to reconnect self with society.[4] To enact this project, we must avoid hollow celebrations of information availability and movement during a time of xenophobia, terrorism and asylum seekers. We value the movement of data, but we fear the movement of people. The solution to this disparity for many of the contributors to this book is an attention to education, whether in formal settings of schools and universities or through community-based programmes. But the goal that unifies all the contributors is a desire for change, not to the digital environment but to social lives. At its most basic, Noam Chomsky captures the rationale for this desire:

> As for activism, that's just elementary. There is an enormous amount of human suffering and misery, which can be alleviated and overcome. There is oppression that shouldn't exist. There is a struggle for freedom all the time. There are very serious dangers: the species may be heading toward extinction. I can't see how anybody can fail to have an interest in trying to help people become more engaged in thinking about these problems and doing something about them.[5]

If this book required a justification, then Chomsky – probably the most famous intellectual in the world – provides it. We ask all who read our words to 'have an interest' in thinking about building social relationships and empathic understandings of injustice and inequality.

We need such an interest now, as digitisation shadows the structural exclusions of terrorism. The separation of insiders from outsiders, the web-literate and the excluded, ensures that not only are hierarchies of power perpetuated, but the nodes and sites of injustice are increased. The concern with many of the theories of the knowledge economy, derived from Clinton and Blair's Third Way ideologies, was the assumption that digitisation intrinsically and inevitably initiates democracy. Tom Bentley, for example, has stated that:

> formal knowledge has always been contained and enshrined in institutions – libraries, monasteries, factories, universities, schools. But increasingly, knowledge is accessible from outside these institutions, because of the processing and communications power of technology, and because the most valuable knowledge is carried by increasingly mobile vessels – people. The purest example of this is the internet, which literally exists nowhere – in 'hyper space'.[6]

If *The Revolution Will Not Be Downloaded* has a single aim then it is to disrupt the unproblematised mantra that presumes that information is freely available for all through the internet. Such a mantra increases the disrespect and denial of expertise held by librarians, teachers, journalists and academics. This book – to deploy Mike Kent's phrase – focuses on the creation of 'cultware', the building of an information scaffold for the digitally disempowered to discover strategies for education, learning and social change. The aim is to align the hypertext non-linear delivery of web content with the (often analogue) political aspiration for social connectivity and interdependence.[7]

The critiques made in this book are not attacks on digital convergence, downloading, the internet or the web. Instead, we have questioned whether analogue injustices can be solved or even lessened through a digital panacea. In the context of education, Michael Arnold has addressed this problem:

> The question asked by post-Fordists, and answered by the mainstream computer in education literature, is not why, whether, and where technology should be employed in schools, and to what end, but rather, how to make the most intensive use of high-technology, and how to integrate the computer across the curriculum ... Both the sociology of education and the sociology of technology are marginalized by the computer-in-education literature.[8]

We affirm and welcome Arnold's critique of technocentrism. We ask that much more attention be placed on 'the why' of digitisation, rather than 'the how' of computing. We have also brought the sociology of technology back to our studies of popular music, love, sex, death, terrorism and education. Downloading pornography, blogs, music or even news will not transform social inequalities. Effective policy, political interventions and increasing the agency and consciousness of the empowered and disempowered will address historical injustices. Hoping that e-mails, blogs and government websites will intrinsically lubricate democratic government is a flawed argument, agenda and ideology.

Hoping that the siren's call of downloadable digital content would drag the underprivileged, disempowered and poor to the screen was a mistake. Instead, proactive policy is required for all groups in society, rather than simply the school children targeted in documents such as 'Connecting the UK'.[9] As the web has become another place to shop and blogs have become another way for the overconfident to spread their personal desire for micro-celebrity to a wide audience, democracy is being lost through the flattening of debate. A few people have far too much to say and the web is increasing their avenues for expression.

If we sit alone at our computer – satiated in the glow of our back-lit screen – then we are not only complicit in our own empowerment, but the disempowerment of others. The meritocratic illusion that if we work hard then we can be successful in public life it is not only incorrect, but incredibly damaging. We must carry forward our anger at the injustices of class and race being not only perpetuated but reified through digital convergence. *The Revolution Will Not Be Downloaded*, as a title and project, asks that we finally move away from a focus on access and content for the few and grant attention to the lives and context of the many.

Notes

1. Leadbeater, C. (1997) *Civic Spirit: The Big Idea for a New Political Era*, London: Demos, p. 5.
2. Commentary on *PopArt: The Video* (EMI Records, 2003).
3. Pink, D. (2005) *A Whole New Mind: Moving from the Information Age to the Conceptual Age*, New York: Penguin, p. 51.
4. David Boyle has argued that, argued that 'part of the solution is going back to the local to find the very real resources that we tend to ignore there, while continuing to hold on to a global vision of the world'. See Boyle, D. (2004) *Authenticity*, London: Harper, p. 289.
5. Chomsky, N. (2005) *Imperial Ambitions*, London: Penguin, p. 183.
6. Bentley, T. (1998) 'Learning beyond the classroom', in I. Hargreaves and I. Christie (eds.) *Tomorrow's Politics*, London: DEMOS, pp. 80–95.
7. This project is explored in Mulgan, G. (1997) *Connexity*, London: Chatto & Windus.
8. Arnold, M. (1996) 'The high-tech post-Fordist school', *Interchange* 27(3–4): 225–50.
9. Prime Minister's Strategy Unit with the Department of Trade and Industry (2005) 'Connecting the UK', London: Stationery Office.

Index

Al-Qaeda, 219
  – *see also* terrorism
Anderson, Benedict, 149, 152, 197
  Imagined Communities:
    Reflections on the Origin and
    Spread of Nationalism, 197
Arnold, Michael, 226–7
  'The high-tech post-Fordist school'
    226–7
Aronowitz, Stanley, 8–9
  Education Under Siege, 9
  The Knowledge Factory, 8
  – *see also* education
Arquilla, John, 216, 222
  'The advent of netwar: analytic
    background', 222
  – *see also* netwar
Aspin, Lois, 14, 20
Austen, Jane, xvi, 171, 186
Australian Broadcasting Authority,
    137, 143
Australian Recording Industry
    Association (ARIA), 106,
    111–13, 127–8, 132

Baudrillard, Jean, 220, 222
  The Gulf War Did Not Take
    Place
Bellhouse, Sonia, v, ix, xvi, 11, 22
Bennett, Rebecca, vi, ix, xvii, 153,
    206

Berners-Lee, Tim, 94
  – *see also* World Wide Web
Berg, Nick, 214, 220
Blair government, 25–6
  third way ideology, 26, 225
Blair, Tony, 64–5, 67–8
blog/blogging, vi, xvii, xxi, xxii, 7,
    68, 135–44, 153–61, 203,
    206–7, 226
  Columbine High School massacre,
    138
  journalism, 135, 139, 206–7
  weblog, vi, 153–61, 206
  – *see also* Australian Broadcasting
    Authority
  – *see also* paedophilic activity
  – *see also* pornography
Bourdieu, Pierre, 90, 95, 98–9
  – *see also* cultware
Brabazon, Tara, v, vi, ix, xii, xiii,
    xxii, 8, 16, 21, 45, 73, 86, 152,
    166, 170, 223
  Digital Hemlock, 8, 16
  Ladies Who Lunge, 170
  Liverpool of the South Seas, xxii
Bragg, Billy, 130, 132
Brown, Gordon, 65
Bush, George, W., 6

Carr, Nicholas, xviii, xxiii
Chavez, Hugo, xv

Chomsky, Noam, 207, 211, 225, 227
   Imperial Ambitions, 225, 227
Clarke, Arthur C., 3, 8
   'Technology and humanity', 8
Clinton, Bill, 6, 225
Coates, Tim, 44, 70
Coelho, Paul, 11, 19
   The Alchemist, 19
Community Development Western
   Australia, Dept. of, 32, 34,
   68–70
computer knowledge, 13–15, 18
   for aged, 46–66
   Nannanet, 65
Cope, Bill, 4, 8
   Multiliteracies, 4, 8
copyright, 92, 105, 107–9, 115–16,
   120, 122–3, 128, 131, 207
copyright lawyers, 123, 131
Cross, Michael, 65, 71
   'Class consciousness', 65, 71
Cull, Felicity, v, ix, xv, 106, 123
cultware, 89–91, 93, 95–8, 166, 191,
   226
cyberspace, 98–9, 144, 154–6, 181,
   196, 201–3, 215–21, 224
   cyber attacks, 216, 218
   cyber-audiences, 156
   cyber-bullying, 138, 144
   cyber-cafes, 26
   cyber chat room, 137, 139, 142,
      172, 174, 177–86, 195
   cyber-communications, 181
   cybercrime, 215–16
   cybercultures, Japanese, 152
   cyber-desperados, 187
   cyber-encounters, 181
   cyber-estate, 203
   cyber gay community, 188, 196
   cyber homophobes, 188
   cyber-junk, 203
   cyber-literacy, 181

cybernaut, xvi, 202–3, 205
*Cyberprotest: New Media, Citizens
   and Social Movements*, 211
cyber punks, xix, 92
cyber sex, 185
cyber sluts, vi, 171, 177, 186
cyberspace revolution, 201–2
cyberterrorism, xiv, 213, 215–19,
   221–2
cyber-thieves, 203
cyber-threats, 218, 222
cyber-topia, xiv
cyber-wars, 211, 216, 218, 221–2
   – *see also* Gibson, William
   – *see also* Jordan, Tim
   – *see also* Lewis, James
   – *see also* Loader, Brian
   – *see also* McLelland, Mark
   – *see also* netwar
   – *see also* Nixon, Paul
   – *see also* Rucht, Dieter
   – *see also* Stephenson, Neal
   – *see also* Taylor, Paul
   – *see also* Van De Donk, Wim

diaspora, 187–97
   – *see also* globalisation
digital divide, 4, 6, 11, 19–20, 22,
   24, 46, 51, 56, 65, 67, 98
digitisation, xv–xvi, xix, xxi, 13–15,
   22, 26, 28, 45, 65, 92, 96, 103,
   105, 202–3, 225–6
   digitised environment, 96
   digital underclass, 11, 90, 97–8

Eastbourne, UK, vii, xvi, 33, 40–4,
   70
   East Sussex County Council, 41
   Sussex Careers Service, 41
   Central Library, 41–3
eBay, vi, xv, 7, 163–70, 223
   – *see also* Omidyar, Pierre, 163

e-ducation, xiv, 80, 83
education, 73–87
    education export, 75, 85
    – *see also* Monash University
        Malaysia, 75, 84–5
    flexibility, 74–5, 78–9, 85–6
    higher education enrolments,
        76–80, 83–4

Facebook, xviii, 142
Felten, Edward, 118–19, 121
    – *see also* file-sharing
file-sharing, 103–4, 106, 110,
        115–20, 124, 126–31, 207
    – *see also* Felten, Edward, 118–19,
        121
Flickr, xiv, xviii
Florida, Richard, 35
Fukuyama, Francis, xxi, xxiii
    The End of History, xxi
Fulton, Kathleen, 7–9
    'Learning in a digital age: insights
        into the issues', 7–9
Fyrst, Valentin, vi, ix, xvi, 201

Gaydar, vi, xvii, 187–97
Gibson, William, 98
    Neuromancer, 98
    – *see also* cyberspace
Giroux, Henry, 8–9, 164, 170, 207
    Education Under Siege, 9
    – *see also* education
globalisation, 153–61, 209
    global cultural diversity, 189, 192
    global cyberspace, 155–6
    global gay diaspora, 187, 189–97
    global gayness, 189–90, 193
    global power, 155–6
    global tourism, 154, 158, 160
Gottlieb, Nanette, 152
    Japanese Cybercultures, 152

Guardian, The, xiv, xxii, 66, 70–1,
        111, 113, 132

Hafner, Katie, xxiii
Hall, Stuart, 207
hardware, 11, 16–17, 55, 59, 65,
        89–96, 98
Hewitt, Patricia, 25, 67–8
Hoffman, Donna, 71
    'Bridging the racial divide on the
        internet', 71
    – *see also* internet usage

internet usage, 27, 32, 40, 43, 71,
        137, 140–1
    regional areas, 15, 26, 33, 41, 62,
        121
    online banking, 17, 49, 52, 59–61,
        65, 140–2, 144
    – *see also* Hoffman, Donna
    – *see also* Lenhart, Amanda
    – *see also* Marsden, Rhodri
iPod, 43, 46, 48, 58, 109, 124,
        126–9, 131
    Apple Computers, 112–13, 129
    – *see also* music
Iraq conflict, 205–6, 213–14, 220
Irish Republican Party, 219
    – *see also* terrorism

Japanese Cybercultures, 152
Japanese 'Supreme Truth', 219
    – *see also* terrorism
Jordan, Tim, 211
    *Hacktivism and Cyberwars: Rebels
        with a Cause*, 211
    – *see also* cyberspace

Kalanzis, Mary, 4, 8
    Multiliteracies, 4, 8
Kay, Peter, 23, 65–6

Keegan, Victor, xiv, xxii

Kent, Mike, v, x, xv, xvi, 19, 89, 103, 155, 191, 202, 226

Klein, Naomi, 207

Koprowski, Gene, 132
   'The web: The effect of illegal downloading', 132
   – *see also* music

Kurdish Workers Party, 219
   – *see also* terrorism

Kusek, David, 115
   – *see also* music

Leadbeater, Charles, 44, 70, 223, 227
   Overdue: How to Create a Modern Public Library Service, 70

learning, xxiii, 5, 8–9, 19, 24, 27, 29, 35, 37–9, 41–4, 63, 70, 73–5, 78–87, 92, 140, 226–7
   e-learning, 73–5, 78, 80, 85–7
   learning communities, 37–8, 44, 70
   online learning, 73, 75, 84

Lee, Christine, vi, x, xvi, 213

Lenhart, Amanda, 8–9, 67, 69, 71, 98–9
   'The ever-shifting internet population: a new look at internet access and the digital divide', 8, 67, 98
   – *see also* internet usage

Leonhard, Gerd, 115
   – *see also* music

Lewis, Garan, vi, x, xvi, 205

Lewis, James, 218–19, 222
   'Assessing the risks of cyber terrorism, cyber war and other cyber threats', 218–19, 222

– *see also* cyberspace

literacy, xi, xvi, 3–8, 11, 13–14, 16, 22, 27–8, 35, 44, 47–50, 53–5, 58–9, 61–2, 65, 67, 70, 73–5, 78, 89, 92–6, 104, 136, 155, 164–9, 203
   computer literacy, 4, 12, 15–16, 28, 52, 93
   critical literacy, 5, 7
   cultural literacy, 95
   cyber literacy, 181
   digital literacy, 7
   eBay literacy, 165
   fashion literacy, 165–9
   information literacy, 4, 7, 70, 92
   internet literacy, 36, 62, 65, 67, 159, 164
   teaching literacy, 3–4
   techno literacy, v, 3, 7, 155
   web literacy, xx, 28, 41, 58–9, 61, 164
   – *see also* Macken-Horarick, Mary, 5, 8

Loader, Brian, 211
   Cyberprotest: New Media, Citizens and Social Movements, 211
   – *see also* cyberspace

Locke, Kathryn, v, x, xvi, 3, 12, 22

Lowe, Chris, xiii, 223
   Pet Shop Boys, 223

Macdonald, Kevin, 214
   One Day in September, 214
   – *see also* terrorism

Macken-Horarick, Mary, 5, 8
   'Exploring the requirements of critical school literacy: A view from two classrooms', 8
   – *see also* literacy

Mandurah, W. Aust., xvi, 33, 35–41,
44–5, 48–9, 51, 54, 62, 64, 70
Newman, Mark, (CEO, City of
Mandurah), 37–8, 70
Senior Citizens Centre, 38–9
Marsden, Rhodri, xxiii
– see also internet usage
Matthews, Joel, vi, xi, xvii, 145
McLelland, Mark, 152
Japanese Cybercultures, 152
McRae, Leanne, v, xi, xv, 73
media, 3, 7, 11, 20, 39, 48, 52, 63,
67, 97, 99, 111, 115, 120, 131,
135–43, 148, 205–22
computer mediated, 25, 28, 64, 69
entertainment media, 18, 141
home-based media, 34, 63
Indymedia, 210
news media, 138–40
Meikle, Graham, 163, 170
Metcalf's Law, 99
'Metcalf's law and legacy', 99
– see internet
Monash University Malaysia, 75,
84–5, 87
– see education
Morley, David, 34, 45, 69–70, 195,
197
Home Territories, 45
Morley, Paul, xx, xxiii
MP3, 43, 104, 106–10, 112, 126
music, ix, x, xiii–xvii, xxii–xxiii,
57–9, 62, 92, 106–8, 110, 112,
115–21, 123–32, 163, 172, 207,
223, 226
copying music, 92, 103, 105–7,
109–10, 115–18, 120, 123, 127,
131, 142
copyright, 92, 105, 107–9,
115–16, 120, 122–3, 128, 131,
207

declining sales, 106
downloaded music, 107–8,
110–12, 116–17
file-sharing, 103–4, 106, 110,
115–20, 124, 126–31, 207
iPod, 43, 46, 48, 59, 109, 124,
126–9, 131
iTunes, 107, 129, 132
P2P (peer to peer) distribution,
104–8, 116–22
Petrillo, Caesar, American
Musician's Union, 128
Radiohead, In Rainbows, 110,
113, 124
record companies, 104–5, 110,
115, 120, 123–5, 127–9, 130–1,
222
Recording Industry Association of
America (RIAA), 108
– see also Koprowski, Gene
– see also Kusek, David
– see also Leonhard, Gerd
– see also Yorke, Thom
MySpace, xviii

Napster, 104, 108, 120–2, 127, 130,
207
netwar, 208, 216
– see also Arquilla, John
– see also Ronfeldt
– see also cyberwar
New Musical Express, xx
Nixon, Paul, 211
Cyberprotest: New Media, Citizens
and Social Movements, 211
– see also cyberspace
NOFX, xv, xxii
'The Marxist Brothers', xvii
Norman, Donald, A., 3, 8
The Design of Everyday
Things, 8

Novak, Thomas, 71
  'Bridging the racial divide on the
    internet', 71

OhmyNews, 208
Olympic Games, Munich, 214
  – *see also* terrorism
Omidyar, Pierre, 163
  – *see also* eBay
online banking, 17, 49, 52, 59–61,
  65, 140–2, 144
online dating, 171, 174–9, 181–2,
  186–8

P2P (peer to peer) distribution,
  104–8, 116–22
paedophilic activity, 137, 143, 184
  – *see also* blog/blogging
Palestine Liberation Organization,
  214
  – *see also* terrorism
Petrillo, Caesar, American Musician's
  Union, 128
PEW's Internet and American Life
  Project, 6, 8–9, 12, 19–20,
  22–3, 25, 33, 36, 55, 64, 66–70,
  90, 97–9, 143–4, 205
Pink, Daniel, 224
  A Whole New Mind, 224, 227
podcasts, xv, xvii, xxii
popular culture, ix–xiii, xv, xxii, 122,
  124, 148, 174
Popular Culture Collective, ix–xii,
  xv, xxii
pornography, 90, 137, 226
  – *see also* blog/blogging

Radiohead, 110, 113, 124
  In Rainbows, 110, 113, 124
  – *see also* Yorke, Thom

Reagan, Ronald, xxi
Rheingold, Howard, xiii, xxii
  – *see also* World Wide Web
Ronfeldt, David, 216, 222
  'The advent of netwar: analytic
    background', 222
  – *see also* netwar
Rucht, Dieter, 211
  *Cyberprotest: New Media, Citizens
    and Social Movements*, 211
  – *see also* cyberspace
Rucker, Rudy, 92, 99
  wetware, 92

Schumann, John, 128, 132
Scott-Heron, Gil, xiv, xv, xxii
Smith, Carley, v, xi, xv, 108, 115–18,
  124
Smith, Joanne, vi, xi, xvii, 135, 206
Smoove, xv, xxii
software, 16–17, 40, 55, 58, 65, 67,
  85, 89–96, 98, 108–10, 112,
  116, 121–2, 127, 136, 142, 202,
  207, 210, 215, 224
Stephenson, Neal, 98
  Snow Crash, 98
  – *see also* cyberspace
students, ix, xi, 4, 6–8, 67, 73–83
  e-learning, 73–5, 78, 80, 85–7
  international, v, vii, xi, xv, 73–81,
    83, 85–7
  mature-aged, xi, 18, 73
  teaching 'face to face', 74–5, 80–2,
    84–5
suicide, online, vi, xvii, 139, 145–52,
  184, 218
  group, 146–52
  in Japan, 145–52
  practices, xi, 145–52, 218
  website, 150

Taylor, Paul, 211
  Hacktivism and Cyberwars: Rebels with a Cause, 211
  – *see also* cyberspace
Tennant, Neil, 223
terrorism, vi, 63, 171, 199, 205, 215, 217, 222–6
  – *see also* Al-Qaeda
  – *see also* Irish Republican Party
  – *see also* Japanese 'Supreme Truth'
  – *see also* Kurdish Workers Party
  – *see also* Macdonald, Kevin
  – *see also* netwar
  – *see also* Olympic Games, Munich
  – *see also* Palestine Liberation Organization
Thomas-Jones, Angela, vi, xi, xv, 163
tourism, 153–4, 157, 159–60
  gay tourism, 191
Turkey, John, W., 91, 98
  'The teaching of concrete mathematics', 98
  – *see also* software
Turkle, Sherry, xiii, xxii
  Life on the Screen, xxii
  – *see also* World Wide Web
Turner, Graeme, 141, 144

Van De Donk, Wim, 211
  Cyberprotest: New Media, Citizens and Social Movements, 211
  – *see also* cyberspace
virtual communities:
  virtual chat-room, 137, 139, 142, 172, 174, 177–86, 195

virtual communication, 172–5, 178, 180–4
virtual environment, 24, 178, 182, 186, 190
virtual gayness, 191–4, 196
virtual intimacy, 171, 174, 179–80, 184
virtual relationships, 171–86
virtual shopping, 27, 163–70, 223
virtual terrorism, 215, 221, 224

Web 2.0, xvii–xix, xxii–xxiii
weblog, vi, 153–61, 206
  travel weblog, 153–60
  – *see also* blog/blogging
wetware, 89–96, 98–9
  – *see also* Rucker, Rudy, 92, 99
Wikipedia, xvii, xix, xxi–xxii, 144, 153
  – *see also* Wales, Jimmy
World Wide Web, v, xiii, xx, 11, 21–2, 24, 41, 45, 48, 63, 94, 96, 136, 163
Wurman, Richard, 3, 8, 13, 20
  Information Anxiety, 8
  – *see also* education

Yorke, Thom, 110
  – *see also* music
Young, Melinda, vi, xi–xii, xvi, 171, 188

Zapatista movement, 208, 219
  – *see also* terrorism